Authors Access
30 Success Secrets for Authors and Publishers

Irene Watson
Tyler R. Tichelaar
Victor R. Volkman

Authors Access: 30 Success Secrets for Authors and Publishers
Copyright © 2009 by Irene Watson, Tyler R. Tichelaar, and Victor R. Volkman
All Rights Reserved.

Individual articles in this collection retain the copyright of their original authors.

First Printing, March 2009

Library of Congress Cataloging-in-Publication Data

Authors access : 30 success secrets for authors and publishers / [edited by] Irene Watson, Tyler Tichelaar, Victor R. Volkman.
    p. cm.
 Includes bibliographical references and index.
 ISBN-13: 978-1-932690-98-9 (pbk. : alk. paper)
 ISBN-10: 1-932690-98-0 (pbk. : alk. paper)
 1. Authorship. I. Watson, Irene, 1946- II. Tichelaar, Tyler, 1971- III. Volkman, Victor R.
 PN137.A97 2009
 808'.02--dc22

                            2008043930

Modern History Press   Tollfree 888-761-6268
5145 Pontiac Trail   Fax: 734-663-6861
Ann Arbor, MI 48105   Email: info@LHPress.com

Modern History Press is an imprint of Loving Healing Press

Table of Contents

Acknowledgements iii

Foreword v

Chapter 1 – The Craft of Writing 1
    "Put Your Best Prose Forward" by Jane Toombs and Janet Lane Walters 1
    "Don't Murder Your Mystery" by Chris Roerden 13
    "Discovering the Elements of Story" by Joan R. Neubauer...................... 21
    "The Myth of Writer's Block" by Mark David Gerson 28

Chapter 2 – Genre Writing 31
    "Writing About Forensic Science and Criminal Law" by Andrea Campbell 31
    "Writing Effective Regional Fiction" by Tyler R. Tichelaar 38
    "Five Tips on Writing Romance" by Sylvia Hubbard 47
    "Paperback Writer: A Memoir of Gay and Lesbian Fiction" by Victor J. Banis
    49

Chapter 3 – Children's Books 59
    "Rules for Writing Children's Literature" by Lila Guzman......................... 59
    "Publishing a Children's Book? Better Get a Child's Opinion First" by Tyler
        R. Tichelaar 64

Chapter 4 – Editing Your Work 69
    "Editing Tips for Authors" by Kenneth J.M. MacLean................................ 69
    "Editing: The Second Pair of Eyes" by Bob Rich, Ph.D.............................. 75

Chapter 5 – Elements of Book Design 87
    "Five Keys to a Better Book" by Michele DeFilippo 87
    "Smart Self-Publishing" by Jim and Linda Salisbury.................................. 93

Chapter 6 – Exploiting the Writing Market.................................. 101
    "Exploring Ghostwriting, Co-Authoring, and Collaborating" by Ami
        Hendrickson... 101
    "How I Became a Successful Freelancer" by Yvonne Perry 110

Chapter 7 – Building Buzz with Book Reviews 115
    "Everything You Need to Know about Book Reviews" by Irene Watson.. 115

"Creating Bound Galleys and Advance Review Copies" by Tyler R. Tichelaar and Irene Watson 121

"Negative Book Reviews: How to Avoid them and How to Use Them to Your Advantage" by Tyler R. Tichelaar 124

"Elements of a Quality Book Review" by Tyler R. Tichelaar 127

Chapter 8 – Marketing Your Work 135

"Promoting Your Book with a Publicist" by Maryglenn McCombs 135

"Branding: It's a Book Thing, Too" by Paul McNeese 142

"What Can Author and Publisher Associations Do for You?" by Tyler R. Tichelaar 154

"Amazon Adventures: Staring Down Earth's Largest Bookstore" by Victor R. Volkman 162

"Twenty-One Mistakes to Avoid when Publishing and Promoting Your Book" by Patrick Snow 170

"Twelve Things Under Ten Bucks You Can Do" by Victor R. Volkman ... 174

Chapter 9 – Making the Most of Technology 177

"Successfully Selling Your Book Online" by Brad Grochowski 177

"Promoting Your Book with Social Media and Web 2.0" by Deltina Hay and Neil Kahn 192

"Revolution: Audiobook" by Toby Heidel 199

"Book Marketing on MySpace" by Tyler R. Tichelaar 206

"Amazon Kindle: Lighting a Fire on eBook Sales" by Victor R. Volkman 210

About the Editors 215

Bibliography 217

Index 219

Acknowledgements

A big thank you to every author who has been on our program; you have made this the Earth's most informative and entertaining podcast about publishing. Also, the moderators of Self-Publishing@yahoogroups.com who have been essential in allowing us to get the word out.

Special thanks to my stalwart co-host Irene Watson, who managed the scheduling and handling of more than 75 guests as well as recruiting them to contribute to this book. Tyler R. Tichelaar also became an essential part of our team, backing us up when needed and appearing as an expert in his own right. Tyler stepped up yet again to do a complete copy edit of the final draft. My own role in the production team has been primarily as co-host, audio engineer and webmaster. Any typesetting errors in this volume are entirely mine.

In alphabetical order, the contributors to this First Edition, this book would not be here without you: Victor J. Banis, Andrea Campbell, Mark David Gerson, Lila Guzman, Brad Grochowski, Michele DeFilippo, Deltina Hay, Toby Heidel, Ami Hendrickson, Sylvia Hubbard, Kenneth J.M. MacLean, Maryglenn McCombs, Neil Kahn, Paul McNeese, Joan R. Neubauer, Yvonne Perry, Robert Rich, PhD, Chris Roerden, Jim Salisbury, Linda Salisbury, Patrick Snow, Tyler R. Tichelaar, Jane Toombs, Janet Lane Walters, Irene Watson.

Victor R. Volkman
November 6th, 2008

About the Cover

Photo credit goes to NASA Goddard Space Flight Center Image technicians Reto Stöckli and Robert Simmon as well as a host of contributing team including MODIS, the USGS, and the Defense Meteorological Satellite Program.

This spectacular "blue marble" image is the most detailed true-color image of the entire Earth to date. Using a collection of satellite-based observations, scientists and visualizers stitched together months of observations of the land surface, oceans, sea ice, and clouds into a seamless, true-color mosaic of every square mile of our planet. These images are freely available to educators, scientists, museums, and the public.

Learn more about this imagery at The Visible Earth http://visibleearth.nasa.gov/

Foreword

Authors Access, originally titled "Publisher's Open Forum" was conceived in August 2006, in an extended brainstorming session between Irene Watson and myself. My own personal motivation was that as I was bringing on more and more authors into my publishing business, (Loving Healing Press Inc.) I was finding it ever more burdensome even to help them find the ropes, let alone teach them the ropes. At the time, most books I found were either solely about self-publishing or marketing and didn't seem to find the right niche I wanted. Podcasting seemed like the obvious solution; little did we know that we'd end up coming full-circle and producing our own book about the subject.

Although our initial plan for the show was roughly to cover the lifecycle of a book, just as we do in this volume, we were quickly diverted into all kinds of interesting side paths. Truth to tell, I wouldn't have predicted in my wildest dreams that we would go on to record 75 shows and reach an audience of 500 authors and publishers each week.

Again, when we started in 2006 there weren't a lot of publishing podcasts out there, so we stepped in to fill the void. Along the way, I learned a ton more about audio production, the marketing of podcasts, and got to meet the luminaries of the independent publishing movement. By no means is this the end—podcasting is still the most economical, fast, and fun way to get the word out. It's been a heck of a ride and I hope you'll enjoy this book as much as we've enjoyed making it available to you.

Victor R. Volkman
Modern History Press

1   The Craft of Writing

Put Your Best Prose Forward
Jane Toombs and Janet Lane Walters

The last word of the story has been typed. As the author, feeling a rush of accomplishment, you're ready to send the manuscript to an editor or an agent. Or are you? A final check will make sure the prose shines bright enough to spark the agent or editor into enthusiasm for your project.

You may be fortunate enough to have a critique partner or a group who can point out the flaws. What if you don't have these resources? This was our primary reason for writing *Becoming Your Own Critique Partner* from Zumaya Books. Summarizing our entire book into a single chapter is impossible, but here are a number of steps you can take to make sure you've put your best prose forward.

The reader's interest must be captured from the first word. This interest must be held through the middle to the end. But if the opening chapter doesn't intrigue the editor, agent or reader, a meaty middle or a dynamic ending won't matter. Here are some ways to check the first chapter to make sure of that interest.

1. Do you have your main character or characters in trouble of some kind right away, or make it clear one or both might be headed for trouble? You'd better!

Does this mean you have to have a slam-bang opening with action galore? Not really. A sense of danger or a hint of a problem will pull the reader into the story. Be warned, though: If the opening is too exciting, keeping up the pace may prove impossible. Here's an example of an opening with a promise of something to come.

> "A flash of lightning brightened the sleeping chamber. Ash woke with a start and burrowed into the pillows. The scent of trouble rode the air currents that threaded through the open window slats."[1]

Here's an opening that begins with a mixture of mystery and excitement.

---

[1] *The Henge Betrayed* by Janet Lane Walters (Mundania Publishing)

"He floated in darkness, the tiny flame of his awareness the only light in the Stygian gloom. The flame flickered, fading, he had no will to keep it aglow. As he drifted closer to the dark shore of no return, a beam of blue energy seared across the blackness. Drawn to the power, his life force flared anew, growing as it fed on the surging fountain of energy."[2]

2. Do you have a lot of backstory at the beginning? Take it out and drop it in later in dribs and drabs when necessary. Just not a chunk of it in Chapter 2, or you may stop the action cold. Never do that.

Often writers use backstory as their way of learning who their characters are and how they react. This information is needed by the author, but not the reader. Readers don't need to know much about a main character's past right away. Only when some such information affects the present action does the writer need to drop that tidbit into the story.

For example: when Mary was three, she was locked in a closet by her older brother. If nothing in the present story makes this incident from the past have an effect on what's happening to her now, there's no reason to mention this. But if Mary has to hide in a dark place during the story, how she reacts may be governed by the incident from her past. Then and there the reader needs to know.

Another example: The main character in *Under The Shadow* wakes injured on a California beach during gold-rush days. He doesn't know who he is, where he is, or how he got there. So he has no past. Neither he, nor the reader learns anything about his past until an injury halfway through the book restores his memory. So there is no back story at all until that point. Even then, a flashback shows (not tells) where he came from. Then he's immediately thrust into action with no huge chunk of back history dropped in.

3. Is it clear where and when the action is taking place? That is, do readers know by the second page where in the world (or galaxy) they are? If not a contemporary story, do they know what year it is? See that you tell them in some way where and when they are. Do remember that just mentioning a local landmark is not telling a reader from another part of the country or world where the story is set. Of course if you use the Empire State Building that is enough of a landmark so most

---

[2] From *Under The Shadow*, the book #1 of the Moonrunner Trilogy by Jane Toombs (New Concepts Publishing electronic).

readers will recognize where they are. Is it day or night? Hot or cold? Indoors or out? Readers need to know.

One way of letting the reader know where or when is to state it at the opening of the chapter. For example. "Dover England, August 1811." This will show where and when, but there are other ways of weaving the place and time into the story.

> "The sun rose above the distant hills. The August day promised to be a scorcher. Once again she had come to the Dover docks. For a moment, she felt a chill and wished she'd worn a pelisse."

This example shows much of the same information as given in the dateline but draws the reader into the story.

> "The palace of the wizards rose on the horizon. The setting sun colored the crystal spheres in iridescent rainbows."

Here the sample shows we are in a different world and the time is evening.

> "Andrea Sullivan skirted a small stand of pine and stopped, staring at strangely familiar ivy-covered ruins dead ahead. She'd never set foot in Gatineau Park before—or Quebec Province for that matter—but Sherri's long ago description of the McKenzie King ruins had proved to be marvelously accurate."[3]

In the above example Canada is not mentioned, but the reader picks up the clue from "Quebec Province." Since no date is mentioned, the reader assumes it's contemporary, which is well established as the chapter goes on.

4. Do you have talking heads? Readers need to see characters in some kind of surroundings and performing actions that give clues to their nature. Be sure they do.

Long passages of dialogue with no action or sense of place are fine in a movie or a play. In those forms there are visual components. In a book the writer needs to show the reader who is speaking, show where they are, and by their actions give a hint to the kind of person they are.

5. Are you positive of the meanings of all your words? Have you loaded the chapter with *ing* words, *ly* adverbs and too many adjectives? If so, rewrite without them. Are you sure you know the difference between words such as affect and effect? Are you positive *it's* means *it is* and *its* is a possessive? Are you sure you haven't mistyped a word, such as loin for lion?

---

[3] *Moondark* by Jane Toombs, a paranormal romance from Amber Quill Press.

Using *ing* words, or adverbs and adjectives isn't wrong but they can muddy the prose or throw your words into a whirlpool pattern. Do vary your sentence structure. Try not to fall into a predictable pattern such as the one below.

Example: "Standing on the pier, she stared at the rushing waves. Waiting for her first sight of the ship, she sighed. Hoping he would arrive this time."

After a while this kind of pattern can cause the reader to fall asleep.

Adverbs, especially ly ones are often used in tag lines. Don't.

> "In your dreams," she said laughingly. *Poor*
> She laughed. "In your dreams." *Better.*
> "Shut up and get out," he said harshly. *Poor.*
> "Shut up and get out." His harsh voice rasped the words. *Better*

Another problem is strings of adjectives.

> She saw a tall, broad-shouldered, dark, curly haired, green-eyed man. *Poor*
> She saw a tall green-eyed man. To add to his attractiveness he had an athletic build and dark curls. *Better.*

Try not to throw in the entire description with one adjective after another instead of sprinkling the prose into the description.

6. Do you ever have the heroine running her fingers through her long blonde wavy hair? Please don't. Unless you're really unusual, YOU never think of the color of your hair or whether it's curly or straight when you run your fingers through it. Neither should she.

Any description of a character is best coming from another character's observation. Or the character can think something similar to this: Shannon ran her fingers through her hair, wishing for nth time it was long and blonde and straight instead of a frizzy mass of red curls.

7. Have you done a search and find on all those plaguey little words that creep in unnecessarily? Words such as: it, that, almost, very, just, thing, then, finally, suddenly, seem and seemed—to mention some of them. If so, have you found a way to eliminate a good many of them? A bit of rewording usually allows you to do this.

Very tends to sneak in without us noticing.

> She was very angry. *Poor*
> Fury gripped her. *Better*
> The vase was very unique. *Wrong.*

The vase was unique. *Correct.* Unique means one of a kind, so adding very to it accomplishes nothing.

Words such as *it, thing, that, something, somewhere* are vague and don't add to the story. Example:

"What is it?" She pointed to the thing in the corner. "You know that one. It's something I've seen somewhere."

Instead, try:

"I can't make out what that strange spiked object is." She pointed to a corner. "I might have seen one in a museum once, but don't recall the name."

8. Do you try to make things simple for readers? Easy to understand? Without, of course, using clichés. Never paint a picture so confusing the reader has to stop to figure out what you mean. This might accomplish something you'll regret. The reader may be jerked out of the story and decide not to return.

Example: "The moon rose, so bright a yellow it resembled a gigantic round lemon hanging from the tree of the sky." This is unusual enough to make a reader pause to think that lemons aren't round and the sky isn't anything like a tree. Many readers are literal-minded. Don't confuse them.

9. Are you sure of your dialogue punctuation? Are you certain you haven't used laughing, smiling, or snorting, etc. as tags? While characters can do all of these things, they can't do any of them while speaking.

"Where are you going," Mary smiled. *Wrong.*
Mary smiled. "Where are you going?" *Correct.*

Another kind of tag can cause amusement such as hissed. If there aren't a lot of *esses* in the dialogue, hissing is hard to do unless the character has a speech impediment.

"Sam, you're nothing but a cobra," she hissed. *Wrong*
"Sam's a slimy snake," she hissed. *Passable.*

10. Is your point of view (POV) always clear, so the reader knows which character is speaking?

Do you try to keep to one POV per scene? Or if a long scene and you switch, do you refrain from switching back? Do you, as the author intrude with your POV? Don't.

Some authors are able to switch POV with ease but with others the reader can feel as if a ping-pong match is occurring. The purpose of POV is dual. One is to help the reader identify with the character and the other is to give the reader insight into the character's nature. If POV shifts too often in a scene, the reader isn't sure who is the star of the scene.

Most of the aforementioned ten items that you should check when you edit your beginning, should also be applied to the rest of the manuscript. As you go on, you need to check this next list for other irregularities that may doom your writing.

Ten Irregularities of Doom

1. Editors believe readers do not like long paragraphs. Heed this and keep yours short. Part of the problem with lengthy stretches of prose is the purpose of the paragraph can be lost or muddied. Along with long paragraphs, there is the runaway sentence. While grammatically perfect, the phrases and clauses bury the point beneath a heap of verbiage.

2. Do the hero and heroine in your story have inner conflicts and outer conflicts that will hinder a relationship between them? Do the inner conflicts arise from their life experiences and how they feel about themselves? If not, why not? Neither inner nor outer conflicts should be trivial and thus easy to conquer.

An inner conflict should be strong enough to carry the plot throughout the story. If characters cannot grow enough to realize their inner conflict is keeping them from happiness and from what they really wish to accomplish, then they haven't reached their potential.

If you also have a villain, he or she needs inner and outer conflicts that may both speed and/or hinder the person from accomplishing his or her evil deeds.

Are your inner and outer conflicts for major characters real ones? Difficult to overcome? If not, the plot is weakened and readers may lose interest. Example of inner and outer conflicts:

> Heroine: Twenty-five-year-old Elsa is a non-dominant identical twin. Her sister has directed all her life choices, sometimes against Elsa's own inclination, until her sister married and moved to China. Elsa's first on-her-own decision when she followed the advice of a devious man landed her in both trouble and danger. She's lucky to have survived. Now she's afraid to trust any man and determined to be her own decision-maker.

Hero: Mark, thirty-two, is an ex-Marine, used to making quick decisions. Sometimes too quick since they may affect other people.

So Elsa is not going to trust Mark and will have to learn that mutual decisions are possible. Mark has to learn to understand where Elsa is coming from and not try to run her life, even when he can see trouble ahead for her. He, too, has to learn to work on mutual decisions. These inner conflicts are complicated by an outer, dangerous conflict, where they're at odds.

Fred Martin is the villain in *Obsessions* by Janet Lane Walters (Hardshell Word Factory). His inner conflict is his love for his mother and his feelings for the heroine of the story. His mother died during a Code and he blames the nurses and doctors who were present for her death. He intends to punish them by killing them. But the heroine was his mother's favorite nurse. The outer conflict involves both the police and the heroine. How can he keep them from learning the deaths are connected before he achieves his goal?

3. As a resolution to outer conflict, have you wimped out? Have you used the old Greek *deus ex machina*—the just-in-time rescue by an outside force? If an outside force to rescue is used, make sure at least one of your main characters has created time for that force to arrive by some clever maneuver. Or maybe by overcoming an inner conflict or trait. Or both.

As an example, the villain in Obsessions has cornered the heroine after a chase through town. She has used her heavy stethoscope to break a window of a house where a party is in progress. This alerts the hero and the police. The villain finally catches the heroine on an overlook above the Hudson River as police sirens sound. She's the last of those who had been at his mother's Code. I won't give away the ending, but the event is played out step by step in short scenes using three POVs, hero's, heroine's and villain's.

4. Check for sections of telling, not showing, where it's important to show because otherwise you're cheating the reader. Rewrite to show. Don't forget telling can show up in dialogue as well as narration—as when one character tells another what they both already know. Sometimes you do have to tell. Be sure you know the difference between these times and when you should show. Think of the following example as being in the 1800s at an isolated farm. Emma is eighteen and Mary is eleven and they're alone at this farm.

Mary had never seen anyone in labor before and didn't know what to do. She'd heard you always boil water, so she went to the kitchen and put the kettle on.

Telling—and in the doing wimping out by omitting the birth scene. Compare with a longer treatment:

Emma cried out and clutched her abdomen, grunting in pain. "Help me," she begged.

Mary stared at her in dismay. "What's wrong?"

"Can't you see I'm having the baby now? Way ahead of time." Emma sobbed.

Mary wrung her hands. "I don't know what to do."

Emma grunted again and screamed.

Scared out of her wits, Mary ran from the room to the kitchen. The only thing she remembered about babies being born is hearing someone say you had to boil water. So she put the kettle on the stove, then covered her ears so as not to hear Emma screaming.

This shows what's happening instead of telling. It's easy to see which is more likely to grab a reader's attention

Also check for good balance between narration and dialogue and correct where necessary.

5. Check for spots where inadvertent POV changes may have been made. Don't forget that when the author sneaks in a POV of his or her own, that's usually a no-no. Rearrange wrong POVs.

Statements such as "If she had known" usually means author intrusion.

Or "Meanwhile, the folks on the farm were sitting down to dinner." Once again, the author has stepped in.

7. Is your black moment (crisis) really dark enough? When a character reaches this point in the story, he or she has to believe all is lost. He or she faces a dilemma where there seems to be no way out of the situation. The hero knows he can't have the heroine. He despairs. Try not to have the sort of ending to the black moment that is suddenly resolved. Play the moment to the full until the character realizes something has to change if he or she is to reach the goal.

8. Got at least some of the five senses in here and there? Sight, sound, smell, touch and taste add depth and details to a manuscript. Here's an example.

Her nose wrinkled at the odors rising from the pit. Bile burned her throat. Taking care not to plunge into the dark ooze, she reached for the wooden cover. As she pulled the cover closed, the grating sound made her shiver.

The sharp tang of ammonia bit her nose and she gripped the side of the old wooden door so hard a splinter poked her palm.

9. Any padding? (Unnecessary or repeated words, scenes and ideas.) If so, take it out. Any awkward place and time shifts? If so, smooth them out.

One place to look for padding that may have sneaked past you is in moving characters from one scene into the next. Instead of taking a character step by step from one place to another, use a space break and add something such as this:

Twenty minutes later a breathless Joe reached town.

Later, at the office, Natalie found a stranger at her computer.

10. Do either of your main characters seem to be lacking motivation? (This includes any villain.) Give them more. What does your hero believe his goal is? Why is he motivated to seek it? The same for the heroine. And villain. During the plot action, the reasons for striving for a goal may change. For example, if the hero pursues the original goal, he may lose the heroine's love. Let's say the theme of the book is "Learn to compromise." In which case both the hero and heroine will have to modify or alter their goals to reach happiness.

Villains' motivations may not be logical.

Fred in *Obsessions* is motivated by his mother's death. Even though she was very ill when she coded, he cannot accept that her death was natural. When he was a child, she made a promise. "I'll never leave you. They'll have to kill me first." These words have become a litany for him and trigger his actions.

11. Read dialogue out loud if necessary to check if characters are speaking appropriately for who they are. Reword any that isn't working.

A person's speech patterns are influenced by many things including age, where they were born and grew up, their sex, education and job or profession. Remember to consider these factors when putting words into your characters' mouths. And whether in modern times or the past, almost all people, when they speak, use contractions such as I'll, you're he's, etc. Don't bog down historical characters with I will, you are, he is, etc. Yes, they wrote without contractions because writing was formal in the past. In fact, the reason some seem to think Native Americans in the old days spoke formally is because an educated person of the times translated their speeches into written English *of the times*. Always remember that men and women almost always use different speech patterns. Listen! Note the differences.

Don't inundate the reader with too many local patterns of speech. Dropping in the occasional odd word or spelling is better than having every other word in a sentence differ from basic English. For example, if your character leaves an ending g off his words, you may irritate a reader by using too many ing words with a dropped g. Think around this. Gonna substitutes nicely for goin' ta. Gonna is not a word, but is used so commonly that readers accept it.

12. Look for your theme. If you discover it, have you emphasized the theme as well as you could? What is theme? In music, theme is the basic melody of a composition. In writing, theme is a melody repeated again and again throughout your story—sometimes faint, sometimes loud and clear. Dean Koontz tells us, "Theme brings purpose and meaning to the plot." At the same time, do remember that each genre has a given theme. Romance is "Love conquers all." Mystery is "Justice triumphs." Or perhaps "Good conquers evil", which is also the theme of many fantasies. Your individual theme when writing these genres is your particular spin on those general themes.

In *Obsessions*, each of the major players in the story has an obsession. Fred, the villain, is obsessed with revenge. Susan, the heroine, after the death of her overprotective husband is obsessed with having complete control of her life. Trish, one of the major players is obsessed with drugs. The three doctors each have an obsession, one for power, one for reputation and one for a woman. The first character to die is obsessed with gossip. The heroine's best friend is obsessed with a man. The hero is obsessed with keeping Susan safe.

13. How about pacing? Do some sections seem to drag? Determine why. Perhaps in the action scene, the sentences are long and flowing when a staccato pace is called for. Is there too much chit-chat with no advancing of action? Too much explaining? Too much research material thrown in as a lump? Minor characters stealing scenes? These all either bore or confuse readers.

Do your characters' eyes wander around the room or fasten on someone or something? Do disembodied hands touch people? Hearts drop to the floor? Keep body parts attached to their owners. Eyes can gaze, or look, etc., but they never leave the person. Hands always belong to a specific person unless a character can't see because of darkness or a blindfold or some other reason and feels a hand touch her. In such cases, she wouldn't know who the hand belongs to right away.

Cars can be another problem. Cars do nothing by themselves. They have drivers. A car doesn't turn onto the off-ramp unless the driver makes it do so.

Here's an example that also shows distancing, which is another problem. Distancing is almost always passive writing.

> Barking was heard in the night. *Wrong.*
> Somewhere in the darkness a dog barked. Right

The passive ing word has been removed and the bark reattached to the dog.

15. What is voice? There's a lot of talk these days about voice. Nothing more than your individual way of telling a story. But be careful not to decide edits for clarity and grammar will destroy "your way" of telling a story. Writers sometimes fear that changes to a manuscript may alter or mute their voice. Don't be one of them. A grammatically correct, well-edited manuscript is the best way to showcase your voice. Unless you edit and re-edit, over and over until the story loses its original verve, your voice will not only survive, but come through all the clearer if you apply these guidelines to your writing.

Finally, after you've considered all these points and made the needed changes, check one more time for spelling and grammatical errors and word choices. Then you can send your story to the agent or editor knowing you have put your best prose forward.

About the Authors

Janet Walters is both a nurse and a novelist. She has published 28 novels and four non-fiction books over a 30-year writing career, three of these written as a ghost-writer. Janet has written in many genres including: Romances from sweet to spicy and from contemporary to historical. She has written paranormal and fantasies, cozy mysteries and suspense.

In 2003, *Becoming Your Own Critique Partner* (with Jane Toombs) won the EPPIE award for non-fiction. Jane Toombs is the author of more than eighty published books and fifteen or so novellas or short stories. She writes in all genres except men's action and erotica, though paranormal is her favorite to read and write.

Podcast Airdate:	June 21st, 2007
Podcast URL:	http://authorsaccess.com/archives/62
Author's site:	http://www.newconceptspublishing.com/janetlanewalters.htm http://www.janetoombs.com/

Don't Murder Your Mystery
Chris Roerden

The following transcript is from a broadcast of Authors Access with special guest Chris Roerden. Chris is a member of Mystery Writers of America and served six years on its Southeast regional board. She is also a member of Sisters in Crime and Romance Writers of America.

Chris: When I hear other writers talk about their colorful early careers—bartender, blackjack dealer in Las Vegas—my career might seem boring. I started as an editor right out of high school, and have worked at almost nothing other than teaching writing and doing community organizing. While my editorial roles change, I've always been in communication and publications in one way or another.

Irene: We are certainly happy to have you here talking to us and sharing all of your wonderful skills and ideas and experiences. First, congratulations on your huge win of the Agatha Award. My goodness, that's big.

Chris: Thank you. I was convinced I was not going to win, so when my name was called I was speechless. I managed to make my way to the stage and stumble a few words of thanks, but afterward I was amazed that I'd stood before 600 readers and writers with a live mic and never thought to pitch my next book!

Irene: Oh, you're funny! Your current book is *Don't Murder Your Mystery,* and we are going to delve right into that. Why did you write this book?

Chris: I wrote it because I have forty-four years of editing experience, and it seemed a waste to take all of it to my grave. I've also been a managing editor, but I didn't like that because there was no time to work on manuscripts. So I left my last position in 1983 and took the risk of going out on my own. My goal has always been to share what I know about writing and publishing to help writers succeed.

Most writers have no idea what it takes to submit work to a literary agency or publishing house. Too many writers leave clues all over their opening pages that reveal what the industry calls amateur writing—which I call average writing. Those clues tip off the first reader very quickly that the level of writing is not professional enough for an agency or a publisher to invest money in.

The vast majority of manuscripts are rejected immediately. The most common explanation—when one is given at all—is: "We are looking for a fresh, new voice." We'll get into voice a little later.

Irene: So Chris, what is the first clue that the first manuscript reader looks for?

Chris: The first clue has nothing to do with the writing but everything to do with the packaging and appearance of the manuscript, which takes common sense and the ability to follow directions. Recently a manuscript arrived in a big box, and when I opened it, popcorn jumped out—that awful foamy stuff that flies all over and clings to your clothing, desk, and everything else. The manuscript had not even been placed in its own envelope inside the box. I had to shake out the pages and try to get all that miserable popcorn to let go. I can tell you that anyone else would have tossed the whole thing, removing only the first couple of pages so they could record who'd sent it. No one would sit there for fifteen minutes trying to pick clingy popcorn off their clothing and hands. An error like this shows that the author gave no thought to how the manuscript would be received. I've received manuscripts so reeking of smoke that they lived in the garage for a couple of weeks airing out before I would look at them, and I'm being paid to look at them, unlike an agent or publisher.

If writers have no awareness of how their submissions are received, how intuitive can they be in weaving stories that create a desired effect in a reader? This is where the independent editor comes in, suggesting revisions so the first reader, who comes at the writing cold, experiences the story at its best, without distraction by techniques that don't work effectively. To experience a story, the first reader has only what the author paints a picture of—for instance, setting the scene. Often, writers begin a story with no indication of location or even whether it's day or night. Conversely, some mystery writers include too much detail about the setting.

I could go on with all kinds of stories about the unfortunate way that manuscripts are prepared. I can tell you that receiving any piece of mail typed all in capital letters won't be read. I could talk about the typographical and grammatical errors that insult the recipient, showing that the writer didn't care to get the manuscript cleaned up so the agent or editor could focus on the content and not be distracted by mechanics.

Victor: I get a lot of unsolicited manuscripts, and I know what you mean. I can't read them without the red pencil in my hand.

Chris: True, though I don't use red because it's the color of danger and blood and anger, and I think red is received by the writer as being too strong or too critical. I have to anticipate how my suggested revisions will be received, so I use a pencil with a soft, dark lead. I'll remember not to send you something of mine that might come back with red all over it!

Victor: That's another great point. Good editors have to be diplomats in trying to not hurt the delicate feelings of writers.

Chris: You're right. Those feelings are raw. It's almost impossible not to engender a negative reaction, especially since I edit very closely. I am likely to have ten or twenty marks on a single page of manuscript, which is a lot for any writer to deal, but what's this all over my pages? She must be lying to me and I'm a worse writer than I ever thought." The writer feels misused and hurt.

Victor: Exactly. Let's stop for a second before we get into more details of editing. In the mystery genre what would you ideally like to see in the package? What goes into the cover letter? Does the author need to send a résumé or a competitive analysis? What are all the key elements that would be in the ideal package that you may never even get?

Chris: A competitive analysis of the market is necessary for nonfiction, as well as a platform—how your credentials, background, and contacts support your marketing of the finished book. For fiction, credentials are less important, unless the work is, say, a medical or legal mystery. Then it helps to mention a background in medicine or law in the query. Today, some mystery writers are being asked for a platform, too. More important, submitting a query or cover letter, and finding the right people to send it to, involve more than a few quick words of advice. One size does not fit all, so research pays off. There are so many books available on how to submit, how to format, and how to find the right agent, there's little excuse for anyone's getting those things wrong. One book I recommend is *Making the Perfect Pitch: How to Catch a Literary Agent's Eye* by Katharine Sands, because many agents quoted in her book tell precisely what to include in a query letter. For nonfiction there's *How to Write a Book Proposal* by Michael Larsen. Jeff Herman regularly updates his *Guide to Publishers, Editors and Literary Agents.*

As for the manuscript, which must be ready to send when the successful query does its job, the first thing an agent sees is the same as the first thing I see: appearance. In two seconds, the agent decides whether the submission looks professional or amateur. In my case, in two seconds I see whether the format facilitates or inhibits editing. Is the manuscript double-spaced, Courier 12, with adequate margins for my notations? When the font is proportional, such as Times Roman, it's not only harder to read but harder to slide a correction between tightly packed letters.

One of the biggest mistakes writers make is feeling arrogant, believing their story is so good it cannot be improved, format isn't important, and everyone who sees it will want to publish it. Not true. Agents and publishing houses are overwhelmed with manuscripts.

Victor: Let's get into some of the specifics of things where you can really add value. Is it things like the plot and characterization or dialogue? Where are some of the key areas?

Chris: Definitely plot and character development, when I edit, and other big-picture, whole-book elements as well as details of dialogue, narrative, forms of expression, and everything else on every page. For the writers who self-edit, who do not hire their own manuscript editors, I have put as much advice as possible in my books for writers, in which I analyze most of the same elements—the opening hook, motivation, pacing, conflict (and conflict, as you know, is essential in all fiction), dialogue, tags, action, creating tension and suspense, raising the stakes, regrounding characters in their settings, density, texture, how to effectively use description, backstory, flashbacks, body language, regional speech, names, figures of speech—and on and on. I support my advice with excerpts from authors who do right what most writers get wrong.

And I deal with voice. Because ninety-percent of manuscripts land in the "no" pile quickly, without being read past the first one or two pages, saving a submission from that common fate is not character or plot—the development of which cannot be seen in a few pages. It's the writer's voice and the use of craft and technique.

What I call the *hobbled hook* is the opening intended to shock that instead rambles off into something else, usually description and backstory. The writer who puts backstory on page one doesn't realize that the way to do it is to sneak a little hint of background in with the action. Instead, most new writers stop the action and start to tell each character's history.

I once edited a mystery which told the history of five victims, from birth to death, taking at least four pages *apiece!* None of it was germane to the story. There are other ways of letting us know a villain was abused as a kid without going through three generations of family. You've seen it. I hear you laughing.

Irene: Oh yeah, I'm totally with you on this.

Chris: Then there's the description dump. For example, it's after midnight and there's a loud knocking at the door. Jack rushes in. He is wearing a blue suit and a white shirt with a red tie, and his dark hair is combed straight back....Who cares about all that? Here is a character arriving after midnight, in a hurry, which surely indicates some urgency. Letting us know his wardrobe isn't urgent. The first reader questions how valid this emergency is and how skilled is the writer who doesn't continue the action once it starts?

Victor: Exactly. Are there other things beyond chapter one, or are most of the deadly things happening in chapter one?

Chris: Enough clues show up on page one, or at most, page two, that the first reader doesn't have to read any farther. It's already clear that the quality of the writing is not good enough to publish—no matter how interesting the story's content seems to be.

One indicator of voice is the overuse of modifiers. "A tall, lean blonde walked into the dark, dingy bar and sat at a small, round table." Not only do we have this pile-up of adjectives, a disorder I call *adjectivitis*, most are not necessary, at least not all at once. Details can be worked into the action—if any action ever gets a chance to occur. What's happening here is that the writer with adjectivitis has set a rhythm going. There are two adjectives for each noun. Tall lean, dark dingy, small round. You could almost dance to the rhythm.

Victor: Yes, the waltz.

Irene: Chris, you mentioned something I had to kind of smile to myself about—that many writers think they have a best-seller, and don't understand why agents and publishers aren't interested. As a book review service, we run across a lot of books, particularly those that are self-published and not edited. I think that what happens is the writers have no money, whatsoever, to hire an editor. They go through a spell check, maybe, and they self-publish a book. There are so many errors. One, for example, was sent back to us by the reviewer, who said, I cannot read it, it has so many errors. I randomly took a page and I found twelve errors. I'm not even an editor.

Chris: Unfortunately, very common.

Irene: So tell us more about what people should do who really want to self-publish. What are some major areas they need to concentrate on and why?

Chris: First of all, to self-publish requires a realistic budget, not only for production but also for editorial and marketing. Self-publishing may take less time but it's very expensive. It breaks my heart to hear about writers who send their manuscripts to vanity or subsidy publishers expecting to get an edit, and feel humiliated on learning that their dream is now in print, errors and all. A spell-check is far from an edit. Sometimes the cause is naïveté, sometimes it's arrogance—the assumption that "I'm so good (or I have so many people around me who are good at picking up these things), I don't have to seek professional help." Maybe it's both, as in: "What could be so special about editing? Anyone can do it."

In saying this I am not trying to sell my services; in fact I'm looking forward to retiring. I've cut back a great deal, so I'm certainly not selling anything by saying that not all editors are created equal. There are no standards for hanging out one's editing shingle, no licenses or credentialing. Nothing can replace a hands-on, line by line, close edit by a skilled professional, not to mention the consultation, the advice, the recommendations that come with a good edit by someone who knows how the specific book will be received by its intended audience.

I'd like to share something with you because I find it surprising. Sometimes I get manuscripts that don't identify the genre, that don't say this is a mystery or this is fantasy. I read the first page and can't even tell if it's fiction or nonfiction. So I created a form for writers to fill out telling me where they see their manuscript going next and what marketing plans they have, because I won't take money from people with no concept of how they will sell the result. My questions are designed to help the writer get the right type of editing. When I have to ask if the manuscript is fiction or nonfiction, the writer sometimes asks me, what's the difference?

Next I might ask, who is your ideal reader? "Everyone," they answer. "Well, no, not everyone will be motivated to buy your book. What is unique about it? Who would make up your specific audience?"

"Um, well, I don't know."

If it's a mystery I might ask, for example, "Is it a thriller, is it a cozy, is it a serial killer, is it romantic suspense?" And they don't know. They say, "There is some romance in it and some mystery, too." So my next question is, "Tell me what writers you enjoy reading." Can you guess what the answer is? It's "I don't have time to read." Writing without reading but expecting to get published is arrogance. It's like someone entering a bridge-building contest who knows nothing of engineering. Writing looks easy; let's write a book and get it published.

Irene: Gosh, Chris, you have given us so much information, and I'm sitting here and I just looked up at the clock and it's like oh my goodness, we're running out of time, and I know that you have tons more information and I'm sure that a lot of it is in your book, *Don't Murder Your Mystery*, and obviously it is because you've got twenty-four fiction-writing techniques in there.

Chris: I should mention that *Don't Murder Your Mystery* was made a Writer's Digest Book Club alternate selection. And *Don't Sabotage Your Submission* is a rewrite of the same book.

Irene: Great book. I'm so happy you are putting something out there like that because *Don't Murder Your Mystery* looks like it's more for mystery, but obviously the points you make are interchangeable with other genres.

Chris: The reviewers have been extraordinarily complimentary, and I'm excited about the libraries that keep adding my books to their permanent collections. I also drive about 15,000 miles a year taking my workshops to writers' groups and conferences to teach the techniques that make up the fresh, new voice publishers are looking for.

Irene: Oh that's great! Again Chris, thank you so much for taking the time to be with us, giving us all of these pointers. I know our listening audience is going to be thrilled with all the pointers you gave us.

Chris: My pleasure.

About the Author

Chris Roerden, who, in May 2007, won a major award for best nonfiction: the Agatha Award—named, appropriately enough, in honor of Agatha Christie. The title of Chris's new book is *Don't Murder Your Mystery: 24 Fiction-Writing Techniques To Save Your Manuscript From Turning Up D.O.A*. This book was also a finalist for three additional awards, ForeWord magazine's Reference Book of the Year, the Anthony Award from the largest mystery readers' convention in the country, and the Macavity Award from the largest mystery readers' organization in the world.

Although *Don't Murder Your Mystery* is about writing fiction, reviewers are saying it is a book for all writers. So her publisher, Bella Rosa Books, had Chris write a new version of it, called *Don't Sabotage Your Submission*, for writers in any genre. These books have grown out of a large body of experience; Chris has been a full-time manuscript editor of both fiction and nonfiction for more than forty years. The last twenty-four years she's been independent, she has edited authors who have been published by St. Martin's Press, Berkley Prime Crime, Midnight Ink, Intrigue, Rodale, Viking, Walker & Co., and many others, as well as authors who have self-published. Chris has also had a hand in those authors winning twenty-two awards of their own.

In addition to editing, Chris ghosted four books for clients of the eleven books and a game she has written. She received her Master's in English from the University of Maine, where she served as president of the graduate student body and was invited to stay on as an instructor of writing. In the mid-nineties she was elected president of Mid-America Publisher's Association, a ten-state trade association for publishers founded by John Kremer. She initiated the first series of night classes in publishing at the University of Wisconsin-Milwaukee, which she taught for eight years.

Podcast Airdate:	May 24th, 2007
Podcast URL:	http://authorsaccess.com/archives/52
Author's site:	www.bellarosabooks.com

Discovering the Elements of Story
Joan R. Neubauer

We love stories. In childhood, we loved to hear stories of all kinds. Some of us may have even made up some of our own. I'm sure we all had our favorites, such as *Sleeping Beauty, Cinderella,* or *Beauty and the Beast.* Very young children relate to stories such as *The Three Little Pigs, Little Red Riding Hood,* or *Goldilocks and the Three Bears.* But no matter how simple a story, each of these fairy tales has something in common: they all contain the elements of story.

Put more simply, they're not chronicles of events, such as, "The first little pig was born in Chicago in 1820. When the Pig family moved to Dallas in 1825, the second little pig was born."

Rather, each takes only a certain portion of the complete story and gives it a complete structure, with no expectation of anything else to come when you finish the story. That complete structure has a beginning, middle, and an end. In addition, it has the basic elements of narrative, characterization, dialog, plot, and conflict. If you think about it, the fairy tales from our childhood have all these elements, and end with "happily ever after."

Let's use *Goldilocks and the Three Bears* as an example. As a believer in the KISS principle (Keep It Simple, Stupid), I think if we can understand how something simple works, we can use that information to understand something far more complex, like a novel. Understand how Goldilocks works, and you can understand *War and Peace, Gone with the Wind,* and the novel you're working on at the moment.

In the Beginning...

At the beginning of our Goldilocks story, or any other story, we have an introduction where we meet the characters and get an inkling of the plot. At the very outset, we meet Goldilocks and her mother. We also get a clue about the other characters in the story, the three bears. The story begins with Mama warning her adventurous child.

> "You can go outside to play, but don't leave the yard. There are all sorts of wild animals out in the woods that might harm you."

Of course, Goldilocks, a child after my own heart responded, "Name two."

> Mama said, "I'll name three for you, that Bear family over on the other side of the woods: the Mama, the Papa, and the Baby Bear. I hear they're a mean bunch."

So, now, we've met two characters, and have learned of the existence of three more. Next, Goldilocks goes outside to play in the yard, but the world beyond her gate beckons. She wants to cavort with the squirrels and chase the butterflies through the forest. Little by little she wanders closer to the fence to gaze longingly at the woods that hold the promise of adventure. We can all relate to this. We crave the forbidden fruit. We all struggle with what we want to do as opposed to what we should do, and therein lies one conflict, the inner conflict. Goldilocks reacts by rationalizing and taking the wrong path, exactly what characters do in novels.

> "I know I shouldn't leave the yard, but it would be so much fun to go exploring. Just think of all I could learn and all the creatures I could meet."

Eventually, she gives into the temptation and disobeys her mother. She opens the gate and steps out of the safety of her yard. If she obeyed her mother, we'd have no story. However, since she chooses to do otherwise, the plot moves forward.

The Middle

With an awareness of our characters and the conflict, our plot begins to take shape. Goldilocks does indeed leave the yard and begins her exploration of the woods. Now, we must set the scene with description and narrative.

> As Goldilocks ambled through the woods, the canopy of trees dimmed the sunlight, and cast ominous shadows. Goldilocks looked over her shoulder hoping that no creatures followed her. A strange sound caught her ear and she wrapped her arms about a tree in fear. Her mother had told her about bears, and she hoped this sound had not come from one of them.

You can also take this opportunity to build tension.

> An animal's growl captured her attention and he froze on the spot. What was that? She suddenly wished for the safety of her yard, but had no idea which direction to go.
>
> "I'm lost," she whispered in a shaky voice.

The Craft of Writing

In the meantime, while poor little Goldilocks suffered the pangs of guilt and fear, the Bear family began their day. As in the case of introducing any group of characters, you need to define the dynamics of this group. Dialog works nicely. Through dialog, you can show who really runs this family and how they interact.

"Breakfast!" Mama Bear shouted.

"We'll it's about time," Papa Bear groused.

"Porridge again?" Baby Bear whined.

Or...

"Come and get it! We've got breakfast on the table," Mama Bear trilled.

"Thanks, Honey. We all appreciate your efforts." Papa Bear gave Mama Bear a kiss on the cheek.

"Oh, boy, porridge again! My favorite," Baby Bear squealed.

You get the idea. Have fun. Play around, but let your dialog reveal important things about your characters. Then, when the bears sat down at the table and they each agreed that, *"This porridge is too hot!"* who suggests that they go for a walk to allow the porridge to cool, and what is their tone of voice? Try to see how many different combinations you can come up with. Have some fun here.

So while the Three Bears are taking a walk, Goldilocks finds the cottage of the Three Bears, an inviting little place nestled in the woods. Of course it has the requisite white picket fence surrounding it and a little mailbox out in front. To Goldilocks, it looks like any other house and she feels saved.

Sure she can get some help here; she approaches the house and looks inside, but doesn't see anyone. She knocks, but no one answers. She tries the door. Eureka! She swings it open and walks inside to find a kitchen table with three bowls of porridge. We come upon another conflict here.

Goldilocks knows it's wrong to walk into someone's house uninvited, but she's afraid of being in the woods any longer. She's also hungry and tired, and when she finds three bowls of food that belong to someone else, she chooses to sate her hunger anyway.

She tasted the porridge from the biggest bowl and said, "Oh, this porridge is too hot!"

Then she tried the porridge from the medium sized bowl and said, "Oh, this porridge is too cold!"

Finally, she tried the porridge from the smallest bowl. "This porridge is just right," and she ate the whole thing.

Then, she decides to explore the house and comes upon the living room. She sees three chairs of three different sizes which she decides to sit in. Again, take this opportunity to demonstrate something about the characters with dialog and description.

Goldilocks walked over to the first chair with its tall, straight back, and sat in it. "Oh, this chair is too hard."

She quickly scooted over to the next chair and settled into its soft, pink upholstery. She felt as though it swallowed her up and she immediately stood. "Oh, this chair is too soft."

Then she spotted the smallest chair and sat in it. "Oh, this chair is just right," and it splintered into a hundred pieces.

Now, we should have a very guilty feeling Goldilocks. She has entered someone's house uninvited. She's eaten their food, and she's broken a chair. But she's overcome with fatigue and goes looking for someplace to lie down, and she comes upon the bedroom where she sees three beds. At this point, I'll bet you can predict what she'll do.

Goldilocks decided to take a nap in the biggest bed in the room, but of course, she couldn't get comfortable, and said, "Oh, this bed is too hard."

Then she spied a slightly smaller bed and tried going to sleep there, but that didn't last long. She left it saying, "Oh, this bed is too soft."

Then she noticed the smallest bed in the room and tried that. "Oh, this bed is just right," she said, and quickly fell asleep.

Please notice, that we've got the Rule of Three in action here: three bears; three bowls of porridge; three chairs; three beds. Also, Goldilocks never succeeds the first time, or the second time. Only her third attempt brings satisfaction. The same holds true for characters in fiction. They must fail twice before they achieve success. Each failure builds sympathy for them and helps the reader further identify with them.

The End

Now we come to the end of our story where we must have a confrontation, a resolution to all conflict, and tie up all the loose ends. The bears come home and immediately discover something amiss.

> Papa Bear says, "Someone's been eating my porridge."
>
> Mama Bear says, "Someone's been eating my porridge."
>
> Baby Bear says, "Someone's been eating my porridge, and they ate it all up!"
>
> Very upset that someone has invaded their home, the Bear family walks into the living room and Papa Bear says, "Someone's been sitting in my chair."
>
> Mama Bear says, "Someone's been sitting in my chair."
>
> Baby Bear says, "Someone's been sitting in my chair and they broke it all to pieces!"
>
> By now, Papa Bear feels the need to defend his family and picks up Baby Bear's baseball bat as they head for the bedroom.

You see the tension building here for the climax? In each little scene we notch it up a bit.

> When they reach the bedroom, Papa Bear says, "Someone's been sleeping in my bed."
>
> Mama Bear says, "Someone's been sleeping in my bed."
>
> Baby Bear says, "Someone's been sleeping in my bed, and there she is!"

Please note the story continues to use the Rule of Three, and it has built tension to the breaking point. Now the hens (or bears as the case may be) have come home to roost. Goldilocks must face those she has offended.

First, she takes on the bears. With all the noise and consternation, she wakes up to a family of bears staring at her. The poor girl, frightened out of her wits, and feeling very guilty, runs as fast as she can, out of the house, into the woods, and finds her way home.

Second, we still have the conflict to resolve with Mama.

> By this time, Mama has looked all over for Goldilocks and is frantic with worry. She can't find her anywhere. Then she looks up to

see Goldilocks running toward her from out of the woods. Mama rushes to meet her at the gate with a big hug.

"Mama, Mama, I'm so sorry! I went into the woods, and I got lost, and tired and hungry, and then I found the house of the Three Bears, and I ate porridge, and I broke a chair, and fell asleep, and they all came home and found me! I woke up and I ran and ran all the way home. Mama, I promise I'll never disobey you again!"

Mama gave her a big hug. "Of course I forgive you, but I'm glad you learned your lesson."

This is where the story ties up all the loose ends and we have conflict resolution. Goldilocks has learned her lesson and vows to obey her mother in the future. We sympathize with the characters on their losses, and rejoice in the lessons they have learned. We don't know for certain what the Bear family did to recoup their losses, but if the story were written today I'm sure they would have hired an attorney to sue for damages. In this way, they could be made whole again and we have a satisfactory end to the conflict.

While this may seem like a very simple story, once you tear it apart and analyze its parts, you'll find that they're the same pieces that we need when we put together the puzzles of our own writing. Whether fiction or nonfiction, good writing is good writing and the same things apply. Goldilocks and the Three Bears may not be your favorite story, so think of another simple story that you particularly like. Tear it apart into all its constituent pieces, identify them, adapt them appropriately, then put them all back together to tell your story. You'll find that you'll have all the necessary pieces: beginning, middle, end, narrative, characterization, dialog, plot, and conflict.

Now that you understand how to do this, go home and write!

About the Author

Joan and her husband Steve Neubauer own and operate WordWright.biz, Inc., a publishing house in Alpine, Texas. "We're an author incubator," Joan says. "We want to nurture authors and help them develop into the fine writers and promoters they can become." Joan takes her own advice and is making a name for herself, her publishing house, and her authors. WordWright has acquired a reputation as one of the finest publishing houses to showcase new authors. Since 2000, WordWright has published over one hundred fifty titles for new authors.

Joan continues to write books, articles, and columns. She also travels extensively to promote her books and her publishing house. She is available to speak on a variety of subjects for writers groups, corporate functions, civic and service organizations, and schools.

Podcast Airdate:	December 21st, 2006
Podcast URL:	http://authorsaccess.com/archives/23
Author's site:	http://www.wordwright.biz/

The Myth of Writer's Block
Mark David Gerson

There is no writer's block. There is only fear. When we stare at the blank page, the only marks on it the beads of saltwater sweat that drip from our stressed, frustrated brows, we're not experiencing a lack of talent. We're experiencing a fear so primal it has probably been with us at least since childhood.

It has probably been with us since that first time someone judged us harshly or devalued us in some way. It happens all the time and it happens, more often than not, from a misapplication of love than from love's absence.

Whatever the past created, the present can transform. Writing can transform your pain into joy, your fear into love...into freedom.

Why do you feel blocked? Because you fear to travel where your pen would guide you. Because you're afraid to surrender to the unknown gifts that await you. Because you're afraid to let go of all the controls that bind you to a place that feels safe but isn't.

Meet Annie. Annie was in her late fifties when she attended her first class of mine. Short, with close-cropped graying hair, she had a pixie's frame but lacked a pixie's spark.

"I want to write a memoir," she announced when we introduced ourselves, each word measured, controlled. "But I have writer's block. I have had it for a decade."

She struggled with the early exercises, struggled against the controls she had placed on her self-expression. She wanted to avoid going where her pen was taking her, wanted to force her pen in other directions.

Yet as she surrendered to her pen and, perforce, to that pixie part of herself that was now, at last, finding expression, she had everyone in the room laughing so hard at the absurdities of her Earth Mother alter ego, we couldn't stop crying.

Annie, and that's not her real name, didn't have writer's block. She was afraid to embrace the part of herself that was light, funny, bizarre and uncontrollable. Once she did, her self-described block dissolved in a rush of daily writing—just for the pleasure of seeing where it would take her, just for the joy of surrender.

As Annie discovered, there is no writer's block. There is no need for a blank page to remain blank. There is no reason for words not to flow. They may not be the words you would choose from your personality mind. That's not a block. That's a choice.

Unfortunately, unless you allow the words that yearn to flow room and space, no others will likely flow. No others worth mentioning. No others that will have the power and impact and emotion and life and heart and truth of those you denied an exit visa from your heart to the page.

Let them go. Let them free. Let yourself free. When you do, there are no blocks.

So, set the tip of your pen to the page and begin. Just begin.

Don't stop. Don't think. Don't question. Don't second-guess. Don't criticize. Don't judge.

Don't stop for any reason.

Allow. Allow the pen to move you. Allow the words to flow. For they will.

It may feel difficult at first — just as it was for Annie. But that's the same difficulty you experience in childbirth. You push and you push and you push. You strain and you strain and you strain. Then, suddenly, creation is freed and flows through you.

The strain in writing is not your brain straining to find the right words. It's your brain straining to hold you back from the right words.

Don't let it stop you. Don't let anything stop you.

Write any time and at all times. Write when you would rather be sailing. Write when you would rather be cleaning your bathroom. Write when you would rather be cleaning your neighbor's bathroom. Write whenever you feel the slightest resistance to writing. That resistance is the power of your words trying to surge past the barriers you have erected against them.

Tear down the barricades, just this one time. Tear them down and let the flow surge from you. Try it once. Then try it again. And discover that the block you thought you had has not dissolved because it was never truly there. The words were always there because the words *are* always there.

All you have to do is allow them free reign over you. Give them the keys to the kingdom of your dreams, your visions, your truth. They will not let you down. They may surprise you. They may scare you. They will empower you.

About the Author

Mark David Gerson has taught writing as a creative and spiritual pursuit for more than fifteen years in the U.S. and Canada. Through classes, workshops, coaching and consulting, Mark David has guided groups and individuals to connect with their innate wisdom, open to their creative power and express themselves with ease.

Author of *The Voice of the Muse: Answering the Call to Write* and of the award-winning novel, *The MoonQuest: A True Fantasy*, Mark David has also recorded *The Voice of the Muse Companion*, a 2-CD compilation of guided meditations for writers.

Podcast Airdate:	October 18th, 2007
Podcast URL:	http://authorsaccess.com/archives/85
Author's site:	http://markdavidgerson.com http://lightlinesmedia.com

2 Genre Writing

Writing About Forensic Science and Criminal Law
Andrea Campbell

I came into forensic science through the back door. In the late 80s, I studied graphology, handwriting analysis, with Father Tony, a Catholic priest. He had a degree in psychology and used it in his services at a men's prison, a girl's private school, and with counseling couples. I didn't know it then but graphology to forensic scientists, who work with Questioned Document Evidence, is kind of like reading a horoscope. Most times they consider graphology no better than an occult reading. But it was a beginning for me.

I went on to study more handwriting analysis by taking a course given by the American College of Forensic Examiners (ACFE). I became a member and very good at the discipline. But I still was unsatisfied, and I went to community college at night for a degree in criminal justice, attended professional workshops through ACFE, and studied lots of other disciplines. Following that, I went on to study forensic art. I learned how to create a bust from a skull by studying at the Cleveland Institute of Art with someone I consider the world's best, Betty Patricia Gatliff. She was a pioneer for the industry. And soon I found myself studying comprehensive composite art (what could be called, "eyewitness drawings") with another of the world's premier artists, Karen T. Taylor.

Another professional membership ensued—The International Association for Identification (IAI)—and lots more workshops, conventions and seminars, until I became an expert in just about everybody's business from behavioral profiling to crime scene photography.

I've written books about forensic science and criminal law and am considered an expert in both areas. Currently, I'm working on a historical biography for Overlook Press and I'm very excited. It's about the world's first detective. His name is Eugène Francois Vidocq and he lived through the French Revolution, was a fugitive, a prison spy and eventually, the founder of *le Sûreté*, the world's first detective bureau.

How Much CSI Stuff is Real?

I have a Web site devoted to that phenomenon (See: www.the-CSI-effect.com) and I can tell you there are major differences between TV crime drama and real life. I often give presentations on it and the staging concepts are lively: I make an audience member suit up in PPP—personal protection equipment—and, I can assure you, it's a great deal different than what you see on Caleigh Duqueane in CSI Miami. But, you can't fault the producers. They only have forty minutes for their crime dramas; they have to make the victims and perpetrators attractive (I've never seen Miami *so clean*), but you cannot get good information from television.

Tips for Success

1. Make Internet connections with forensic science and criminal justice experts

Expert	Web site
Zeno	http://forensic.to/forensic.html
Carpenter	http://www.tncrimlaw.com/forensic
Reddy	http://www.forensicpage.com
Kruglick	http://www.bioforensics.com/kruglaw/forensic.htm
Pitsco's	http://www.askanexpert.com

If you are seeking publication you must dig further.

2. Stay abreast of local law enforcement happenings in your community by reading the police blotter and meeting the court reporter for your area's newspaper

3. Attend courtroom trials to see justice in motion—it is your Constitutional right; our Sixth Amendment right to a fair and public trial by a jury in the state in which the crime took place.

I have had jury duty three times and it is a fascinating walk through the criminal justice system. There is always talk about "getting out of jury duty" but I think that's a mistake; it should be every citizen's duty to attend. In Arkansas, you

Genre Writing

are subject to the jury pool selection in connection with your driver's license registration and voter registry.

4. **Take a criminal justice course at your regional college, university, or with an online school.** You can even get an Associate's degree online. One such course is: Online Forensic Graduate Course: http://www.forensicscience.ufl.edu/ My book, *Legal Ease: A Guide to Criminal Law, Evidence and Procedure* (Charles C. Thomas Publishers) is being used as a college/university textbook because it's extremely thorough. Check it out. There is another version of this book specifically for writers, written by me, of course—it took me two years to compile—called: *Making Crime Pay: The Writer's Guide to Criminal Law, Evidence and Procedure* (Allworth Press).

5. Keep a clipping file on important law, Supreme Court, and case files from the news.

6. Locate government sites for the best documents and statistics, and use them in your writing (your tax dollars at work).

Government/Legal Sites	URL
Forensic Science Communications	http://www.fbi.gov/hq/lab/fsc/current
National Institute for Science & Technology (they publish Tech Beat)	http://www.nist.gov/
Supreme Court & Cases (USA TODAY often features the results of yearly decisions, watch for it.)	http://www.supremecourtus.gov/
Find Law (Thomson)	http://www.findlaw.com/
Department of Justice	http://www.usdoj.gov/

7. In addition, Court TV (now TruTV) has a terrific site called Crime Library and there are case histories, interviews, and information about disciplines all online. http://www.crimelibrary.com/

8. **Don't forget these professional magazines:**
Forensic Magazine (Vicon Publishing) http://www.forensicmag.com/
Evidence Technology Magazine http://www.evidencemagazine.com/

9. **Stetson's University College of Law** publishes *The National Clearinghouse for Science, Technology and the Law* (www.ncstl.org)

10. **Look for individuals who have great Web sites about their field.** My friend, Scott Doyle has the best site featuring ballistics (the study of firearms, ammunition and its properties). (www.firearmsid.com)

11. **You can also get information sent to your e-mail box by using Google Alerts;** head to their Web page and type in your characteristics and you will get regular updates. (www.googlealert.com)

Tip: A great spider is an essential tool to getting what you need on the web. www.ixquick.com is one that provides a very thorough search box to bring you the best results without repetition.

Researching for Noir

The noir era can be a real challenge! To begin, you have to make sure that the era details are intact. For example, if you're writing about a crime that took place in the late 1940s, you need to remember that the suspect won't be read their rights (i.e. Miranda), a practice that didn't come to fruition until the 1960s. For suggestions on where to find information, use courthouse historical documents of the region; look to the National Clearing House of Science, Technology and the Law; the Supreme Court history online, law libraries locally (the same ones the prosecutors and attorneys use) and finally, look to West's journals.

If you are writing about nonfiction, whether that would be about a discipline or a historical character as in a biography, make sure that you use stories. A feature on ballistics will take on a much more interesting character when it's based on a case. For example, in my children's book *Detective Notebook: Crime Scene Science* I wrote about the case of the dancing bullet. It goes like this:

Case Story: The Dancing Bullet

Used bullets are sometimes difficult to find. FBI agents were involved in a shootout inside a house in St. Louis, Missouri. The suspect fired five shots. One bullet killed an FBI agent, and two other agents were wounded. Four bullets were recovered, but the fifth one, which had injured an agent's leg, could not be found.

A week later, the stray bullet was found at last—in the kitchen sink, under six inches of water. After uncrunching the bullet, firearms examiners at the FBI lab determined that the bullet had struck the agent's leg, gone through some indoor-outdoor carpet, hit the floor, bounced up through more carpet, struck a chair leg that deflected it up, bounced off the ceiling, and landed in the sink.

Use your connections

Professional organizations cannot be underrated as a primary source of information. Not only will you gain knowledge from their training, but you also make friends in the process. Most of the professional organizations also make it easy for students to join. If they are actively pursuing their education, there are often reduced membership fees. Meet people who are on the frontlines. Two good associations I mentioned previously are the International Association for Identification (IAI) and the American College of Forensic Examiners International (ACFEI). Also look to the American Academy for Forensic Sciences (AAFS).

Inspiration for Characterization

Once I went to an ACFEI conference in San Diego and was very excited about meeting John Douglas, FBI Special Agent (ret.) and one of the founders for the behavioral profiling unit of the FBI, and the originator of the first handbook for the Behavioral Sciences Unit (BSU) on the subject of behavioral profiling. I had thought that that was something that might interest me. But, after seeing John's slide presentation with its sexual elements, grisly crime scenes and even impaling, I decided it wasn't for me. Still there are some great books written by these amazing men such as: *Journey Into Darkness* by John Douglas, *Whoever Fights Monsters* by Robert K. Ressler & Tom Schachtman, and *Signature Killers* by Robert D. Keppel, Ph.D. with William J. Birnes. Warning: if you have weak or sensitive sensibilities, these books are not for you.

How true crime writers do what they do

I am here to tell you that it takes a special type of writer. I rely on advice from my good friend and Edgar-nominated colleague, Diane Fanning, whom I have interviewed for my author's e-newsletter, *Soup's On*. Diane says it is often difficult to gain access to certain records—that you have to be prepared to dig into lives that would rather you left them alone. They may have already been victimized and if they suffer the stigma of accusation, they lose the support of family members, their jobs, and any income they may have had due to hefty court costs and attorney fees.

So you need to know going in, disturbing lives to write true crime will test your mettle. True crime writers like Diane Fanning, Ann Rule and Corey Mitchell among others, immerse themselves in others' lives by visiting the crime scene, interviewing the principles, looking for court records, autopsies—and you will need finances for travel in order to stay in the venue, and remember, people will be reticent about talking to you. As if these problems weren't enough, often, publishers will make you sign an indemnification clause, which is typically, not author-friendly, leaving you liable and open to lawsuits in a very litigious United States. Diane's advice would also be, read, read, read in this genre.

I teach a distance-learning course on book proposal writing. The book proposal is a sales document that agents depend on in order to get an overview for a book. This cannot be a "wing-it" type sales pitch either; you will need to have your ducks all in a row before any type of query or presentation to a literary agent. You can write to me at andreascampbell@gmail.com for more info on my intense, 8-week e-classes.

Other tips

- Try to get first-person information (avoid hearsay).
- Question more than one person about each fact.
- Keep good author's notes: contact information, Web site links, phone #s
- Find criminal law cases to highlight important points.

About the Author

Andrea Campbell's latest title is *Legal Ease: A Guide to Criminal Law, Evidence and Procedure* (2nd Ed.), a reader-friendly book that is now a college law textbook published by Charles C. Thomas Publishers. She is the author of ten nonfiction books on a variety of topics, but specializes in forensic science, criminal law, and entertaining with interactive parties. Andrea is also Editor for the *Arkansas Identification News*, a quarterly that goes out to forensic scientists and law enforcement, whom all belong to the International Association for Identification. A trained forensic artist, Andrea is capable of building a bust out of clay from a skull and can do cadaver drawings and fugitive updates. A Diplomate and Fellow with the American College of Forensic Examiners International, Andrea frequently attends forensic science training conferences and blogs on several topics. Currently, she is working on a book about the world's first detective for Overlook

Press. To subscribe to her free, bi-monthly author's e-newsletter, *Soup's On*, send an e-mail to: andy1349@aim.com

Podcast Airdate:	November 1st, 2007
Podcast URL:	http://authorsaccess.com/archives/87
Author's sites:	http://womenincrimeink.blogspot.com/ http://www.the-CSI-effect.com http://www.thecsieffect.blogspot.com http://www.ehow.com (search for "AuthorAndrea" and my article list will come up)

Writing Effective Regional Fiction
Tyler R. Tichelaar

Understanding Regional Fiction

The first question a person must ask when planning to write regional fiction is "Why will anyone want to read about this region?" That was the question people asked me when I first told them I was writing a series of novels set in my native Upper Michigan. My response was, "Why do we read novels set in Paris or London or Mexico or Australia?" No one thinks twice about reading a novel set in a major city—many of us have never visited New York City, but so many novels have been set there. I know Upper Michigan is just as interesting as New York City, and by focusing on what makes the region unique, I convince my readers to agree with me. Since the regional fiction I write is set in Upper Michigan, I will use examples from my own experiences writing regional fiction, but they are examples that can easily be applied to any locale by any author.

First and foremost, a regional writer must make the region attractive to readers, whether or not they are already familiar with the place. This attraction requires a universally appealing story line mixed with an emphasis on what makes the setting distinct and interesting. Regional writing is similar in this respect to historical fiction. Historical novelists interest their readers by focusing on the way life has changed since the time they are writing about and what was distinct about that period. Setting a novel in the past is no different than setting a novel in a unique place with its own culture and customs. The past is a strange and fascinating place to us—Isn't it curious that women in 1866 wore hoopskirts? Isn't it bizarre how people wore mourning for two years when a loved one died? Isn't it mind-boggling how they could wear all those clothes during a hot summer just because modesty was more important to them than comfort? What a different world 1866 was compared to the world we know in the early twenty-first century. It is this same focus on the distinctiveness of a specific location that makes regional fiction interesting to the reader.

Regional fiction's origins are really the origins of American literature. Early American writers wanted to distinguish their work from their British counterparts. They differentiated themselves by focusing on what was unique about America. James Fenimore Cooper set his novels in the great forests of New York and brought the Native American element into his novels. Nathaniel Hawthorne used the wildness of the forest as a symbol for human temptations that interfered with the strict Puritan code. Vast and frightening forests had long since ceased to exist in Great Britain, so they were an asset to American literature's originality. The wild animals and Indians that dwelt within them were frightening to Cooper and Hawthorne's characters and exciting to their readers. The forest was used to advance the plot and illuminate the motivation of the characters. American and European audiences were fascinated because American literature was unlike anything that had come before it—its regional setting became its distinctive element.

Willa Cather took regional fiction a step further by making the region not only the setting but the protagonist, a character in the story. In my opinion, Cather is the finest American writer of regional fiction—the title of my first novel, *Iron Pioneers*, is a tribute to her masterpiece, *O Pioneers* (1913). In her own words, Cather began writing regional fiction because:

> I had searched for books telling about the beauty of the country I loved, its romance, and heroism and strength of courage of its people that had been plowed into the very furrows of its soil, and I did not find them. And so I wrote *O Pioneers!*

Finding a Readership for Regional Fiction

Willa Cather's great insight was that if she wanted to read books about the region she lived in, others would as well. Regional writers have a great advantage because their audience is right in their own backyard. And believe me, people want to read about where they live.

I always felt Upper Michigan was someplace special, but I did not realize how special until I moved away. Then I began to miss the long winters, the blankets of snow, the stunning beauty of Lake Superior, the incredible autumn colors—so many priceless aspects of the area. Living away from Upper Michigan for six years allowed me to distance myself from it, to see it afresh and come to appreciate it in new and greater ways; that appreciation helped me to depict Upper Michigan in a manner attractive not only to local readers but also to those not familiar with the area. I felt Upper Michigan, its history and its environmental influence on people, was a significant part of the American story that must be told, just as Cather wanted to record as valuable the life of Nebraska's pioneers. My readers have told me again and again I was right, that they enjoy reading about the place they know and love.

A comment I frequently receive from readers is that now they pay attention to the buildings in Marquette as they drive around the city—they try to pick out the sandstone structures built in the 1800s, and they try to imagine what the city looked like back then. My fiction helps them see the region in a new way, teaching them about the area, and encouraging them to find out more about their own family connections to the place.

I have been especially struck by local people's responses to the cover of my book *The Queen City*. The cover photograph depicts the 1949 Marquette Centennial Parade. It never fails at my book signings that someone will say to me, "That's my grandpa there in the crowd" or "My grandmother was on that float." Senior citizens buy the book because sixty years ago they stood that day watching the parade on the corner of Washington and Front Streets when they were young and all of life was before them. They are proud they were part of that significant moment in Marquette's history. Their grandchildren buy the book because Grandma is in the photograph, and so they too feel connected to that place and moment in time. Upper Michigan has shaped who they are, and to discover books written about it, written about people like themselves and their forebears, makes them feel their lives are important. These local readers are my core audience, the people who love and revere Upper Michigan as I do.

Marketing regional fiction to readers outside the area is not as easy as selling it to the locals, but it can be just as rewarding. Tourists enjoy bringing home books about the places they visit; if they enjoy the books, they tell their neighbors and friends. Furthermore, a host of expatriates from the region are homesick and longing to revisit it through the written word. I get book orders from all over the United States from people who want to read my novels so they can revisit the home of their childhood. They tell their friends—people who have never visited Upper Michigan—about my books, and soon word-of-mouth, the greatest selling point, expands my readership outside Upper Michigan.

People who have never visited Marquette enjoy my novels because they identify with the characters, with the basic themes of love and survival, with the difficult decisions the characters must make—the reasons for why we read and enjoy any good novel. Think of *Gone With the Wind*—I first saw the film and read the novel when I was only twelve years old. The impression it made upon me is immeasurable—in fact the first novel I ever wrote, although completely in my head, was a sequel to *Gone With the Wind*. The power of that novel lies in its depiction of a specific region—the Old South—and the distinct way of life in that time and place, a way of life all the more fascinating because it has vanished. The land, especially the plantation of Tara, plays a key role in the story's setting and theme. Early in the novel, Gerald O'Hara emphasizes the land when he talks to Scarlett:

> Land is the only thing in the world that amounts to anything…for 'tis the only thing in this world that lasts, and don't you be forgetting it! 'Tis the only thing worth working for, worth fighting for—worth dying for…And to anyone with a drop of Irish blood in them the land they live on is like their mother…'Twill come to you, this love of land. There's no getting away from it, if you're Irish.

This focus on the land makes *Gone With the Wind* regional fiction. That is what the novel largely boils down to. The fight for home, the Confederates' attempt to keep their land and control their property by living the lifestyle they choose. While today we are appalled by slavery, Margaret Mitchell still makes us sympathize with her plantation owning characters. The novel's themes resonate with readers because they are the very elements we all feel strongly about—the values of home, the threat of your way of life being destroyed, the determination to survive amid all odds, loving someone you cannot have—these elements have made *Gone With the Wind* one of the most successful books of all time. It was twenty years after I read the novel that I finally visited Atlanta, but I did not need to visit the South for Margaret Mitchell's world to come alive for me because she effectively depicted it through her words. Through her characters and descriptions of the events and places, I vicariously lived through the Civil War. Effective regional writing will take a reader to that place, whether it is Atlanta, Nebraska, or Upper Michigan. If a reader can identify with the characters and feel he knows the setting, then any region can be of interest.

Personifying the Region as Protagonist

Willa Cather's greatest contribution to regional fiction was that she altered the region's role from being simply the setting to becoming a character or even the protagonist of the novel. *O Pioneers!* is told in third person through the eyes of Alexandra, but the real hero of the novel—the book's dynamic character—is the land that changes from being dry windswept plains to rich, productive farm country.

The protagonist of regional fiction can be farmland, or equally, a city, county, state, lake or river. An example of depicting a region as a character occurs in my novel, *Iron Pioneers*. In the following passage, set in Marquette in the winter of 1884, Agnes Whitman has taken her children sledding. She is waiting for them to walk back up the hill when she looks out upon Lake Superior.

> The children were climbing back up the hill, but Agnes still had a couple minutes before they would reach her. She continued to look out at the half frozen, silent lake, so serene this afternoon; a flood of warm sunlight made its iced surface sparkle like diamonds. Some days that massive lake roared like a bellowing monster; some days it was cruel, as when it had taken Caleb and Madeleine. But the lake was a constant in Agnes's life, something that never failed to revive her spirits when all else came and went. The lake was always there, almost like a family member, someone to quarrel with one day, but ultimately, even if begrudgingly, to love as a familiar extension of herself, its very water flowing inside her. The lake was a part of her as was the snow, the trees, and these hills she loved so well.

This passage personifies the lake—Agnes realizes she has a relationship with Lake Superior as if it were a family member—it is a love-hate relationship—her siblings have drowned in the lake, but she cannot help but admire its beauty, and its very water feeds her body. My *Marquette Trilogy* covers a century and a half, so the human characters come and go throughout the story, but Lake Superior is a constant throughout the books, a character in itself and one that ties together the novels.

The Strength is in the Details

Writers always say the best advice about writing is to write what you know. I am from Upper Michigan; I know it well so I write about it. I could not write as effectively about London or Paris or Florida, all places I've visited but do not know as thoroughly.

A regional writer is already the expert on the area—no one is better qualified to tell the story of that place. But to make the story interesting to people from outside the area, the author needs to determine what is unique and appealing about the region. An effective way to emphasize the region's attributes is to focus on the sensory details, the way the characters experience the region through their senses. In my third novel, *Superior Heritage,* the main character, John Vandelaare, has moved home to Marquette. He wants to write about his native land, and in preparing to do so, he awakens to his own memories and sensory experiences of the region.

> As autumn approached, he became aware again of the Upper Peninsula's special environment. That year, the autumn colors appeared more brilliant than he had remembered them in past years. In the mornings, the smell of rotting leaves gripped his nostrils with a comforting feeling he had not known since childhood's countless autumn walks with [his dog] Dickens. The sunlight sparkling on orange and yellow foliage reawoke a sensitivity to light and color he had long forgotten. Soon, the snow would come with its blinding reflections, its cold, its white wonderland possibilities. One evening, he heard the harmonious honking of the Canadian geese on their southern flight. He looked up into the cold northern sky as darkness spread across it. Quickly he tried to count the V of geese—twenty-six, twenty-seven—he was not quite sure how many, but they were a miracle.
>
> His senses had reawakened to the voices of birds and the wind, the beauty of leaves and the lake, the smell of snow and an approaching rain shower, the taste of blueberries, the bitter cold biting at his cheeks and fingertips. The singular elements of this land began to mold his imagination, to heighten his senses and his aesthetic appreciation. He had been isolated from Nature's powerful influence while downstate. If he moved away again, he would not have this oneness with his environment that was so essential to his writing; he refused to let himself again forget these little details that made life so splendid. This land had shaped seven generations of his family, until it had seeped into his being, claiming him as its native son.

This passage demonstrates John's experiences with the region, and vicariously through John's senses, readers themselves sense how it feels to live in Upper Michigan. It is by highlighting what the characters experience through their senses that the region comes alive for the reader.

The power of regional fiction lies in the details, but writers should be cautious because too much attention to detail can be disastrous. I am often asked about writing dialect in regional fiction. Yes, we have a unique dialect in Upper Michigan—the Yooper accent—a mixture of the accents brought by immigrants to Upper Michigan in the nineteenth century from Scandinavia, New England, Canada and Italy. The accent is similar to that of Northern Minnesota—a slightly exaggerated version of it can be heard in the films *Escanaba in da Moonlight* and *Fargo*. Dialect and accents are amusing to listen to, but they are not fun to read. Use them sparingly and only to emphasize a point. In *Iron Pioneers*, I have characters who come to the newly founded village of Marquette from Germany and Italy. They speak broken English with an accent, but I only allow them to speak in short sentences. A long string of dialect will slow down the reader who wants to enjoy the story and the plot; readers do not want to translate dialect that is written as if it were almost another language. If you have ever tried to read the Uncle Remus stories, you will know what I mean. They are a perfect example of how not to write dialect. In their day, the stories were commended for capturing slave dialect. Today they are a nearly unreadable curiosity. Leave dialect to the linguists.

Local customs are also something you want to make interesting, but not to the point of boring the reader. It is fine to mention a single unique food from your area, such as the pasty—a meat and potato type pie brought to Upper Michigan by the Cornish miners—but if your book is set in Louisiana, details of a dozen different Cajun foods your readers are not familiar with will not interest them—pick one you want to emphasize and no more. Unless a meal or a food somehow advances the plot or enlightens us about a character, it is unnecessary information.

Do not bore readers with the details of processes. In Upper Michigan, many people are involved in the iron mining industry. In writing my novels, I spent considerable time reading about how iron ore is mined, melted down, made into pellets, transported by railroad to ore boats and then carried to the steel mills in Pittsburgh or Buffalo. I needed to understand the process of mining and shipping iron ore so my novels were accurate, but my readers do not want to know the temperature required to melt the ore, what the miners' tools looked like, or the dimensions of the ore boats. I only give my readers a taste of a character's experiences working in the iron ore industry; hopefully my readers will be interested enough to find history books to educate them further on the process, but I do not want them distracted from the story by such details.

I provide only the details necessary to develop the character or plot, to make the reader understand the psychological impact of the hard work, the feeling of the heat from a furnace, the dirt and grime of underground mining and why a character may feel frustrated working in the mine, or how working on the ore dock makes him look out over Lake Superior with a longing to travel upon it. The details are less important than how the situation affects the character. My novels have frequently been compared to those of James A. Michener, but the comparison is not always flattering because Michener tended, especially in his later novels such as *Caribbean*, to fall into writing encyclopedia articles in the middle of his stories. Remember, if details do not advance the plot or develop the character, leave them out. Broad brushstrokes will provide your regional fiction with attractive local color without putting the reader to sleep.

Write What You Know

It's been said a million times, but it's still the best advice any writer can receive: "Write what you know." If you live in the Black Hills of South Dakota, don't write a regional novel set in Florida's Everglades. Write about your hometown, your farm, the place you know the best. You are already an expert on that region—no one else is better qualified than you to tell your story. Draw on your own experiences—go back and remember all the events, memories, feelings you have experienced that are directly related to living in that place. Place your memories and feelings into the minds of your characters—if you can relate to your characters, your readers will relate to them.

Find that quiet but passionate place in your heart that is your personal romance, your own love affair with your land, your town, the lake you live upon—that is the love story that should inspire you and will make your story come alive. Then your readers will feel that the region you write about is home to them, the characters you write about become people your readers half expect to meet in the grocery store or wish they could invite over for dinner.

To allow readers to journey to another place through your words, to make them feel they have actually visited that place—that is the key to writing successful regional fiction.

About the Author

Learn more about Tyler R. Tichelaar, Ph.D. in the About the Editors section beginning on p. 215.

Podcast Airdate:	March 23rd, 2007
Podcast URL:	http://authorsaccess.com/archives/41
Author's sites:	http://MarquetteFiction.com http://SuperiorBookPromotions.com

Five Tips on Writing Romance
Sylvia Hubbard

1. **Develop strong characters.** Bring in strong characters that are real! Characters should be bigger than life because they have to be created in the reader's imagination. This doesn't mean flawless characters, just ones that the reader can identify with or understand their strengths and weaknesses. You should be able to tick off the three predominant traits of all your major characters.

2. **Stick with no more than two Points of View.** Readers don't want to go into more than knowing what the main protagonists think. The more time the reader spends inside of the head of one character, the more real the person seems to them. Similarly it is jarring to switch viewpoints so the beginning of a new chapter is the ideal place to shift, if necessary. MTV-style jump cuts don't work on paper.

3. **It's okay to cross genres when writing romance.** Romance can be a key element within the plot of a Mystery, Science Fiction, Historical, Paranormal, or almost any other type of fiction. Don't feel like you just have to live on one shelf. Romance adds an extra spice to other genres that helps pull along readers who might not be plot-detail oriented.

4. **Join writing organizations!** Networking and staying close to the business of writing keeps you grounded to your genre. Get involved in a local group or start your own. Reading and critiquing other writer's works makes you a better writer. Check your library or try www.meetup.com.

5. **Research your topics, no matter what the subject.** Make sure you know all your facts and figures about your characters and plots to give as much reality as possible. Use www.newspaperarchive.com to find out about trends and controversies. Use online maps, aerial photos, and street-level photos all available for free from Google Maps (maps.google.com).

About the Author

Detroit Native Author, Sylvia Hubbard, is a romance suspense writer of four paperback and over ten e-novels. Crowned "Cliffhanger Queen" by her readers, her stories are enjoyed all over the world. Always urban and contemporary styled, her writing is enjoyed all over the world by all nationalities. In the upcoming year, she will be featured in several anthologies and will be publishing another paperback and four more eBooks. She has a degree in Marketing/Management and minored in journalism, broadcasting (Specs Howard), drama, html programming, teaching assistant, customer service specialist, and commercial art.

Podcast Airdate:	September 7th, 2007
Podcast URL:	http://authorsaccess.com/archives/79
Author's sites:	http://sylviahubbard.com http://hubbooksliterary.homestead.com/ http://michiganliterarynetwork.com/

Paperback Writer: A Memoir of Gay and Lesbian Fiction
Victor J. Banis

Okay, that's not quite the truth, that *paperback writer* business. Over the years, I have written both hardcover books and paperback books, eBooks and short pieces, in English and various other languages; but it is primarily as a paperback writer that I am remembered, so I thought the title appropriate. And, since I am always asked in interviews how I became a paperback writer, I thought it best to start here with a little personal history.

I began writing when I was a child, five or six years old, I would guess; I remember only a story from the point of view of a blade of grass, being eaten and processed into milk in a cow's udder. As I recall, I got high marks for originality—and not a word from the Pulitzer people.

I started writing professionally in 1963. In the forty-five years since, there have been more than 150 published books, as well as numerous shorter pieces, both gay and straight, in almost every genre imaginable: fiction and nonfiction, humor, romance, mystery, fantasy, science fiction and most recently, a cookbook.

Oh, about the vagueness of that number: At last count, I have 156 books on my personal shelf, though some of those are anthologies in which I am only one of the contributors—and there are several books, perhaps a dozen, that I don't have in my collection. So, impossible to give an exact count, but "more than 150" isn't far off the mark.

Many people are surprised to learn that I did not start out writing gay material and that the number of gay books that I wrote number far fewer than the straight ones. Nonetheless, it is as a gay writer that I am most known today and, indeed, in the world of gay publishing I have become something of an icon. William Hewitt, Ph.D., labels me "One of the Grand Old Men of Gay Publishing." Thomas Long, Ph.D., has referred to me as the "godfather of modern gay fiction." Dewey Wayne Gunn calls me "one of the foundational writers of gay literature." I could go on in that vein, but the point is, yes, I can be considered an iconic figure in the history of gay publishing, a fact for which I am happy.

The earliest writing of any consequence that I did, however, was not in any sense gay, but a series of Nancy Drew-ish mysteries, written in junior high and high school. I had a crush on a classmate (Carol Peters, now Carol Cail, and a fine writer herself) and I began writing these stories featuring her as the teen detective, and she began to illustrate them, and they were very popular among our classmates—but did nothing, I am afraid, for my romantic longings, which in time I came to realize were misdirected anyway. I rather think she knew before I did, but we were good friends then and happily remain so to this day.

These stories, however, were written for my pleasure and hers, and that of our classmates. I had occasion to read one of them recently and I think after all they were probably in part to blame for the failure of my romantic longings. Still, they were a part of my youth, and the sole example I have remains very special to me.

I did not really even think about publishing any of my writings for more than a decade. In 1962, the Swiss gay publication, *Der Kreis* (published also as *Le Cercle* and *The Circle*), advertised an English language short story competition and, more on a whim than anything else, I entered a story, *Broken Record*. It came in 4th, and was published in the magazine—my first taste of the thrill of seeing one's words in print—like a drug to any potential writer, I'm afraid, and one to which he all too quickly becomes addicted.

Emergence of Paperback

In 1963, I walked into a paperback bookstore. Now, the concept of "paperback bookstore" was in itself new in 1963. Up till that time, paperback books were distributed along with magazines and newspapers, and sold mostly in drugstores, bus stations, train stations and such, but not in legitimate bookstores.

But by 1963, the socio/sexual revolution that would explode in the middle and late sixties was already beginning to stir. A handful of publishers had begun publishing and distributing sexy magazines and periodicals, and in time, they added paperback novels to their wares. As these grew in popularity, bookstores devoted to them began to open in major cities like Los Angeles and New York City.

This particular one was in Los Angeles and I stopped in as much out of curiosity as anything else. To my disappointment, there was no gay male fiction, a rarity in any book form in those days, but there were a great many lesbian books. Leafing through a few of them, I thought to myself, "Gosh, I could do this."

I bought a handful of books, seven or eight, as I recall, took them home and read them. On a whim, I sat down at the typewriter and wrote a proposed novel, and sent the manuscript off to the publisher who seemed to offer the best variety and quality.

In a matter of weeks, I had a contract with Brandon House Books, and soon thereafter, my first novel, *The Affairs of Gloria*, was published in 1964.

And very quickly ran afoul of the law. The book included a couple of very tepid (by today's standards) lesbian scenes—anathema, as it turned out, to the Federal watchdogs of the day. The U.S. Postal Service charged the book as obscene and I was indicted along with ten others, including publisher Milt Luros, on conspiracy to distribute obscene material.

Later, I came to realize that my presence in this legal wrangle was more or less incidental. Milt Luros was one of those who by this time was making money hand over fist with both sexy magazines and sexy paperbacks, and the Federal authorities wanted to put him out of business. They pursued this end aggressively by bringing about trials around the country, mostly in Midwest venues where they thought conviction would be easier to obtain than in the major metropolitan centers (ours was in Sioux City, Iowa), and by including in the indictments as many defendants as they could. Since Milt had no choice but to defend everyone, the expenses were staggering. It was thought, no doubt, that if nothing else they could drive him out of the business by means of financial ruin.

After a long and scary trial, during which I had the prospect of ten years in federal prison looming over my head, I was acquitted on a legal technicality. The other defendants were convicted, but those convictions were eventually overturned on appeal.

Ironically, though the governmental censors must have thought that indicting me would discourage me from anything further in this vein, the actual effect was quite the opposite. Had it not been for my indictment, I probably would not have pursued this path of writing any further; but I was incensed at what I considered a violation of my free speech rights as guaranteed by the U.S. Constitution. Plus, presumably annoyed that I had been acquitted, the federal authorities continued to harass me in ways subtle and not. My mail, e.g., was generally delivered open and out of the envelopes, so that I would know it had been read. Big Brother definitely had his eye on me.

So, I was determined to write something further, if only to show that I had not been intimidated. The difficulty was, I wanted to write a gay novel, and the climate was not at that time favorable for gay male fiction. To the U. S. Government, anything that showed gay or lesbian behavior in a favorable light was in and of itself obscene. In 1963, two Fresno, California publishers, Stanford Aday and Wallace de Ortega Maxey, were sentenced each to twenty-five years in prison for distribution of a line of paperbacks that included some gay novels; so there was a chill on the industry. Moreover, at that time, no one had any sense of the potential market for gay fiction. I was asked often, "Who would buy them?"

I persisted, however, and in time the manuscript for my novel, *The Why Not*, reached the desk of Earl Kemp at the then fledgling publishing house, Greenleaf Classics, in San Diego, California. Although himself heterosexual, Earl loved the manuscript and contracted for it before he had finished reading. The book was published in 1966, to excellent reviews even in the mainstream press. The sales, too, were excellent, and Earl asked if I had anything else to send him.

Up to that time, gay fiction had mostly been what I have dubbed "the sad young men" school of writing. With rare exceptions, gay protagonists had to die in the end or, less often, be cured and converted to heterosexuality. By this time, however, I had become a gay activist. I wanted to write something different, something happy and positive.

I wrote *The Man From C.A.M.P.*, with gay undercover agent Jackie Holmes who, so far as I know, was the first protagonist in a gay novel to be openly gay and proud of it—a jumping off point for the whole concept of gay pride. The book was humorous, an obvious spoof of the James Bond books and movies, and the television series, *The Man From U.N.C.L.E.*; and it had a happy ending.

Forging a New Genre

Different though it was, Earl Kemp gamely published this as well. It created nothing short of a sensation, and spawned eight sequels—the first gay mystery series, as it happened. And it spawned, as well, an entire new style of gay fiction, with heroes of all sorts in every genre, happy endings as well as sad. No more skulking about in the "twilight shadows," as those earlier books so often put it.

The demand for this new style of gay writing was so great that for several years I not only turned out dozens of my own books, but I trained other writers as well and acted as a *de facto* agent for them. There was a joke in the industry then that the gay publishing revolution had mostly occurred at my kitchen table, and there was more than a grain of truth in that. It was a rare afternoon that did not see several of us consulting around that table.

So, I had become a celebrity of sorts in this field, and for a time, this new field of gay publishing flourished. Gays took with great enthusiasm to these new images of themselves. Some historians say it was this sudden appearance of shelves upon shelves of these gay paperback novels that first created a sense of community among gay men, and fostered the spirit that eventually led to the uprising at Stonewall, and the whole gay liberation movement. I think they are probably right.

Eventually, of course, the newness of having these books available to us began to wear off. Sales dropped, and the publishers began to succumb to the endless persecution by the governmental agencies. Standard were lowered, the quality of the writing suffered, sex became the raison d'être of the genre. After a few years I more or less dropped out of gay publishing, and focused once again on my straight writings.

By the early eighties, I was writing straight fiction for hardcover New York publishing houses, with some success and to critical acclaim. Unfortunately, I was having far less fun. I had a clash with one of my publishers, St. Martin's Press—mostly, a breakdown in communications.

I signed up with another publisher, Arbor House, and here too I had a particularly unpleasant experience. The editor did a major rewrite of my novel, *San Antone*. I did not learn of this until the book was in galleys, too late to make extensive corrections, but I begged him to let me at least rewrite three of his scenes which I thought were embarrassingly bad. The book was published, unfortunately, as he had written it, and the very first review, in *Kirkus Reviews*, ridiculed one of those very scenes I had begged him to let me change. I was devastated. What he had done was probably illegal, and certainly immoral, but I had not the resources to take on the Hearst Corporation. I was frustrated and unhappy—and, frankly burned out.

Taking Time Out

The result of all this was that I took a very nearly twenty year hiatus from writing for publication. I continued to write for my own pleasure, sketches, character studies, and such, but no novels, no complete stories. And no attempt to see anything published.

It was not, in fact, until 2007, that I again published a novel, *Avalon*, a straight love story; and soon after, *Longhorns*, a gay cowboy novel. Since then, *The Astral: Till The Day I Die* (straight); *Drag Thing* (hmm, kind of mixed, really); and *The Pot Thickens* (a cookbook, which I think you'd have to categorize as neutral); plus, about two dozen of my older books have been reissued in the past two years.

Still, there you are, as I said earlier, my straight writing far outweighs the gay material, but it is as a gay pioneer that I am mostly known today. *Longhorns* (Running Press) has been followed by a number of other gay novels, most recently

Lola Dances and *Deadly Nightshade*, both from MLR Press, and *Angel Land*, from Regal Crest. And of course I have done quite a few short stories as well, in both categories.

The truth is, however, I no longer give much thought to the gay or straight orientation when I write today, and frankly, I don't much like labels anyway. I like to think of myself simply as a writer, a teller of tales. I am somewhat inclined to think those labels do a disservice to one's writing, and perhaps to readers as well. As an example, my short story, *If Love Were All* (in the anthology, *Hard Working Men*, MLR Press) is about two damaged individuals trying to make a connection, which seems to me to be a universal theme. But because the two individuals are male, I am resigned to the fact that it will be considered (and dismissed by some) as gay fiction. Which it to say, there are probably many who would enjoy reading it and perhaps bring something away from it, who will never come across it because they do not investigate or read gay fiction. I think some of them may be the poorer for this failure.

As I say, though, I just don't much worry about that kind of categorization. I've been doing this so long, I more or less do it on automatic pilot, as it were. I let the stories come to me—or, more accurately, the characters come to me, and they dictate genre and style and orientation. But, I don't really sit down with the intention to write a gay or a straight novel.

Contemporary Trends in Erotica

The same is true of erotic content, which is often linked to gay fiction. Of course, since those early books in the sixties were published by houses that specialized in sexy material, there was often (though not always) a strong erotic element—more so in the realm of gay male fiction than in the lesbian material. My friend Ann Bannon, who is truly the queen of lesbian fiction, discussed this at a book event a few years ago. Many of the early lesbian novels were in fact written by men, for men, and those stories went from orgasm to orgasm, whereas in the books written by women, romance was more important.

There is a parallel to this in today's male fiction. There is a hot new trend of male to male (M/M) fiction written by heterosexual women for heterosexual women who happen to enjoy reading about two men together. In these woman-oriented stories, the emphasis is on romance rather than the erotic element that dominates in much gay fiction written by men for men.

It was to some extent the erotic element in gay male fiction that brought the genre perilously close to extinction. Historically, the unceasing campaign of the federal authorities did succeed in driving those early publishers out of the business, but with an opposite effect to what they must have intended. The businesses were mostly taken over by the Mafia, and abandoned all pretenses of good fiction, becoming for the most part just hard core erotica. At the same time, detecting the scent of money on the wind, the New York publishing houses got on the gay bandwagon, but they went in the opposite direction, publishing "literary" works with virtually no sexual element in them. Not only did the characters in these novels not have sexual relations, they often read as if the characters did not even have genitalia. In too many of these novels the effect was very "ho-hum."

Which proved to be unattractive to the gay male reader, who was left without anything much to read that would offer him both a good story and the sexual content he wanted. Large numbers of gay men stopped buying books, or they bought erotica and mostly shunned the high tone offerings from the major houses. Only recently have a few publishers begun to bridge that gap, and more gay men are reading today than in the last couple of decades; but the numbers tell the story: in the sixties, sales of 50,000 or even 100,000 copies of a gay novel were commonplace. Several of mine sold in the 150,000 range. Today, 4,000 copies is a best seller.

Overcoming Writer's Block

I am asked often about writer's block, and about my writing techniques and habits. Obviously with my output, writer's block has never been much of a problem. That "vacation" I took was not about my inability to write, but rather my disinterest at the time in working with publishers and editors. Once stung...

As for habits, I early on trained myself to a business-like discipline. From the first, I treated my writing as a job. I had a partner in those days and he would go off in the morning to his office at the bank and I would sit myself down at the typewriter and write until lunch break, and then back to work until the cocktail hour. Most of those old gay paperbacks that I did were written in four, maybe five days, but they were long days of continuous writing.

Since I've mentioned the cocktail hour, I should mention as an aside that I strongly advise writers against having a drink while they write. Alcoholism has been called "the writer's disease." A drink does indeed loosen the inhibitions that can cause writer's block, and allow ideas to flow more freely. Alas, over time, it takes more and more of the juice to get the juices flowing, and eventually, the only idea one can focus on is having another drink. So, always, my writing day ended with the cocktails.

Writing a novel in four or five days, however, means writing mostly off the top of the head—not a lot of editing or rewrite. I am surprised, indeed, when I read some of those old works, to see how well they read, all things considered.

Later, as I moved into the straight romance genre, still paperbacks, but for major New York publishing houses and for a bit more money, I began to take my writing more seriously, and spent more time on each book, writing and rewriting. Eventually, I moved into the realm of hardcover books, and spent even more time on each effort. *This Splendid Earth*, for instance, took me nearly a year and a half in research, and six months to write.

Still today I tend to sit down each morning first thing and get my writing done, whether it's a page or ten pages, before I turn my attention to anything else. *Longhorns,* for instance, was written in just two weeks, but it was two weeks of total immersion, in which I was completely taken over by the story and, especially, the characters. There is a cattle stampede in that novel, and I tell people of the night about halfway through the book when I was awakened by a lightning storm and sat up in bed, saying, "Oh, no, the cattle will stampede." Of course, I don't have any cattle. So, the point is, I was totally living in the time frame and locale of the novel.

But, that early discipline has paid off for me many times over. Other writers often ask how I can turn out so much material. The answer I give them is always the same: I write.

As to technique, as I said earlier, most of what I write today I do on an unconscious level, and I mostly try to get me out of the way. It's much like learning to drive a car. When you first start out, you consciously have to think about the various things you need to do with brakes, clutch, gears, etc. After a while, though, that all becomes automatic and you just drive without thinking about it.

So, I tell writers that it is important to learn the rules first. Grammar and spelling, of course, and the elements of plotting and pacing and characterization, until you reach the point where you no longer have to think about those things. Someone once asked Picasso why he was so successful when other abstract artists weren't and he replied that it was because he had learned to draw first. Once you have mastered the rules of your craft, then you are free to bend them or break them as you wish, but the point is, you no longer consciously have to think about them.

So, today, I give very little thought to the technical questions—point of view, person, or what have you, which I know many writers agonize over. I do work from time to time with other writers, however, beginning writers, and then I have to go back and think about technique, which is good for me, because it's sort of a refresher course in the basics. Unlike old dogs, old writers can continue to learn. I have grave doubts that I will ever reach the stage where I know everything there is to know about writing. Mostly, I continue to discover anew how little I really do know.

Working with Editors

I was lucky, I think, in starting when I did, just as that whole field of gay fiction was ready to explode. And lucky, too, in working with some wonderful editors. I was pretty much self-taught, but at every major step up in my career I was influenced by an editor who took an interest in me and my work. Earl Kemp, for one, and he and I are still good friends after all this time. Gil Porter, who was with Sherbourne Press, was a friend and mentor as well, and I was fortunate to work with Hope Dellon at St. Martin's Press. More recently I have worked with editors like Lori L. Lake, with Regal Crest; Maura Anderson and Kris Jacen at MLR; and Anne Stuessy at Sniplits, and consider all of them friends, whose input has greatly improved my writing. I like working with a good editor and am always open to suggestions.

On the other hand, I don't take a lot of guff from editors. I don't like editors who try to tell me how to write a book or want it written in their words rather than mine. Once I've rewritten the story, including your suggestions where I find them appropriate, that's pretty much it—my story. I'm not going to rewrite it into your story. So long as it is my name on the cover, the words have to be mine and I must approve any changes. If you are not happy, you always have the option of turning the manuscript down. You don't have the option of rewriting it yourself.

I can afford to take that attitude, of course, where a beginning writer might be reluctant to do so. When I came back to writing a few years ago, I promised myself I would henceforth write what I wanted to write, when and how I wanted to write it, and that is pretty much how it has been. I hardly need another book added to my resume.

Anyway, I have no problem getting books or stories placed, so if someone doesn't want it as it is, there is generally someone else who will. I have no particular desire to be on the *New York Times* bestseller list, or make millions of dollars.

Today, I write primarily for my own satisfaction. I tell people that I am drunk on the magic. I'm like an old racehorse eager to get into the box. I get up in the morning, read the paper and do my crossword puzzle, and by the time I'm halfway through a bowl of cereal I'm gobbling it down so I can get to the word processor. The point is, I am doing what I love more than anything else, and that is a terrific place to be in life.

The Magic Carpet

Now, writers are always asking me for advice, so here is the number one piece of advice I offer writers at every opportunity: Have Fun! Most people live one life and few of them do more than barely scratch the surface of that.

But writing is a magic carpet. You can be and do anything you like. You can be a courtesan, a pirate, an astronaut, a cowboy; not just a villain or a hero, but *both* the villain and the hero. You can live a hundred, a thousand different lives.

And I tell them, too—and this is ever so important—if you aren't living those lives while you are writing them, you aren't doing it right. Don't just write about someone riding his horse across the prairie, get in the saddle and go a-gallop.

That is the magic carpet, and the most important element of all in your writing—without it, you can only plod, with it, you can soar: your imagination.

Writing is all about setting it free. Your imagination, and the reader's.

About the Author

Victor J. Banis is the critically acclaimed author of more than 150 published books and numerous shorter pieces, both gay and straight oriented, in almost every genre: fiction and nonfiction, humor, mystery, romance, fantasy, sci-fi and even, recently, a cookbook.

Podcast Airdate:	March 6th, 2008
Podcast URL:	http://authorsaccess.com/archives/99
Author's sites:	http://www.vjbanis.com

3 Children's Books

Rules for Writing Children's Literature
Lila Guzman

Writing for children looks easy. After all, a picture book is only thirty-two pages long. How hard could it be to crank out something that size?

Writing for children requires special skills and presents unique challenges. A middle-grade novel comes in at 25,000 words while Young Adult (YA) novels range from 40,000–60,000 words (about 250 double spaced pages). That's roughly half the size of an adult novel, but the writer has to give young readers the same thing older ones want: a great story with interesting characters. In a children's book, every word counts. Material must be condensed and conveyed in a short space whereas an adult novel has some rambling room. A juvenile biography, for example, tells a person's life story in about 20,000 words.

Know Your Market

The five most common divisions of children's literature are:

Book Format	Age / Developmental Range
Picture Books	Roughly, Birth to Kindergarten (0 – 5)
Easy Readers (	Kindergarten through Second Grade (5 – 7)
Chapter Books	When the child is mature enough to read a book divided into chapters
Middle Grade Novels	Ages 8-12
YA Novels	Ages 11-14. After the age of 15 or so, young adults usually read adult-level books.)

Children and young adults like to read about characters that are slightly older than they are. If the main character is thirteen, the target audience is probably nine to twelve years old.

Children's literature consists of the same genres as adult writing, except for erotica and pornography. Some genres tend to be more popular with young people than others. Fantasy and science fiction are favorites. Historicals are not, although librarians and teachers tend to be fond of them.

An adult-level book has one intended audience: adults. Children's books must appeal to both adults *and* children. Before a book gets into a child's hands, the author must first navigate through a sea of adults:

- Literary Agents
- Editors
- Librarians
- Teachers
- Book Reviewers
- Book Store Managers
- Book Distributors
- Other adults (curriculum specialists, book festival coordinators, etc.)

What is the children's market like? Right now, it is red-hot. Some authors are getting six-figure advances. J.K. Rowling is richer than the Queen of England.

The market has tightened for adult authors. To get into the big publishing houses, a writer must have an agent. Publishers of children's books often take unsolicited manuscripts, so a literary agent is not a "must have."

What subjects interest young readers? That depends on the age group. For a young adult audience, the following are hot topics: sports, steroids, cheerleaders, vampires, the prom, teen pregnancy, drugs, cutting, excessive dieting, and, of course, sex. Middle grade novels are usually devoid of sex because girls are still considered "yucky" and girls often think boys are "dumb."

Some topics are always hot: horror, blood, gore, elves, witches, warlocks, the magical. Young people can't seem to get enough of vampires. Darren Shan, Stephanie Meyers, and Cynthia Leitich Smith have built careers on these bloodsuckers.

Boys tend to like action, but, generally speaking, they don't like to read. Girls are fond of romance, relationships, and horses. Many publishers are looking for action-adventure books for boys with a fast-paced plot. Girls will read "boy" books but most boys won't read "girl" books.

Today's children know all the latest technology. They use cell phones, text each other using a unique language ("R U there?"), download music to MP3 players, and send instant messages. In some ways, children today are like yesterday's. *Harry Potter* and *The Wizard of Oz* are separated by decades, yet they both involve wizards and magic. The mantra of many literary agents and editors is: "We want more of same, only different."

Like adult-level writing, books are either fiction or nonfiction. The nonfiction market is enormous, with great earning potential. Publishers constantly need books about current events, one of the driving forces behind children's nonfiction. When a new administration comes into office, for example, a new line of biographies opens up.

There tends to be more money in the nonfiction market, but fiction gives the writer more freedom and a greater chance to be creative. However, fiction is a harder market to break into.

Rules When Writing for Children

1. Kill the parents. This sounds harsh, but the writer needs to get them out of the way somehow. That is why many children's books have orphans as main characters. If adults are present, they will intrude or give advice. The main character needs to solve problems by himself.

2. Avoid being condescending. Don't write "down" to children. They are small, not stupid.

3. Have frequent hooks and cliffhangers. Don't give the child a reason to put the book down. This means the story should entertain and compel them to turn the page to find out what happens next.

4. Avoid flashbacks. They can confuse the reader.

5. Don't preach. Presenting a moral or a lesson is perfectly acceptable. Just don't make it obvious. *Kichi in Jungle Jeopardy* is about respecting the environment and using only what you need. The readers see the lesson through the eyes of the protagonist, because preaching to children will turn them off.

6. Action! Action! Action! Chapters in young adult novels are often about three to five pages each. This keeps the story moving.

7. Keep it simple. Books are in competition with video games, iPods, and other fun activities.

8. Vocabulary. Stretch their word knowledge without completely befuddling them. Write the story. Then think about vocabulary. If a word like "consternation" pops up, a smaller word might work better. In historicals, children will catch meanings in context. For example: "The blacksmith sweated as he bent over the anvil and hammered a piece of metal into a horseshoe."

9. Voice. What "voice" will the main character use? A child from Massachusetts may not use the same word choice or have the same accent as a child from Texas.

Pros and Cons of Writing for Children

Are there disadvantages to writing for this age group? Yes. Children's writers lose their audience for three months during summer vacation, but the other nine months, children are easy to track down. Publishers take the school cycle into account. While adult-level authors get three or four months of promotion before the publisher moves to the next book, children's books have a longer shelf life. A children's book may catch fire months and months after publication. *Lorenzo's Secret Mission*, published in 2001, was a 2005 finalist for the Golden Spur.

Best of all, school librarians will pay for author visits. The honorarium varies (around $300 for a half day or $500 for a full day.) How many books would an adult author have to sell to make $300 in royalties in one day?

What is the best part about writing for children? Getting an email from a young reader. It's a real ego boost to have a child say, "I love your book! When is the next one coming out?"

It doesn't get any better than that.

For more information about writing for children, visit www.scbwi.org, the Web site of the Society of Children's Book Writers and Illustrators. Most publishers have submission guidelines on their Web sites.

About the Author

Lila Guzman was born in Kentucky and majored in Spanish and French at Western Kentucky University. For three years, she taught foreign language exploratories in the 7th-8th grade and then decided to do her Ph.D in Spanish at the University of Kentucky. In 1980, she joined the Navy and attended Officer Candidate School. She was assigned to the Defense Language Institute (DLI) in

Monterey, California where she taught native-language instructors how to teach their own language.

At DLI, she met Army Lt. Rick Guzman, who was studying French at the time. He later became her husband, co-author, and the person who dragged her into the writing business. Rick is now an attorney in private practice. We've been married for twenty-seven years and have three grown children.

Lila primarily writes children's fiction and non-fiction in addition to young adult novels. She often teaches workshops on various aspects of writing. Her email address is lorenzo1776@yahoo.com.

Podcast Airdate:	January 25th, 2007
Podcast URL:	http://authorsaccess.com/archives/30
Author's site:	www.lilaguzman.com

Publishing a Children's Book?
Better Get a Child's Opinion First
Tyler R. Tichelaar

When writing a children's book, the most important element to consider is your audience. Many first time authors never get kids involved in creating their manuscript—they will write a story and publish a book without a child even seeing it. Then they are astonished when they receive negative reviews from children. While parents, teachers, and librarians may like the book and purchase it, if a young reader does not enjoy the book, there will be no repeat or positive word-of-mouth sales.

Writing a children's book is not a solitary activity. In fact, many of the greatest children's books were not originally intended to be books but simply stories told to children. Lewis Carroll's *Alice in Wonderland* began with stories he told to a little girl named Alice and her friends. L. Frank Baum reportedly told his children and their friends many stories, and it was their reaction to his stories with expressions of "oh's and ah's" that inspired the name of Oz, and so *The Wonderful Wizard of Oz* was born. Without the children's reactions, Carroll and Baum would not have realized they were on to something or have written books that have delighted generations of children.

The Reader Views Kids page (www.readerviewskids.com) is full of reviews by children. The site is family-friendly and an excellent place to find books that are sure to appeal to children because children are having their own say about what they like. The value of children reviewers for authors is an honest opinion and for parents and teachers a reliable recommendation of what children will enjoy.

Children can be very discerning readers, and they can be brutally honest. They are eager to pick up on every typo or grammatical error and any place where the logic breaks down. We all know children are infamous for asking "Why?" So when they ask, "Why did that character do such and such?" the author had better have an answer. No writer wants holes found in his storyline, which is why a smart author will ask children's advice before the manuscript goes to a publisher.

Here are a few examples of complaints children have had about books they have reviewed. These are clues for what authors should watch for and avoid.

One thirteen-year old reader complained about lack of logic in a book. The example she gave referred to a boy standing over a girl whose eyes were shut. The girl opened her eyes when she realized the boy was standing over her. The thirteen-year old reviewer asked how the girl knew the boy was there if her eyes were closed.

We have also received negative comments about books being too preachy. Children want to be entertained, not forced to read something that's "good for them." One of the worst complaints a child reviewer will give is "This is something my mother would want me to read."

Children also don't want the same-old same-old. We often get complaints about how a book is too much like another recently popular children's book. Kids appreciate originality.

One of our ten-year old reviewers resigned because she had to review four books in a row she thought were bad. Here are just a few more negative comments we have received from our child reviewers:

> "I just don't get it." – This was a book that got rave reviews from adults and teachers.
>
> "We get a lot of non-fiction/self-help type of books to read for school so I want to read fantasy."
>
> "The illustrations don't look good. It's hard to tell what the pictures are."
>
> "I was shocked that the book said it was for twelve-year olds. Some parts are for a bit more mature audiences."
>
> "To me, X and Y fall in love unrealistically and too quickly. I love the author's other heroines but X lacked depth and the story was over too fast for me really to get to know her."
>
> "Plot-wise, I had a few issues. Sometimes, I felt that there was just too much going on at once and so many subplots that they were rather hard to keep track of."
>
> "I would like to see the grammar and spelling mistakes fixed."
>
> "It is confusing and the sequences are poorly-written. Some books should just have an ending."

Of course, we get positive responses as well. When kids love a book, they show their appreciation:

> "…a hilarious book which had me laughing from cover to cover."

> "Reading this book was like doing all the things the children did right along with them…was a lot of fun to read and was like being in another world."
>
> "Once you pick up this book, you will really want to keep reading it. I hope you will like this book as much as I did."

Authors can receive such positive responses if they get feedback from children before their books are published. I asked two authors whose books have been positively reviewed by Reader Views for Kids how they involved children in writing their books.

Debbie Glade, author of *The Travel Adventures of Lilly P. Badilly: Costa Rica* wrote and illustrated her picture book about a millipede who travels to Costa Rica. She included a read-along CD with the book. Debbie, also a mother, knew she needed to have children enjoy the book she was writing. Before beginning, she started asking children what they liked:

> I made sure to talk to kids of several ages about their book likes and dislikes even before I wrote the story," says Debbie. "I had children read different drafts plus look at the illustrations, and I learned something new from readers every time. Children see the world from completely different perspectives than adults, so essentially I had to be able to think like a child in order to write a book kids will love. The most valuable insight I received was from avid readers who were a few years older than my target audience.

One change Debbie made was to delete a detail about Lilly. "Kid reviewers all had different opinions on the age the main character should be," says Debbie.

> I originally had Lilly's age in the book as 10, then changed it to 12. In the end I just left her age out, letting the readers imagine Lilly's age as they wish. One thing I did learn for sure is that readers always want to read about someone a bit other than they are, and Lilly definitely fulfilled that wish.

The children also helped Debbie in illustrating the book. Debbie created all the illustrations on her own, using watercolor pencils and pan watercolors and then outlined many figures with ink so they would stand out. Despite her artistic talents, Debbie still asked for children's feedback. "I completely redid the illustration of Lilly on her bed when she was talking about her fears because several kids said the picture I painted was way too dark and scary. I changed the color of the background, which was formerly a deep red/pink, and lightened Lilly up a little bit. But I kept the four fears the same."

Perhaps most importantly, Debbie made a point of reading the book out loud to children and watching their reactions. "I watched kids as they were listening to see their emotions and facial expressions and to make sure they were not losing interest." Reading out loud gave Debbie a good indication of what was working in the story and what parts still needed work.

When the book was published, Debbie sent a copy to Reader Views for Kids. Our seven-year old reviewer, Matthew Feliciano, commented "I liked *The Travel Adventures of Lilly P. Badilly: Costa Rica* a lot. It was educational and showed me new things about a new country…this book was really good."

When I interviewed Debbie, I asked Matthew to join me. Matthew surprised Debbie Glade with a question she had never thought about. In the book, Lilly goes to Costa Rica with her grandparents. The book never mentions Lilly's parents. Matthew asked Debbie, "Where were Lilly's parents and why didn't they go on the trip too?" Debbie kept her cool by replying, "That is a great mystery that will be revealed some time in the future." Later, Debbie admitted to me, "I actually had never thought about anyone asking me what happened to Lilly's parents. When Matthew asked me about it, I was both surprised and impressed by his curiosity. It left me with a great opportunity to resolve the mystery in a future book."

Melissa Strangway also knows the value of having children read her manuscripts. Her novel *56 Water Street* tells the story of two children who solve a mystery concerning an old house the children can see but which is invisible to everyone else. Again, seven-year old Matthew Feliciano was asked to review the book. He commented, "I couldn't put the book down and it kept me wanting more. The kids were just like any other kids and were curious about this house. It made it easy to read a story with regular kids doing interesting things."

Matthew identified with the characters because they were regular kids like him. Melissa was able to make sure her kid readers would identify with her main characters, Derek and Ravine, because she got children's comments before she published the novel.

Melissa told me she decided to get children's advice as the result of her friend, David, asking her why she wrote. She replied that she wrote to share stories with children. He challenged her then to show children her writing, and she decided to take his advice.

The process began for Melissa when she brought the manuscript of *56 Water*

Street to her son's school for an evaluation. "The principal handed it out to five students. It was the hardest thing I had to do," says Melissa, "but the wisest. Children are honest, brutally honest, which is what you need when sharing your story with them. Plus, who better to evaluate a children's story, other than a child? After you get over the fear of having them read it, you realize it's the best thing you can do. After all, the worst that can happen is they say they don't like it. Which means heading back to the computer and making it a better story."

It turns out the students did like Melissa's book. "The students sat down with me after they read it and gave me great feedback," Melissa recalls. "Some constructive criticism and some praise. Everything that was very valuable in making *56 Water Street* the best it could be. One suggestion was to make sure that even though Ravine and Derek are experiencing the same things, almost at the same times, it was important to make sure their personalities were completely different."

While Melissa says she benefited from the criticism she received from children, she feels they also benefited from the process. "The children in turn always seem pleased when I ask for their opinions and input. And why not? The story is for them."

In getting feedback, authors can begin with their own children, their children's friends, or their nephews and nieces. Children love to be read to. Visiting a classroom to read the story and have children respond to it is a great way to get responses from the potential audience and make children feel important as well.

Authors can also seek out children's evaluations. For manuscript evaluations, Reader Views sends children's stories to both an adult and a child reader. And of course, Reader Views will assign a child reviewer if a book is already published.

Children should be included in the process and joy of writing. It helps them become better analytical thinkers, and it helps an author prepare a book children will enjoy for a long time to come. If you're writing a children's book, go find your audience. They're ready to welcome you and give you all the help you need.

About the Author

Learn more about Tyler R. Tichelaar, Ph.D. in the About the Editors section beginning on p. 215.

4   Editing Your Work

Editing Tips for Authors
Kenneth J. M. MacLean

Are you an author who wants to get published?

Whether you will market your book independently, or sign a standard publishing contract, you need a polished manuscript that will interest your readers and clients. Last year, there were over 400,000 new titles published in the United States alone, and that doesn't count those that were submitted and rejected. Professional publishing houses receive dozens of manuscripts every day, and most of them get tossed into the trash. Why? Because a professional editor can tell almost at a glance whether your book is worth going beyond page one.

Before you even think about book cover designs, press releases, and marketing, you need to get your content up to snuff.

Here are some valuable tips that will enable your book to pass muster and see the light of day, and save you hundreds of dollars in editing costs.

Line Editing vs. Content Editing

First of all, you have to know the difference between line editing and content editing. If your manuscript is poorly written, with many grammatical and syntactical errors, and poor sentence structure, your editor may have to rewrite almost every sentence. This is called substantive editing, and will cost you, on average, $5 per double-spaced page, or up to five cents per word. That's a lot of money![4] If you think the cost is unreasonable, consider what your poor editor is going through! A good editor will slave over your prose, trying to keep your writing voice and your message intact, while at the same time, attempting to make your prose smooth, coherent, and interesting to the reader. That's a big job. I have spent over half an hour on just one page of a manuscript!

---

[4] Fee structures for professional editors may vary widely.

A line edit is for manuscripts in good shape. An editor is looking for, inter alia, grammar and punctuation errors, formatting, syntax, and repetitive writing styles, and will correct these and make suggestions. A line edit may cost you $10 – $30 for every 1,000 words.

A poorly written manuscript of 10,000 words may cost you several hundreds, to well over a thousand dollars for a substantive edit, whereas a well-written document may run you $300 or less.

Therefore, if you want to save yourself a bundle *and* make sure that your unique writing voice (and your story) remains intact, take some time to do the following:

1. A Hard and Fast Rule of Thumb: The Rule of Verbalization. Read your prose out loud! Or, even better, have someone else read it out loud.

Wherever you pause or stop, there is a problem, either with grammar, sentence structure, punctuation, dry or stilted dialogue, or plot inconsistencies. This rule is valid almost without exception. If you do nothing else, follow the Rule of Verbalization and you will catch at least 50% of the errors within your manuscript, right off the bat.

2. Think of your reader when writing your sentences! Personally, I never write unless I am feeling inspired. That old saw about writing every day even if you don't feel like it is garbage, in my opinion. Who wants to write (or read) insipid, trite, colorless prose? Not me, and certainly not your readers! Inspired writing will not always be syntactically and grammatically correct, but it will be exciting, and express your creative voice.

3. Avoid re-use of the same word in the same sentence or adjacent sentences. Use your thesaurus and make your language interesting and exciting! Continuing to use the same verb, the same tense, the same voice, is guaranteed to put your readers to sleep.

Example: "First she went to the gym, then she went over to her friend's house, and then she and her friend went out to dinner."

How DULL is that?

How about: "Dianne drove to the gym for a brisk half-hour workout and a shower. She arrived at her friend's house hungry and refreshed, and they enjoyed a fine meal and a chat at Mateo's, their favorite restaurant in the city's Italian quarter."

You don't have to be Ernest Hemingway to write good prose.

4. Avoid the use of similar sentence structure. *Every* writer has a writing style; what I'm talking about is use of the same writing pattern over and over again. This is also guaranteed to put your readers to sleep!

Example: "From any perspective, a focus on the standardization of an architecture that provides a standard and evolving foundation will be applied, utilizing existing technology platforms in a united manner."

How about: A focus on the standardization of an architecture that provides an evolving foundation will be applied, utilizing existing technology platforms in a united manner.

Technical language, especially, needn't be so mind–numbingly dull.

Another example: I edited a wonderful book by a Ph.D. with the same sentence structure throughout the book. He would begin with an introductory idea; the body of the sentence would run on, with overuse of commas and dashes, and then conclude. Each sentence was in the passive voice, and he'd make two or three points in every sentence instead of one. I swear, by the end of Chapter One I was sleepy AND angry.

Bad writing obscures good content.

5. Write Mindfully: Pay attention to grammar and the proper use of words. Get a copy of the *Chicago Manual of Style* and study it! Refer to it if you have any questions. For example, there are so-called writing "rules" that you don't always have to follow robotically. One of the most famous rules is that of never ending sentences with prepositions. This is more of a superstition than anything else. Winston Churchill famously said, "This is the sort of arrant pedantry up with which I shall not put." You end sentences with prepositions or not, depending upon how natural it sounds. "Those are the guidelines an author should adhere to" might sound better like this: "Those are the guidelines to which an author should adhere"

Another writing superstition is the false dictum that you should never begin sentences with conjunctions like But or Because.

It depends on your audience. If you are writing for professionals, use professional language. If you are writing Harlequin romances, you probably don't want to sound so stiff.

6. Avoid wordiness! If you want to say something, think about what you are writing before you write it down! And certainly before you send your manuscript to the publisher.

Example: The changes to business processes should not affect the technical architecture, but rather are to be applied only at the highest level, which is the business architecture and less often so too, the information architecture.

How about: The changes to business processes should be applied only at the highest level, and not affect the technical architecture.

Example from a book that I recently edited in which I had to do a structural edit:

"Going well beyond genetics and family, which we may attribute to some of the inherent traits that influence consciousness, largely, our consciousness is formed through unconscious conditioning and is greatly influenced by our early upbringing."

My editing comments: I'm not sure what you are trying to say here — are you?

If you were an editor, how would you make that sentence comprehensible?

Focus and direct your thoughts as much as possible into trenchant and pithy sentences that say a lot with as few words as necessary. Use sentences to present your ideas logically in a linear format. A book is linear, there's no getting around that!

7. In fiction, try to show it, and not say it.

Narration *is* valuable for:

- Setting up a scene. If the character is entering a room and that room is important in the story, telling the reader what is in the room and how it looks can be very helpful. You don't have to spend a lot of time at this.
- Describing what is going on in the character's heads, and supporting your characters. One of the most difficult (for me) aspects of fiction writing is describing how a character is thinking and feeling. When this is done well, it can give the reader, in a few sentences, a very good idea of the character. When it is poorly done, or not at all, your characters are cardboard cut-outs.

Here's a good example of narrative that has one character describing another:

> As Mr. Rivenhall's notion of making himself agreeable in company was to treat with cold civility anyone for whom he felt no particular liking; and as his graces—far from winning—included a

trick of staring out of countenance those whose pretensions he deprecated, and of uttering blighting comments, which put an abrupt end to social intercourse, he stood in far greater danger (Mr. Wychbold said) of being mistaken for a yahoo."[5]

Although you need narrative to describe scenes and characters, readers and editors alike always prefer clever dialogue!

Example: Here is the same author describing a scene between the young Viscount Sherringham, and his uncle, Mr. Paulett:[6]

"You will allow, dear boy, that there is scarcely an extravagant folly you have not committed since you came of age."

"No, I won't," retorted the Viscount. "Dash it, a man can't be on the Town without kicking up a lark or so every now and then!"

"Anthony, can you tell your Mother that there is not a—a Creature (for I cannot bring myself to call her a Female!) with whom you are not ashamed to be seen in the most public of places? Hanging upon your arm, and caressing you in a manner which fills me with repugnance?"

"No, I can't," replied the Viscount. "But I'd give a monkey to know who told you about that little ladybird!"

Consider how this dialogue, and the information imparted to the reader, would sound narrated. I'm sure you'd prefer this clever exchange to mere narrative description. Not only does it give the reader information about events, but it also describes the nature of the characters, in just a couple of sentences. Brilliant.

8. Pay attention to punctuation! A comma where a semicolon should be, excessive use of the comma and the semicolon—which makes for long, unwieldy sentences that are better truncated—unnecessary spaces, and a host of other formatting errors, makes your manuscript look unprofessional, and makes you look stupid. While an editor will take care of this stuff, he shouldn't have to. (And remember, you are paying for it!) Learn the craft of writing, and your manuscript will be much more easy to read. Bad writing obscures good content!

9.) Most important: Go over your manuscript over and over until it sounds *exactly* like you want it! Only you know what you want to write. Don't let an

---

[5] From *The Grand Sophy* by Georgette Heyer
[6] From *Friday's Child* by Georgette Heyer.

editor hack and slash your manuscript, and try to figure out what sounds best. When I wrote *The Vibrational Universe*, I read and re-read (and edited) the entire manuscript over fifty times.

Again, read your manuscript out loud. This will give you an idea of how it will sound to your reader. YOU know what you want to say, but often that knowledge is in your head. It is the job of the writer to communicate effectively. It is the job of the editor to make your language conform to the standard writing guidelines. What I have found is that when you really THINK about what you want to say, your language will sound really good, and it will be in your own voice. An editor can then easily figure out who you are as a writer and edit accordingly.

About the Author

Kenneth J.M. MacLean is the author of six books including *The Vibrational Universe: Harnessing the Power of Thought to Consciously Create Your Life*. He is an expert on collaborative marketing using the Internet through cooperative means including, but not limited to, reciprocal linking, email blasts, monthly newsletters, movie-style trailers, and sharing substantive content with the public. His newest venture is a book editing service bureau.

Other books by Maclean include: *Dialogues: Conversations with My Higher Self* and several eBooks including *What Do You Do and When all Hell Breaks Loose?* and *Life's Little Instruction Manual*. His latest projects involve using Internet flash movies to portray the key concepts of his philosophy. Ken's most recent book is titled simply *I Love You Dad*, an exploration of communication after his father's recent passing. Ken's main area of interest is the relationship between science and spirituality, and his conviction, through personal experiences, that consciousness is not biologically based. He holds bachelor's degrees in both Computer Science and Political Science.

Podcast Airdate:	May 12th, 2008
Podcast URL:	http://authorsaccess.com/archives/103
	http://authorsaccess.com/archives/47
Author's site:	http://www.kjmaclean.com
	http://macleanediting.com

Editing: The Second Pair of Eyes
Bob Rich, Ph.D.

No matter how good a writer you are, your work does need a second pair of eyes. This doesn't necessarily mean a paid editor, but it has to be someone with excellent writing skills, and the ability to give useful feedback. Praise is useless if it overlooks serious problems. Harsh, destructive criticism is counterproductive. The best critique acknowledges all your strengths so that you can build on them, and picks up all the necessary places for improvement.

When I was a beginning writer, I paid for feedback from a professional editor three times, for three different books. On each occasion, I gained a lot more than improvements to that particular book. My skill as a writer soared.

In the same way, as I edit, I am often as much a teacher as a corrector of mistakes.

Nowadays, I still seek feedback for a completed book, and sometimes even for a work in progress, but now I offer a "crit. exchange" to a few writers whose work I respect. I pick up their faults, and they pick up mine.

Why is this necessary?

At all levels, I am too close to my work to notice all my own mistakes. This goes from the most basic typos to the subtle aspects of producing a work of power. During one crit. exchange, the other person noticed that I started a lot of sentences with "Now," as in "Now, he was ready to enter." I'd been completely unaware of this repetition.

There are many components of writing excellence, and mistakes are likely at each level, for all of us. It takes a dispassionate eye to pick them up.

In fiction and creative non-fiction such as journalism, travel writing and biography, some of these more subtle aspects include:

- The balance between action, description and dialogue;
- The point of view from which the material is presented;
- Giving each character a unique "voice," which is different from the author's;
- Using concrete, vivid, sensory language to show emotion rather than telling the reader from the outside.

Even in nonfiction, you want the reader to become so involved in the content that in effect the language becomes invisible. There are tricks of the trade for achieving this.

You have spent a lot of thought, time and effort in producing a book, or even a short story or magazine article. Not getting an independent edit is like buying a car, and then not spending on maintenance.

But isn't that the publisher's job?

On writers' email lists, I sometimes come across the argument that "I'm a storyteller not a technician. When I get an acceptance, the publisher will have it edited anyway."

Dream on! Publishers gets thousands of submissions for every one they can accept. If you want a hope of having even your second page read, then the first page has to be excellent. Basically, publishers have so many wonderful books to choose from that they need to find excuses for rejecting this one. They don't want to spend a lot of time on a book if they can reject it, because there is a pile of other submissions waiting. Any book that's less than top-notch has no hope, unless it's accepted for reasons other than quality, such as the author's fame, or having personal connections.

Of course, there are agents, the gatekeepers to publishers. They are in the same position, of getting a great many submissions for each one they can accept.

You've got to make your work as professional, as perfect as possible before submission.

Besides, "I am a storyteller not a technician" is a copout. Would you engage the services of a heart surgeon who doesn't know scissors from scalpel? Would you have your wedding photos taken by someone who needs to ask another person about the settings of the camera? All art depends on craft. If you are a writer, your tools are words. The current conventions of language define your competence.

I know all about building. When I walk into a room, I can see at a glance whether the person who'd constructed it was a professional or not. For example, joints in architraves should face away from the door. This has no practical significance at all—but it's an in-trade criterion. In the same way, you can communicate your message even if you misuse the past participle, but every person in the book trade, from acquisitions editor to the last reviewer, will know you are an amateur. And, as I said, when competition is tough, that will relegate you to the slush pile, or to self-publishing a book that's unsalable because of its low quality.

There is a whole generation, not only in America, who went through school without being taught grammar, spelling or punctuation. So, there are people who are intelligent, have something worthwhile to say, and they say it well, but they are functionally illiterate. I come up against this a lot.

With such people, editing is a matter of correcting the technical mistakes, and it drives me crazy. I actually need to charge more because it's hard work. It's boring, difficult and repetitious.

My attitude is that such people should do a remedial English course and learn proper syntax and usage. Language is our tool as writers. I wouldn't take my car to be fixed by a mechanic who uses a shifting wrench to adjust brakes.

I have several clients who started like that, but are now competent after I've edited several of their books. I am in the position of teacher with them.

How does editing differ from criticism?

Completely. Say someone sends me a book for a critique. I'll read it, then send back a report, at the most a couple of pages: this is what I like about your book, here are the parts that didn't work for me, and you might consider improving them in this way.

Of course, a bad critic will only focus on the negatives.

I like the Toastmasters' way of doing an assessment: to start with summarizing the good things about the performance, then give suggestions for improvement, then finish with a compliment. That's how I approach a critique.

In editing, I look for all the good things, because these are the points from which the writer can grow. Encouragement assists learning. But my job, what I get paid for, is to find all the things that are wrong and need changing, and all the aspects that could be changed with benefit for the book. I'll point out the errors of punctuation, grammar and the like, and also aspects where a character seems to be acting untrue to the picture the author has painted, or glitches like someone having the wrong name or eye color or relationship to another person. I'll point out places where the story doesn't flow, or tension is lacking, or the characters seem two-dimensional cardboard cutouts.

Similarly, in nonfiction I pick up all the parts of the book that don't work for me, for example a diagram that leaves me puzzled.

Becoming competent

There are many ways of becoming a master craftsperson with words. One pathway is through University courses in literature, journalism or creative writing, and some of these are excellent. However, I know graduates of such courses whose writing is technically poor, or stodgy, or lacks creativity. It does help to be a storyteller, even for nonfiction. I've only ever enjoyed one textbook: the book on introductory chemistry by Isaac Asimov.

When learning how to write competently, tools like style manuals, dictionaries and thesauri are very useful. Strunk & White or the *Chicago Manual of Style*, at least two good dictionaries (because they do differ) and an electronic tool like Word Web (http://wordweb.info/) are excellent investments.

You are likely to make occasional use of such things even after many years of experience as a writer. However, you need to develop an intuitive feel for correct grammar, spelling, word meaning, and punctuation. It's like riding a bike or playing tennis: you can't do it while reading an instruction manual.

The only real way to learn to write is to do it. Write, get feedback, learn from your mistakes, write some more. Every now and then, take out your older productions and assess them. If you now wince as you read, congratulations: you have learned in the interim.

In my case, I wrote three books that never saw the light of day. I learned on them. The fourth book I wrote was published. Other people are better at it, and may have a bestseller with their first book. But generally, you need to learn on the job. Short story writing is a very good process for that, as is nonfiction writing, e.g., articles for your local newspaper.

So, must written language follow the rules all the time?

A beginning cook courts disaster by departing from the recipe. A champion in the kitchen like my wife does it all the time, and this is precisely what lifts her productions above the norm.

One rule of writing is that no rule applies all the time. There are situations in which they should be broken—but you need a mastery of the rules to know when to violate them.

An example is the use of ungrammatical sentences. Every sentence must have a subject, verb and object: "The man opened the box." Each of the three components can be expanded and complicated. In the process, many people fail to include all three elements, so that if the complex sentence were simplified, it might read like

"Opened the box," with no subject, or "The man opening the box," which has no verb.

However, there are situations in which deliberately ungrammatical sentences can be very powerful. One is while the person whose point of view we are following is in a near-dreamlike, musing state, and long, rather rambling sentences carry this mood. Subtly slipping in some ungrammatical sentences can emphasize the unfocused nature of the thoughts.

> "She watched the little ripples on the bigger ripples on the waves, and the sun glinting off them. Glinting, glinting, riding and flashing around like little live sprites, dancing and jumping and sliding on the surface of the water. How she wished to be one of those little glinting sprites!"

Another is in the middle of intense tension, such as a life-threatening situation. Here, language should be short, choppy, staccato, and the hardness can be amplified by having some sentences bitten in half.

> "The footfalls behind her were getting closer. She speeded up, but they kept there. She forced a deep breath and turned. He loomed in the dim light. Almost on her. She saw his mouth open in a savage grin. His hands reached out. Not yet. Now! Drop, forward roll, feet like pistons. They smashed into his leg, just below the knee."

However, if there are ungrammatical sentences liberally strewn throughout the text without particular reason, the impression will be simply sloppiness, even within such passages.

Also, not all text is writing. Email, instant messaging and the like are forms of conversation. If I am talking with you in a social situation, it'll be quite different from how I speak up on a stage, addressing an audience. Conversation contains pauses, ums and ahs, ungrammatical sentences, and it's all right. If I spoke the same way in a speech, it'd sound uneducated, garbled.

I'd never dream of correcting a typo in an email, but this is very different from looking at a sample of the sender's writing. Then it's my job to make corrections.

What makes a book excellent?

Novelty for a start. Given the type of book it is, its genre, it needs to offer something new and different.

In fact, editing a really excellent book has a trap. I can get so drawn into the content that I have to concentrate hard to stay in editor mode.

Second, the author's job is to create a reality, put some characters into it, and then get out of the way. Create a situation, and then have the characters do all the work after that.

Reading is a funny sort of a tradition. It is very different from watching a movie. In a movie, someone else has done the creativity, and you just take it in. In writing, the writer provides the raw material for a special kind of creation by the reader. It is the reader who is the director, sets the stage, and becomes at least one of the characters—the person whose point of view we are following—as well as the audience.

This is even true for some kinds of non-fiction, but not of course for instructional material. It's true for travel writing, when the writer takes you there. But, in journalism, the point of view is always the writer's.

Different Levels of Editing

When a book is ready for publication, the author will be supplied with a galley proof. This is the last chance for correcting simple mechanical errors like typos. Any other changes will cost money. Proofreading is the most basic editing process.

Line editing can involve changes in expression, choice of words, correction of punctuation or the like, but not in content.

Believe it or not, content editing focuses on the content. In a nonfiction book, this may involve examination of whether the target audience is likely to be able to follow an explanation. The editor may suggest that certain points be illuminated by examples. The order of presentation of different topics could be changed, or subheads could be suggested. I've been known to do a bit of research on the web when a claim in a book sounded dubious to me, and then I'd challenged the writer to provide evidence for the claim.

All the same, there is a huge difference between feedback on content from an expert, and feedback on expression from an editor. If you need the technical content checked for accuracy, then you need an expert in the field. This expert need not be a good writer. However, the writing is something else. I have edited a Ph.D. thesis for a lady in Britain. She is an Internet artist. I didn't know the first thing about her field, but I could help her to translate her ideas into English, which she hadn't originally done. Like many highly visual people, she has trouble expressing ideas in words, and her expression was jumbled.

I have edited several books for a professor in Taiwan. She writes about the theory of fantasy. I know nothing about the theory of fantasy. I like reading fantasy books, and like writing them too, but her field might as well have been about a different planet. It meant nothing to me. But I could help her to express her ideas in understandable English.

Similarly, I've been the editor of a textbook for sophomores on nanotechnology. This involves physics, mathematics, and chemistry. The last time I studied such things was in 1962, so I could say nothing about the content. But there were nine authors, and I was the editor, an essential part of the team.

In fiction, the issues will include many features. One is characterization, and whether people in the story act "out of character." If a previously meek, hesitant person suddenly acts assertive, this will surprise the reader, and that destroys the illusion that the story is real.

There can be glitches, like when the principal of the school is Mrs. Dalton in Chapter 3 but Mrs. Bolton in Chapter 37. There are dozens of aspects of creative writing that a good writer will intuitively do—and a good editor intuitively monitor.

One important consideration is style of writing. Each author eventually develops a voice. Of course, part of my job is not to impose my voice, but to keep the author's. This is where some editors err.

Then there are things like description. It should be invisible. If I notice that I am reading description, then it's too much. It's got to be inserted within dialogue, action, a person's thoughts, so that it seems natural and is taken in without being noticed. The idea is that rather than have something described to me, I should experience it.

You can also have too much thinking. I once read a book by a popular author whom I'm not going to name. It was one of a series. He spent the first thirty-seven pages recapping the previous story largely through having people muse about it. I only forced myself to read that far because I wanted to see how many pages he would go before introducing anything exciting. By the time I got to the first bit of action, I was so bored I put the book down anyway.

Paying attention to all these aspects of writing is sometimes called developmental editing, because it is designed to help the author get the very best out of this piece of writing for its target audience.

Editing is a business, and you get what you paid for. All the same, good editors tend to be rather obsessive, and unable to go past something that jars. Often people send me a book for line editing, but I find I need to make so many recommendations for content change that the book ends up needing a rewrite. If I have been involved in a book, I want it to be as good as possible. Excellence is much more important to me than money. Also, this way I am of service to others. So, even if somebody paid me only for line editing, I still make content suggestions.

The Editing Process

Every editor works differently. Editing used to be scribbling special symbols in the margins and writing comments between the lines of double-spaced typescript. As far as I am concerned, that went out with typewriters. I don't even have a red pen. Everybody is different, but I do everything onscreen.

I know others who print it out and work on paper. I am a conservationist. In this world, with all these disasters caused by climate change, you're either a conservationist or a suicide. Even if I must print something out, I'll do it on the back of a used piece of paper, say an official letter or advertisement someone had sent me.

So, people send me a book as an email attachment. I edit it only after turning on Microsoft Word's "Track Changes" feature unless the person wants a different arrangement.

There are lots of advantages. An electronic file is searchable. Say I suspect that the person referred to as Jim on page 92 was in fact John earlier in the book. I go back to the start and check in a few seconds. Imagine doing the same in a paper book. While I don't rely on the spell checker, it is certainly a help. It's a fact that if I edit on paper, I will miss things that I pick up onscreen.

Most editors look for repeated patterns of mistakes. Once such a pattern is identified, it is not considered necessary to point out every new instance, except in proofreading. For example, I might find that a particular writer fails to cut text into suitable paragraphs. I'll explain the need the first time each specific situation occurs, then for a while I'll mark the spot for a new paragraph with //, then after awhile I'll even stop that. The author has the intelligence to write a book, so learning the pattern should not be too difficult.

If there are too many such problems, I'll send the book back, and only charge for the number of words I have edited. The author can then rewrite, and send me a new sample for a new quote. Usually, I ask clients to pay upfront (because I've had a bad experience with a client who never paid for the work done). If I send the book back part done, I either offer a refund or hold the balance in credit for the author.

A Few Things to Look For

Dialogue is the heart of fiction and journalism, and creative nonfiction like biography.

There shouldn't be too much unbroken dialogue. It becomes word ping pong. And it shouldn't go on for too long. There is a balance, with no objective measure, but it depends on the particular situation.

The first thing is to break up dialogue with little insertions: thoughts, bodily sensations, emotional reactions, what the person notices in the environment around, whatever. Each of these insertions is so short that you don't even notice it while reading, but they break up the word ping pong. They are also excellent opportunities for passing on information in an invisible way.

Second, it's essential for the reader to know at all times who says what. If I have to stop and think about the identity of the speaker, then I've been dragged out of the content. This is one of the reasons why it's essential for each person to have a characteristic way of speaking.

Point of view comes in here, as either a help or a mistake. The scene is presented through the perceptions of a character. "His eyes opened wide" indicates that the person referred to is someone the current witness to the scene is looking at. This is a subtle cue to who is speaking. But if the writer makes this statement about the current witness, then it's an outside view when an inside view is needed.

The third thing about dialogue is the word "said." Many writers struggle with it. "He said" and the like are referred to as tags. If your writing is good enough, you should need very few tags. Strive to minimize them. The fewer tags you need the better, as long as you stay unambiguous regarding the identity of the speaker. You should use a tag to eliminate ambiguity, but if you can achieve this without a tag, the writing will flow better.

The tag should not be so fancy that it attracts attention to itself. So, things like "I asserted" are counterproductive. If you must have a tag, "said" is OK, except, that you must always eliminate as much repetition as possible. So, you don't want a page with five or six instances of "said" on it.

Put in too many occurrences of "said," and the reader will start counting them. Have too many cute alternatives, and the reader may notice and start looking for "said." As always, it's a judgment.

Balance is necessary in everything, and there is only one criterion: the reader should stay immersed in the content and not have attention stray to presentation. I've mentioned too much description, too much dialogue, too frequent use of a word. Nothing is good if there is too much of it in one lump.

Point of view (POV) is at the center of creating a reality the reader can move into. It is the major tool for creative writing. It can even be important in nonfiction, because good instructional writing contains case studies and examples.

There is always a point of view. Either it's the author's, or that of a particular character. In fiction, the author should create the setting, the people and the events—and then get off the stage.

Think of a story as a series of scenes. Each has a witness. Present everything about the scene from the point of view of this person. Subtly insert internal events such as thoughts, emotions, bodily sensations, perceptions and memories, to show this person from the inside. Other people's reactions can be shown by reporting what the witness can observe about them.

Structure refers to plot in fiction or the order of presenting information in an instructional book. Some writers meticulously set out this structure, then expand it up into the full book. Others grow the book organically. Both approaches are valid—what counts is the final result. If the structure is sound, the entire book can be summarized in a single sentence. That "tag line" can be expanded into a number of points, which form a logical chain. Each of these points is in effect the tag line for a chapter or group of chapters. In turn, each of these can be expanded, until you have a summary point for each paragraph.

This can be complicated by subplots or parallel lines of development in fiction, necessary digressions into subsidiary topics in a nonfiction book, but the principle still applies for each such component, and their interrelationships.

Finding an Editor

There are many writers' communities on the Internet. Join them, and then use word of mouth. People will recommend editors who have done good work for them.

Enter "editing" or "editing services" in a search engine.

Either way, be sure to check with "Preditors and Editors," a site which lists the sharks: the people out to fleece writers (http://www.anotherealm.com/prededitors).

The best qualification is, "Suck it and see." When somebody approaches me, I edit a sample of 1000 words for free. I time myself, and give a quote according to how time-consuming the job is going to be. But also, the prospective client gets a sample of my work, and will see what they are buying.

Qualifications can be important. Many editors are graduates of relevant university programs. A degree in English doesn't necessarily make you into a good editor, any more than a medical degree qualifies you to be a good doctor. But it's certainly good preparation.

Other people work for years as journalists, or for a publisher, or, as in my case, have years of experience writing, sharpening writing skills by entering short story competitions, being parts of critique groups. I stumbled into editing by accident.

And Finally

An editor needs to be highly obsessive, have a lot of experience with the correct use of language, be happy to respect people whose writing skills are currently inferior, be interested in the client as a person, and motivated to make the book the best piece of writing possible by this author at this time.

About the Author

Bob Rich is a writer, editor, and psychologist living in Wombat Hollow, Australia. In addition to writing, He has been a professional editor since 1999, working his way through two books in a typical week. He has worked on everything from abstruse Ph.D. theses and graduate textbooks to children's picture books, and all genres of fiction.

Bob's services are used by several independent publishers, including Loving Healing Press. However, most of his work is from writers wanting to polish their work before submitting to an agent or publisher (or self-publishing), and comes to him through recommendation from happy clients. He does both line editing and content editing. Bob goes the extra mile by applying his deep knowledge and study of human psychology to each editing project.

Bob is the author of more than a dozen books on a wide range of topics including the *Earth Garden Building Book: Design and build your own house*, now in its 4th edition, *Woodworking for Idiots Like Me*, *Cancer: A Personal Challenge*, and many others. Four of them have won international awards.

Podcast Airdate:	September 13th, 2007
Podcast URL:	http://authorsaccess.com/archives/80
Author's site:	http://www.bobswriting.com
	http://mudsmith.net
	http://anxietyanddepression-help.com

5 Elements of Book Design

Five Keys to a Better Book
Michele DeFilippo

It's far from an easy task to find, evaluate, and work with the number of people you'll need to prepare your book for printing and public release. If you are new to publishing, how will you know whom to choose, and once you choose them, how will you know that they are doing the job correctly? If publishing is a new business that you are trying to manage in addition to a full-time job, the issues can become even more pressing.

I've worked in publishing for thirty-six years, and in that time I've heard a lot of horror stories from my customers, such as that an editor or a designer was not responding in a timely manner, or if he or she did respond, the quality of the work wasn't good. Or that the agreed-upon price was raised in the middle of the job. Or that a deadline was looming and was not likely to be met. My clients were beside themselves with stress and worry. All they wanted to do was to enjoy the process of preparing their book for printing.

There is a great deal more to publishing your own book than meets the eye. In this chapter, I'll share my experience about several key aspects of creating a top-notch book, including

- Choosing a title that sells
- Why your manuscript deserves professional editing
- Creating an effective cover
- The importance of professional-looking typesetting, and
- Understanding the printing process

The Title Must Sell Your Book

Title writing is a unique skill that requires marketing expertise. The author may be an expert in his or her particular subject, but that's a different skill than being able to choose the exact words that will capture and hold a potential buyer's attention.

If possible, it's very useful to have a book marketing expert to evaluate your title. This person knows what works and what doesn't, and after reviewing a manuscript, he or she will present a few alternatives that drill right down to the message that the book's buyer is looking for.

The same skill set applies to the text on the back cover of your book. Often an author will go into great detail about why he or she wrote the book, and what's meaningful about it to him or her. But the buyer is asking only one question—"What's in it for me?" Back cover text that doesn't answer this question causes the buyer to put your book down and choose another. Again, a book marketing expert writes text that not only informs the potential buyer, but also motivates him or her to spend money.

You can find book marketing experts online, you can ask about them in online forums, and you can get references from local publishing associations.

The Importance of Editing

It's a major achievement to write a book. I certainly couldn't do it. But sometimes an author is just too close to the material to be objective. After many rewrites and even more readings, your brain "fills in the blanks" and sees what it expects to see. You may know what you mean to say, but the text may be less clear to someone reading it for the first time. The fresh eyes of an editor can be a real benefit.

Hiring an experienced editor, rather than a friend or relative who happens to be an English teacher, is very important. A good editor does much more than fix your grammar; he or she improves a book's content and structure in a way that preserves the author's style. Just as important, he or she finds and corrects both major and minor errors.

For example, our editor once found a mistake in a cookbook—a collection of easy supper recipes using pre-cooked rotisserie chickens from the grocery store. At the front of the book, the author provided a warning that these recipes were to be made only with cooked chicken, never with uncooked chicken. All well and good. But our editor noticed that within each recipe itself, the list of ingredients simply said "chicken." Of course, the author knew what she meant, but in real life, people flip through a cookbook and don't always re-read the first pages. This one little correction, changing "chicken" to "cooked chicken," probably prevented a lot of bellyaches (or worse).

Having your book edited is money well spent. An editor won't rob you of your style; he or she will enhance your style. Many freelance editors have their own Web sites, in which they outline their credentials, philosophy of editing, and rates. It's important to find an editor who has worked on books similar to yours. (For example, an editor whose expertise is in children's books is probably not the best person to edit your historical novel or economics textbook). Once you've contacted an editor about possibly working with him or her, the editor will generally ask to see a sample of your book. Have no fear that he or she is going to steal your book idea. The editor simply wants to give you an accurate price quote, so that there is no misunderstanding later. In fact, beware of any editor who will give you a quote without seeing at least part of your book first.

After a thorough edit by a professional, your book will stand up to the tough scrutiny of distributors, reviewers, retailers, and libraries.

A Book Cover is Everything

Some people think that book cover design happens in just a few moments, but that's not the case. Before the designer can even begin, he or she must spend time researching other books in your category so that your book's design will fit in as well as stand out. If that sounds like a contradiction, it is. Your book must look like it belongs with others of its type, but it also must look better, and more interesting, so that people will buy your book and not someone else's.

A cover designer will also talk about your target market, so that the design will appeal to the people most likely to read your book. Age, income level, profession—all of these must be considered in the design. There is no such thing as a book that is designed for "everyone."

That's the science part of cover design. Next comes the art part. While it's true that a designer will start by quickly sketching the first ideas that come to mind, an experienced designer will almost always reject these first ideas and strive for something better and unique. A good designer will find the right images, combine them in creative and eye-catching ways, and show you at least three very different designs to give you a clear choice. Then, he or she will collaborate with you on changes until the cover is everything you imagined. After that, the cover design is back into "science" mode—creating the digital file correctly for printing, so that what you see is what you actually get from your printer. All of this typically takes between twenty and thirty hours.

If you look at the samples of low-cost cover designers critically, you can see that they have used a "cookie cutter" approach—changing a photo here, a typeface there, but not offering the client a creative new look.

To find a designer, it's useful, first of all, to review the Web sites of various designers to determine the styles you like and those you don't. However, don't reject a designer if the samples aren't in the same genre as your book. Look for the underlying design skill, which a competent designer can apply to any topic. Second, ask your friends if they know a skilled designer. Third, attend local publishing group meetings, where you have the opportunity to meet several designers. Chances are, if you like each other in a social setting, you'll be successful working together as well.

When you have identified a few designers whose work you like, describe your project in detail in writing and ask them for a quote. Designers who ask a lot of questions are probably more experienced than those who ask few or no questions. Make sure that they respond with the number of concepts that are included in the price and the number of hours of changes that are included. Also, make sure that you will own the rights to the cover design, as well as any licensed images that may be used when the project is complete.

Pay attention to how long it takes the designer to respond to your request for a quote. Slow response times may mean slow service times later. Most of all, avoid designers who are impatient with your questions. Design is a service business, and you're entitled to a reasonable amount of the designer's time as the project proceeds.

Prices that sound too good to be true can mean that the designer is going to give you only a very small amount of his or her time. When comparing designer quotes, be sure to ask how many concepts the designer will present for the price quoted. In the "good old days," it was standard procedure to offer multiple concepts. Now, many designers offer just one concept and revise from there. This takes less time, of course, but it won't give you an opportunity to decide which approach is more eye-catching.

One final note: when a designer follows up with you after sending you a quote, please don't ignore his or her communication. Even if you choose to hire someone else, it's nice to acknowledge the time and effort that was spent in developing a quote, and the designer will learn from your reasons to adjust his or her business practices accordingly.

The Benefits of Professional-looking Typesetting

Today, the tools to arrange words on paper are everywhere, and it's easy to assume that there's nothing difficult about typesetting your own book. Books look easy to do, but they're not. Book typesetting has its own set of rules that must be followed for a professional look. Break even a few of these rules, or lay out your book with word-processing software, and the gatekeepers in the book industry will immediately know it is self-published.

Word-processing software simply doesn't have the same spacing controls available in a page-layout program. And even if you buy the proper software and navigate the very steep learning curve, chances are that you won't get the same results as an experienced book designer who has been trained to create pages that draw the reader in and are easy to navigate.

We have redesigned many covers and interiors at the request of distributors who simply would not carry a client's book as it was originally prepared.

Just as with the cover, a professional interior design helps to establish your credibility to the buyer, who is as yet unfamiliar with your content. A competent designer starts by creating a unique interior design just for your book. He or she takes into account your audience and your subject matter, so that it will begin to appeal to them before they even begin reading. Then the designer and the author work back and forth, making any necessary adjustments. Design is always the result of collaboration.

If the design firm you choose doesn't offer proofreading, then be sure to hire one on your own. And if you think you don't need proofreading because your book was edited, please reconsider. Choose someone with a good amount of experience proofreading books for publishers. Just as with editing, the best results are achieved by a person who has been trained to do the task. Also, generally it's best if a proofreader has some knowledge of your book's subject or has proofed other books in your genre.

The Ins and Outs of the Printing Process

Printing has its own jargon, which can be intimidating if you've never worked with it before. And, as technologies evolve and options increase, it's getting more complicated to figure out exactly which printer is the best one for your particular book.

Each book printer will respond to a request for a quote in its own way, and it's not always easy to compare apples to oranges. Because printing companies are often overwhelmed with requests, it's not uncommon for them to omit an item that you requested. When this happens, their quotes can look less expensive, and you won't find out until it's too late that the final product is not what you expected.

Then, there's the issue of perceived experience. A printer will immediately determine your level of experience (or inexperience) on the first call. If you don't know what questions to ask, you might run into unscrupulous printers who don't bother to explain the difference.

In this area, as in others, asking colleagues for references is a good idea. One idea is to join publishing e-mail forums and ask participants to recommend printers they are happy (or unhappy) with.

Conclusion

Publishing can be an exciting and rewarding venture, if you have the right team on your side, and a nightmare if you don't. As someone once said, "When was the last time you got mad at yourself for hiring the best?" Allocating sufficient funds for quality editorial and design services is one of the best business decisions a publisher can make. Your book deserves it, and your readers will appreciate the effort.

About the Author

Michele DeFilippo has thirty-six years of design and management experience and is the owner of *1106 Design*, an award-winning one-stop shop for book cover and interior design, typesetting, editing, book title writing, back cover copywriting, proofreading, printing coordination and more. As a member of the Arizona Book Publishing Association, Michele has actively shared her knowledge and experience with many first-time publishers, explaining the difference between choices that can help, or hurt, book sales.

Podcast Airdate:	January 13th, 2007
Podcast URL:	http://authorsaccess.com/archives/28
Author's site:	http://www.1106design.com

Smart Self-Publishing
Jim and Linda Salisbury

If you're thinking of self-publishing a book, memorize these words: Be smart. Do the book right!

This is the message Tabby House has been preaching for almost twenty years at seminars, with our clients, and in all three editions of our book *Smart Self-Publishing: An author's guide to producing a marketable book*. Applying these words means the difference between having a credible, marketable product, and one that reeks of amateurism. We believe that it's important to understand and conform to book-trade standards even if you just plan to sell your book on weekends at a local flea market. You want a product that you can be proud of when it's in the hands of potential readers or buyers.

Yes, books are products. So first take off your writer hat and put on your publisher hat.

We've seen many interesting books doomed to failure because the author / publisher didn't do the book right, and yet, he or she may have spent substantial sums in the process.

Doing the book right for retail sales includes: proper editing (using recommended dictionaries and stylebooks), book typesetting, professional cover design, and the use of credentials. Your finished book should not be discernible as self-published, which unfortunately, many are despite the cost of production.

Smart Editing and Proofing

We recommend using the most current edition of Webster's *Collegiate Dictionary* to check spellings, compound words, meanings and hyphenation, plus *The Chicago Manual of Style*. The stylebook tells you when words should be italicized, abbreviated or spelled out, for example, and how to set up a book properly.

It's important to use the latest edition of the dictionary and stylebook because rules change. Make sure that anyone proofreading or editing your book is also using the same references.

Don't date yourself, appear to be guessing or use Web or newspaper style when working on your book! Here's an example we see all the time. "Web site" is properly two words, with "Web" capitalized for book style. Many writers (and editors) assume that it's spelled "website" because they have not opened their Webster's or they have seen it spelled that way in other publications or on Web sites. Similarly, "online" is one word and e-mail is hyphenated. What happens on the Web, stays on the Web, but what happens in book editing should reflect proper style and use of dictionary and stylebooks.

Smart Typesetting

You cannot properly typeset your book using a word-processing program. You'll need to have access to one of the page-making programs, such as Adobe's Pagemaker or InDesign, or QuarkExpress to adjust leading (the space between the lines), and to apply the headers and page numbers appropriately. You will also need to use Postscript rather than TrueType fonts (part of word-processing programs).

Unfortunately, traditional typesetting rules are increasingly ignored by large publishing houses. You, as a small publisher, can still do your book right, if you know the rules. You will also quickly show your publishing ignorance if you have two spaces after punctuation between sentences or use bold face type or all caps for emphasis.

Smart Credentials

You will need to establish yourself as a publisher by first buying your ISBNs through R.R. Bowker; applying for inclusion in the Library of Congress (LOC) Preassigned Control Number (PCN) program to get your LOC Control Number (LCCN) and a barcode with the embedded price and ISBN for the back cover. All of the aforementioned must be completed before you go to press. Of course this particular flow is peculiar to publishers in the USA; in Canada and abroad the responsible organizations will differ.

Do not use your personal name as your publishing imprint. Obtain your credentials before the book is printed. Believe it or not, we've seen verso (copyright) pages with this statement: "Library of Congress Number applied for." We also recommend that the price be clearly visible. People are more likely to purchase a book if they see the price rather than have to ask about it. And, in order to have retail sales, the barcode must be printed on the back cover.

A word about scams: Scam artists are out there. Some may be well-meaning, but others are just after your money. You need to make sure that the people you hire to edit, for example, indeed are familiar with professional book style, and are willing to work on a per-page, or per-project basis. If you agree to an hourly rate, you may lose control of the total cost of your project. Submit a few sample pages for a potential editor's review, talk with him or her, and then negotiate a fair price, but one that will be capped for your benefit. The same is true for illustrations or cover design. Get a "per" price and find out what is included in that. Also make sure you have a work-for-hire agreement with the artist.

We have been told time and again that a book submitted to Tabby House for book-packaging has been "edited." Rarely has the "editor" checked to see if compound words are hyphenated; are one word or two, or has checked facts. One autobiography "edited" by a librarian for a blind woman was riddled with misspellings of the names of cities around the world and of foreign terms, and the foreign words were not italicized on first reference. We could not let it go to press in that sad fashion nor could we tell her she had been scammed because the "editor" was a friend. Instead, we fixed it.

Smart Marketing

Marketing decisions should be made early, before you commit money to any aspect of the production. Think of marketing as being like a clothesline from which decisions about your book will hang.

First, identify who will be the readers and who will be the buyers of your book. If you are writing a children's picture book, for example, typically your buyers are doting adult relatives who are attracted to a clever title about potty training, or such, with cute bunnies on the cover. The book will be a gift to be read to, or with, a child. The text must be age-appropriate, grammar and punctuation must be correct. We've seen sweet picture books (finished) with poor grammar and bad punctuation. Who wants to be responsible for a book that inadvertently teaches kids something wrong?

Or perhaps you have written a book about what men can do to help their wives around the house. Chances are the buyer is female, and the reader (or recipient of the gift) is male. The content and title will attract the buyer, but your decisions about the cover, such as color (avoid pink or lavender) must appeal to the male reader.

Smart Covers

A professionally designed cover is essential to the retail market and is part of your marketing strategy. Covers sell books. Front, back, and spine. It only takes a few seconds for buyers to select or reject a book, and they often base their decisions on the cover. The cover must fit the book's genre and have a contemporary style for that genre. Visit your bookstores to see what current sci-fi or romance, business, biography or fiction covers look like so that yours will be mainstream. Avoid Aunt Emma's free amateur art and spring for a professional cover designer. It's worth the investment if you are serious about retail sales.

The title and the subtitle must define the book. Obscurity, coupled with an unknown author's name, a mystifying title and baffling artwork, equates to lost sales.

You also need to ask yourself how you are going to reach your buyers. That is part of your initial strategy and will affect price and press run. If you plan mostly to hand sell your books through programs and tables at festivals, you will be able to make more per copy than if you sell through a bookstore, the Web, or other retail distribution where substantial discounts must be taken into consideration.

It's important to be realistic about your market. Just because your friends and family tell you that your book is wonderful, don't expect to get on Oprah. And, don't feel that you're a failure if you aren't carried in the chain stores. You can certainly have your book available through the Internet and sell it through your own Web site, but thinking "little" or regional can mean greater success and profits than "thinking big" or national. We recommend participating in the Amazon Advantage program, linking your sales to its site so you can avoid the cost and hassle of having your own credit card capability.

Chain stores are not likely to consider an unknown author, unless you're very lucky or put a lot of money into national marketing programs. The chains will not consider an eBook or POD book because they are inundated with them and so many are poorly prepared. Bad preparation means no proper editing, amateur typesetting, poor cover, and usually the e-printer's ISBN applied to your book. To get into the national market and sustain sales could cost you more than $100,000 for advertising alone. Who's got that money to gamble?

This is where author / publisher effort is essential. When your book is off press, you must be willing to get out there and promote your book relentlessly. No one will do it better than you. It's a commitment you must make. If you aren't willing to set up a table at a festival, sit on porches of convenience stores, give talks or seminars—whatever it takes—then don't expect your book to sell. Just because it has been published doesn't make it a winner!

Writing your book is the easy part. Producing the book properly takes time and hard work, but selling the book is a constant effort, rewarded by replenishing your bank account and by having a dwindling supply of books in your garage or storage area.

As publisher you will also need to have good inventory records, be registered with the sales tax agency in your state and you may need a county license to do business.

Develop letterhead for your cover letters which will accompany all mailings. Know newspaper deadlines and supply them with photos and whatever is needed for your announcement to make the paper or its calendar of local events.

We strongly recommend that our author / publishers become involved in regional and national organizations: Independent Book Publishers Association (formerly Publishers Marketing Association), SPAN, Publishers Association of the South, and your own regional organization, such as the Florida Publishers Association. We've been members of the FPA for a long time (even after we moved to Virginia), and Jim served as its president during its early years. The newsletters, seminars and networking help members become savvier about changing market conditions, and provide tips on new sales avenues to explore.

FPA and other organizations (such as *ForeWord* magazine, and the Jenkins Group Moonbeam Children's Book Awards) offer annual contests. Enter only legitimate contests (there are scams out there), and proudly display winning stickers. Stickers and awards sell books!

Seek Realistic Review Sources

Most major newspapers subscribe to syndicated review services rather than reviewing books that are submitted to them by small presses or self-publishers. Know the rules for submission to trade publications. Some that review for the book trade want to consider books at the bound galley stage, before they are printed and released; others will review only the completed book for the public after it is in the distribution system and is available in stores. Do your homework.

There are Web review sources that can be valuable. Linda's juvenile fiction series, for example, has been reviewed by kids through www.readerviews.com, giving her good feedback on what her target market thinks about her titles. Reader Views also reviews adult titles and has an annual literary awards contest. Linda's also been pleased by another source of reviews for children's books, www.thereadingtub.com.

Smart Printing and Pricing

The convenience of having a book printed and bound by your local printer can be quickly overshadowed by the cost. Most local printers do not have the capability of printing large page-count signatures (signatures are page groups divisible by eight that most books consist of), nor do they usually have bindery capability. Most local printers job out much of the work, thereby adding to the cost. It's better to seek out a reputable book manufacturer that will do the entire project under one roof. Many book manufacturers are listed in the reference portion of *Smart Self-Publishing*.

If you need only a small quantity of books or have a storage problem, consider digital press. The books are more expensive on a cost-per-copy basis, but you may have a smaller initial outlay and can make corrections and reprint quickly.

If your marketing plan and budget warrants a larger press run, get prices for using an offset press. There are economies in quantities. Do the math. The fewer the books, the higher the unit cost. Your retail price needs to reflect trade discounts of up to 70 percent if you will have your book carried by a distributor or wholesaler. Get several bids from book manufacturers and printers that are experts in books.

Smart Publishing

Although Tabby House is essentially a book-packager, producing books for author / publishers around the nation, we also publish and market our own books. We must practice what we preach about doing the book right.

Linda, a former journalist, began writing a juvenile fiction series, the Bailey Fish Adventures, shortly before she retired from a newspaper career in 2004. As of summer 2008, four of the first five books had won five national awards or honors, and the series has received favorable reviews from a number of national sources (including *ForeWord*, the Midwest Book Review, the Reading Tub, and Reader Views). The books are orderable from Amazon.com and BN.com, and are listed with wholesalers such as Ingram, Baker & Taylor, and Follett (library sales).

We made a marketing decision to sell as many books as possible through school programs in our own region, and wherever we are traveling. As an incentive, Tabby House offers retail outlets, including bookstores that buy directly from us, a 50 percent discount, and a 40 percent discount to schools and libraries. When Linda appears at a school or other events, student buyers are offered a discount from the $8.95 retail price.

Intense promotional efforts, quality products, and reader demands for additional books has meant more than 10,000 books sold in the first three years.

Two of the books have been reprinted. The sixth book will be available in time for 2008 holiday season and Linda has also written another juvenile fiction with an environmental twist that will be released in 2009: *Mudd Saves the Earth: Booger Glue, Cow Diapers and Other ~~Good~~ Ideas.* Cartoonist Joe Kohl is the illustrator.

She is especially pleased that all youngsters, boys and girls, can't get enough of the Bailey Fish series. But it takes constant marketing and promotional efforts all year long to build and maintain readership and sales.

An amazing spin-off is the demand for T-shirts with the title of the first book: *The Wild Women of Lake Anna.* T-shirts are a higher profit item than the books. "I'm a Wild Woman of Lake Anna," "My Grandma is a Wild Woman of Lake Anna," and "My Wife is a Wild Woman of Lake Anna" have been big hits locally. Tabby House also has had kids' T-shirts printed that say "Hooked on Bailey Fish Adventures." They are given to folks who purchase a complete set of the series.

The series has a Web site (www.baileyfishadventures.com), and Linda has a blog that she adds to on an irregular basis.

The series concept is a reminder that having more than one book in your genre helps sales and reduces the cost-per-title marketing expenses.

Smart Success

When we wrote *Smart Self-Publishing*, we used tips and stories from other authors, publishers and professionals in the field (with their permission) to underscore and add to our own suggestions. This broadened our message and offered additional perspectives for what works and what doesn't.

One of those authors was Dr. Dennis Fried, *Memories of a Papillion: The Canine Guide to Living with Humans without Going Mad.* Actually, he credits his Papillion, Genevieve, as the author and she "barktates" her tales quite well. Denny reports that his book has been featured or reviewed in *Time* magazine, the *Boston Globe,* and *Dog World* magazine, among others.

We have put Denny's name at the top of the list of self-published success stories. We have packaged three of his books and have been tickled that, through his relentless marketing efforts, more than 20,000 copies of his first book were sold. In 2008 he found an agent (David Fugate, LaunchBooks), and his first book was shopped to major publishers. Denny was offered a five figure advance from Simon and Schuster and the book will be published under its Simon Spotlight Entertainment imprint. We look forward to seeing it in its new form titled *Small Dog, Big Life: A Memoir.*

With new technology, anyone can self-publish a book. The key is to commit to do the book right!

About the Authors

Jim and Linda are authors of *Smart Self-Publishing: An author's guide to producing a marketable book* now in its 3rd edition. The book has been mentioned in both *Newsweek* and *BottomLine Personal*. Jim is the publisher at Tabby House now based in Central Virginia, and was president of the Florida Publishers Association for many years. He and Linda offer self-publishing seminars in libraries, bookstores and for writers' groups. They are members of FPA, Publishers Association of the South, and Independent Book Publishers Association (formerly Publishers Marketing Association). Linda is the author of the juvenile fiction *Bailey Fish Adventure* series, which has won four national honors. The sixth book in the series will be out in late 2008 and she has another environmentally oriented children's book to be released soon. She is a former journalist and a freelance writer.

Podcast Airdate:	July 19th, 2008
Podcast URL:	http://authorsaccess.com/archives/107
Author's site:	www.tabbyhouse.com or tabbyhouse@gmail.com

6 Exploiting the Writing Market

Exploring Ghostwriting, Co-Authoring, and Collaborating

Ami Hendrickson

I got my foot in the door in the publishing world ghostwriting a book for a highly respected expert in his field. The book was published by a very exclusive, niche publisher, and was an instant bestseller both in its genre and with the publisher.

In many respects, I was quite fortunate. The expert agreed to share writing credit with me, so my name appears on the cover. Writing the book was a learning experience in every way—some good; some bad; all necessary.

Helping to make someone else's book become a reality may not be high on many writers' lists. Many writers see ghostwriting or co-authoring as a time-drain that sucks creative energy from their own pet projects.

In my experience, however, ghosting the book was the best thing I could have done for my writing career. I have worked as co-author, ghostwriter, editor, or collaborator on a number of projects since. My involvement on many of those projects can be traced directly back to the work I did on the first book.

My personal experience with ghostwriting, co-authoring, and collaborating has been overwhelmingly skewed in a positive direction. Because I was willing to write for someone else, I've been relentlessly busy ever since. I've also been privileged to work with some fantastically talented people along the way.

Working Definitions

The concept of *ghostwriting* can mean different things to different people. Before I begin throwing words around, it makes sense first to explain what I mean when I say them. That way, we can all meet on common ground—at least for a while.

First, let's consider the experts. It takes many experts to create a book. But at the moment, the two I'd like to discuss are the *Field Expert* and the *Writer*. Both are professionals. Both are experts in their own right.

The Field Expert is the one whose story must be told.

- In the world of *non-fiction*, this person is recognized for his or her outstanding mastery of a particular field of study.
- If the project is a *memoir*, the Field Expert is the person who experienced the events firsthand.
- If the project is a work of *fiction*, the Field Expert is usually the person who originally created a character or a series, or who is a bestselling author with a worldwide readership.

The Writer is the person entrusted with putting the Field Expert's story into a readable manuscript.

There are many variations on the ghostwriting / co-authoring theme. Every situation is slightly different, and any number of idiosyncrasies, exceptions, and special considerations may arise.

Still, putting your talents with the written word at others' disposal probably means that you fall into one of three camps: ghostwriting, co-authoring, or collaborating.

Ghostwriting: (Also called "Ghosting.") The Writer does the work and gets paid, but no credit. In some instances, the Writer may be legally restricted from even acknowledging that he or she worked on the project.

Co-Authoring: The Writer does the work, gets paid, and gets shared credit (usually in the form of "With" or "As told to…"). Depending on the contract, the Writer may also share royalties.

(Note: both Ghosting and Co-Authoring bow to the Field Expert. The writer may make suggestions for "ultimate content," but the final decision lies with someone else. The Field Expert generally holds the copyright on any resulting text.)

Collaborating: A true joint effort between two or more "creatives." The Writer is part of a team. "And" separates the names in the credits. The Writer receives a percentage of the royalties and may hold the copyright. The Writer also has a say in the final content (and may pitch a fit with the best of them in order to keep or cut portions).

Pros of Writing for Others

So many writers write alone. They plug away, day after day, on projects that often receive little support or acknowledgement from anyone else.

This is not the case when writing for someone else. Suddenly, your writing project becomes immensely important to someone other than yourself. This can lead to a whole laundry list of Good Things.

Some of the pros I've discovered that come from writing for other people include:

Benefit	Rationale
Accountability	People support your writing and hold you accountable for producing. Others are counting on you and your abilities with words.
Motivation	You have a deadline. There is a *reason* to write.
Working with a Professional Team	Being the Writer provides an opportunity to form a working relationship with great future resources, including: The Field Expert, the Expert's agent or "people" within the industry, the publisher, the managing editor, photographers, illustrators, book designers, and others.
Minimized Responsibility	If a publisher has committed to an Expert's book, there is reason for that publisher to think the book can sell. If an Expert has committed to self-publishing a book, that Expert probably has plans for marketing it and moving copies. You, the Writer, hold an important piece of the puzzle, but are not solely responsible for the book's ultimate success. Your job is to write the book. If you're a co-author or collaborator, you'll probably also be expected to help market the finished product, but you won't be doing it alone.

In addition to the preceding pros, I've experienced two other unexpected benefits from Ghosting: losing writer's ego and tuning your ear for language.

Loss of "Writing Ego"

Writing for another person means that you are committed to creating a manuscript *someone else* will be happy to "own." You are a sort of surrogate parent to the text. I've found this to be very freeing, in terms of any Writer's Ego I might have had.

Some writers become so married to their words. They almost take it personally if someone suggests editorial changes. They are so close to their writing (in a co-dependent, dysfunctional relationship sort of way) that they are sometimes unable to determine whether a suggested change would benefit the project.

In my experience, that sort of thing goes right out the window when ghosting.

You become able to see your writing as part of a larger whole. You become much more objective when taking editing suggestions. Such objectivity allows you really to focus on creating the best text, without forming an unhealthy emotional attachment to the words.

Developing a Better Ear for Dialogue and Speech Patterns

Since a ghost project must ultimately sound like the Field Expert, it is imperative that the Writer be able to construct sentences with the Expert's rhythms and sensibilities.

If you do your job well, the Expert's personality will imprint every page, and readers will feel as if the Expert is speaking to them.

Writing for others forces you to develop a real ear for dialogue and speech mannerisms. And that translates to creating much more believable characters when you do any kind of creative writing on your own.

Cons of Writing for Others

Writing for others isn't for everybody. It's true that certain "cons" can crop up. Of these, the two most prevalent are shown in the following table:

Negative Effect	Rationale
Loss of Bragging Rights (primarily in ghosting)	You can't tell people you created a book. This can be especially galling if the book does very well.
Risk of Being Perceived ONLY as a Writer-For-Hire	Ghosting doesn't actually build your résumé as you can't prove you've written it. There may be a perception that people who ghostwrite have no creative fire of their own.

Of course it's possible for some to downplay your contribution. It's also possible that a joint project may draw attention away from your individual work.

Your "day job" as a ghost doesn't have to interfere with your own projects. There is nothing to stop you from continuing to polish, and to champion your own work while ghosting.

Set aside an hour or two a day, or take an afternoon a week to set the ghost project aside and work on your own writing project.

Don't just shelve your work and your dreams and rent your talent out to the highest bidder. That only breeds resentment, and it will poison everything you touch with regards to your writing career.

How to Determine if a Ghosting Project is Right for You

Whenever I am faced with a potential project that will involve putting my words to work for someone else, I take the time to analyze it from several different vantage points.

I essentially apply a filter of "Six P's" to the project, and answer the following questions: project, person, publisher, professional development, promotion, and profit.

1. **Project:** are you passionate about the book? Can you stay passionate about it for the next nine to twelve months? Is it worthwhile? Does it appear to be something you will be proud to have been a part of?

2. **Person who is the Field Expert:** is the person someone whose talents or expertise you admire? Or does the person have a compelling life story you would be honored to help tell? (Does the person deserve to have you write his or her book?)

3. **Publisher:** will the final book be a quality product? Is the publisher well-known, or well-respected? If a small publisher, do they have a good distribution system? Does the publisher have access to other Field Experts who may need a Ghost at some point?

4. **Professional Development:** will working on this project give you something you need (such as published credits, a byline, a working relationship with a highly respected Field Expert or Publisher, or exposure within a particular niche)?

5. **Promotion:** is this a chance to learn a thing or two about marketing and promotion? Does the project have a big PR push planned, or a huge marketing machine behind it? Does this provide an opportunity to learn as much as you can about the marketing aspect of the business—so you can then apply what you've learned to your own work?

6. **Profit:** All other things being equal, is it worth your while to dedicate your life to this until the project is finished?

At least one of the "Six P's" (Project, Person, Publisher, Professional Development, Promotion, and Profit) must be enough to bring you on board and *keep* you on board.

If more than one of the "P's" appeals to you, that just makes a project doubly compelling.

If you can't find anything in a project to get excited about—*don't do it*. You'll do yourself, and everyone who *is* committed to the project, a huge disservice.

Where to Find Ghosting Opportunities

If you want to meet a writer, go to a writer's conference. If you want to meet people who *need* a writer, go where the professionals are.

Go to conferences, seminars, workshops, and public appearances featuring people whose abilities you admire.

Go to events that feed your soul—that interest *you*. When people ask you what you do, tell them you're a writer.

Remember, you offer a valuable service. There are any number of experts out there who really *need* a book. Make connections with people who need you.

Before Beginning a Ghosting Project...

Before accepting a writing project that allows someone to access your talent with words, make sure you set yourself—and the project—up for success.

Know you can do it. The Expert looks to the writer for guidance on a book project. To the Expert, *you* are the Expert when it comes to putting his or her words on a page and making those words sing.

You *must* know you can produce. It doesn't matter if you don't have a book *published* before you begin. I really believe you must have one *finished*, however.

You have to know, in your heart of hearts, that you can do what you've been brought on to do. There can be no room for soul searching and second-guessing yourself once the project is under way.

Commit to the project. I cannot stress this enough. You've got to love the project through the inevitable growing pains.

(Remember that I said Ghosting was a great way to lose your Writing Ego? Notice I didn't say anything about any loss of the Expert's Ego).

There will be snags along the way. Life will interfere because—that's life.

Be willing to do *whatever it takes* to get the project done well, and done on time. That means there is no room for "it's not my job." That kind of thinking will bog down a project indefinitely.

Know Your Client. Know who your client is. Is it the Publisher? Is it the Expert? Who is paying your bills? Who writes your checks? Know where your loyalties lie, know who makes the ultimate decisions, and be able to work with that situation.

Know Your Deadline. Publishers are very up front about things like deadlines. Usually there's a reason they want a book ready by a certain time.

If the Expert is self-publishing, chances are he or she has a plan for when to release the book.

Get out a calendar and look at your stated deadline. Count back two weeks and consider that *your personal deadline.*

Then, map out a plan. Schedule blocks of time to compile information, draft copy, obtain the Expert's approval and edits, revise, polish, illustrate (if necessary), and edit the manuscript. Commit to the deadline. Refuse to let anything come between you and it. Period.

Have an Iron-Clad Contract. Have the terms and conditions of your writing services spelled out in detail, including what happens if the book is cancelled before publication. The contract should include things like a definition of what constitutes "satisfactory copy," payment agreement (including royalty splits if applicable), deadlines, and a clear explanation of what services (drafting copy, providing content, editing, photo editing) the writer will provide.

It should also have a clearly stated "escape clause" for both writer and client. The most important thing about any contract is how you can dissolve the working relationship. Have an escape clause, but don't use it unless your life depends on it. I've written books while pregnant, while mothering an infant, and while my spouse was in the midst of a life-threatening medical crisis. I've never invoked an escape clause, but it's always good to know that you *can* if you *have* to.

How to Ensure a Great Ghosting Experience

Answering four key questions right at the outset of a ghostwriting, co-authoring, or collaboration project can help to keep your vision for the project clear. It can help guide you through the unknowns that will arise during creation. Before you write Word One, you must know the answers to these questions:

What do I get out of this? Remember your filter of six *Ps*. Articulate exactly how you will benefit from completing the project. What new skills, credits, or contacts will you have at the end of it?

What do I bring to the table? State your strengths. Know your capabilities. List your assets. Know what you do well, so you can fall back on your strengths when the going gets tough.

What will the audience (my readers) take away? Always keep the end reader before you. Though you are speaking in another's voice, you are still speaking to the reader. Be honorable. Deliver real value. Provide the readers with something that will benefit or enrich their lives.

WHY am I doing this project? Know your reasons for committing to the project. They may be the same as "what you get out of it." They may be different. Be honest with yourself and state why you are willing to give someone else the benefit of your writing expertise. Referring to this "why" as the project proceeds can help motivate you to persevere.

About the Author

Ami Hendrickson is an award-winning screenwriter and bestselling author. She has written for some of the leading horsemen in the world including the United States Hunter Jumper Association (USHJA), hunter trainer and judge Geoff Teall, neurosurgeon Dr. James Warson, and Clinton Anderson, of Downunder Horsemanship. Ami is founder and president of Muse Ink (www.museink.com), an online writer's resource site.

Podcast Airdate:	June 7th, 2007
Podcast URL:	http://authorsaccess.com/archives/55
Author's site:	www.museink.com
	www.amihendrickson.com

How I Became a Successful Freelancer
Yvonne Perry

Writers in the Sky Creative Writing Services, also known as WITS, is my Nashville-based writing and editing services company. I started this company in 2003 with a strong belief that I could create the career I wanted by learning as much as I could about the craft and business of writing, focusing on the positive goals I had set, and doing the work necessary to reach these goals. I started out solo, but since have put together a team to diversify the types of writing services we offer our clients. Today, we have a commercial copywriter, four writers who are also editors, a fiction writer, and a graphic designer. We provide writing and editing for books, professional biographies, blogging services, résumés, articles, memoirs, media releases, Web text and marketing pieces to individuals and businesses. We can help with internal book layout, cover design, company newsletters, and business branding. We also offer author publicity packages that include book reviews, manuscript evaluations, book trailers, and interviews on our weekly podcast. With our blog, podcast, and newsletter, we are able to help writers who are trying to get started with their career.

Before sharing the joys and challenges that come with my chosen career, I would like to start by explaining what it means to be a freelance writer in terms of offering services to others. Freelance writing means that I am not employed by a corporation. Instead, I am self-employed—a writer-for-hire under contract with each client. When I am finished with a writing project, the work belongs to the client who hired me to write or edit for them. Freelance writing also means I don't have a guaranteed paycheck each week, which is certainly one of the drawbacks to any form of self-employment. To me, this potential lack of security is worth it because I love what I do.

Know Your Strengths

The products created by a freelance writer will depend on his or her forté. Commercial copy writing, business and technical writing, grant writing, book and article writing, as well as writing for media outlets are all possible avenues to be taken by freelance writers. It took me a couple of years trying several approaches before I found my niche. Today, I do mostly editing and ghostwriting for nonfiction books, and the promotional writing for the business itself. I am fortunate to have team members with backgrounds and specialties that allow us to provide a wide variety of other material. We provide ghostwriting, editing, and proofreading to make sure books that are heading to the market are in top-notch condition for publishing. We also write query letters and book proposals when needed.

My personal journey with writing began at a very young age. I have enjoyed writing ever since I was first introduced to the crayon, but didn't realize I had talent until my creative writing teacher encouraged me as a senior in high school. All throughout the raising of my children, I wrote stories about the cute things they did. I also wrote songs and poems on a regular basis, so I was familiar with language and painting imagery with words. When I took a job as an executive assistant, I was writing correspondence, press releases, and grants for a living. I have always been such an independent person, and therefore found that I really didn't like the corporate environment and its politics. It occurred to me in 2002 that I might be able to make it as a freelance writer. I spent a year planning and arranging my finances in a manner that would allow me to break away from my day job and give business ownership a try. I paid off every possible debt, saved any extra money that I could for the business, got my Web site up and running and even refinanced the house to get a better interest rate so that my income wouldn't be as needed. These steps gave me the financial freedom to try this new venture. Today, almost five year later, WITS is flourishing.

Getting Started

A blog or Web site is a first priority in today's market. You must have an online presence. Take the time to establish a Web site or a blog, a platform that will showcase what you can do and what you are trying to accomplish. You may want to include a portfolio of writing samples, or a media kit in case someone wants to interview you. You also should have a biography detailing your professional and personal background.

If you are just getting started and do not yet have an extensive supply of writing samples to share with potential clients on a Web site, you might consider registering with online services that match writers with companies and individuals who need writing assistance. I built my writing portfolio through Guru.com. Through this matchmaking service, I had to bid and pitch my skills and services. I wouldn't want to do that now because I have the business coming in from other avenues. But, at the time, it taught me how to write query letters, how to present myself in a positive light to potential clients, and it built my portfolio as I did these small jobs for little pay. I gained a great deal from that experience. A reputable service that matches writers with clients is a really good way for a beginner to get started.

You may be interested in pursuing a career specifically as an independent article writer. In this instance, you want to create a one-page query letter that provides as much information in as few words as possible. Give the content the article will provide. Tell what it will do for the reader or how the magazine will benefit from publishing your article. Offer some specific ideas concerning the topics of articles you would like to send them. Mention how your article fits into the theme or overall message the magazine or newspaper is trying to portray. It behooves the writer to know a lot about the magazine. Read some previous issues and be able to discuss particular stories. Get a list of their publication schedule for the next six months. Magazine editors are always working six to eight months in advance. Rather than sending the entire article upfront, you might first want to make sure the acquisitions editor wants to see your work.

Over the past few years, I have developed a strong background in ghostwriting books for clients. A client may be a public speaker with a wonderful topic on which they are well-versed. People are always coming to their seminars and asking if there is a related book available. A book is an avenue that allows professionals to expand their reach and gain an audience beyond those at any particular conference. Back of the room sales may be the goal of this client. Other clients may be someone who has a great idea but cannot imagine putting together such a large project as a book. It's very time-consuming to write a well-researched book. One of my own titles, *Right to Recover, Winning the Political and Religious Wars over Stem Cell Research in America* took 600 hours to complete due to the extensive research required. Even as writing professionals, it takes WITS four to six months to ghostwrite a book.

Ghostwriting for Books

If a client wants us to ghost a book, our ghostwriter will take information–seminar notes, slide shows, published articles–and begin to formulate an outline of content working with the author every step of the way. We gather information through interviews by phone, fax, email, or in person. Then, we put the book together from start to finish. The client approves the proof we prepare and then we move on to the editing stage, and finally, the proofreading stage. The author's name will be on the cover of the book and we will probably not even be mentioned unless the author chooses to note that we were the editor or ghostwriter. By the time we are finished, the client has a book that is ready to self-publish, send to a publish-on-demand company, or pitch to a conventional publisher.

Selling your articles to magazines and ghostwriting books are just two of the endless opportunities available to those interested in the freelance writing world. I encourage anyone who is considering this path to look at other options such as blogging, business or technical writing, editing and proofreading, book reviews, press releases, and creation of Web site text as exciting possibilities.

Once you've made the decision to become a freelance writer, and you know the areas in which you plan to specialize, you will start your online marketing. Then, comes the task of making sure you are organized as a business entrepreneur. For me, the greatest challenge is cataloging my daily tasks for maximum productivity–not only family time versus work time, but also the time spent during my office hours. I have to balance the time spent on marketing and networking versus the time spent on actual writing projects. To this end, I keep an organizer on my desk that's written in thirty-minute intervals and I know what I need to get done by a certain date. I usually go out to that due date and then work backwards to set up a time line and break the work into manageable daily portions. I keep in mind the due date of projects I am currently working and use that to determine how many more clients I reasonably can accept and when I can take on another project. If a client is in a hurry and my schedule is full, I send the leads to one of the other writers or editors on my team.

Writers in the Sky is able to fill just about any niche in the writing market. If I cannot complete the project or if someone on my team cannot do it, I have an established network of writers across the United States upon whom I can call. We know what our limits are as a team, we know what we can do and do well, and we won't take on a project we don't feel we can complete on time and in a quality manner. By taking the time to develop your networking skills, you will improve your sense of professionalism in the eyes of potential clients and discover opportunities when the favor of a referral is returned.

You Are an Entrepreneur

On a related note, one of the most important reminders I can provide is that freelance writers are also business owners. As the head of a freelance writing team, it is up to me to market the business, bring in new clients, and give these clients the best writing and customer service possible in hopes that they will refer us to others. Writers may not recognize this essential role at the onset. But, take a moment to consider that we have to manage our time and money, promote our business, generate sales, keep records, book the next speaking engagement, and countless other details. A lot of people can write, but selling what you have written is another venture altogether. You have to do both to be successful as a freelance writer. Either you must query magazines and newspapers in hopes of selling an article idea, or you must market and promote your writing services to the world-at-large in hopes of gaining clients. Without the business piece of the job, there's no money in the endeavor. Writing for fun is one thing. Writing for profit is another. Hopefully, a freelance writer can do both.

Do not jump into the world of freelance writing cold turkey. Don't quit that day job and think you're going to have clients tomorrow. I took a year to prepare myself for this professional change, and this career is still a work in process. I build on it every day. Tell yourself, "I'm happy where I am today, but I know I'm going to be in a better place tomorrow." And, even when you don't see the paychecks coming, don't give up or get discouraged by the process. If you're good at what you do and you're persistent at marketing and you can assure clients that you are trustworthy, you will land paying jobs. Be patient and believe in your skills and the products you create.

About the Author

Yvonne Perry and her team provide ghostwriting and editing companies and individuals. Yvonne is also the author of eleven children's eBooks, a humorous book titled *Email Episodes*, which is about mid-life crisis, a paperback book titled *More Than Meets the Eye: True Stories about Death, Dying and Afterlife*, which provides comfort to those who are grieving the loss of a loved one; and *Right to Recover Winning the Political and Religious Wars over Stem Cell Research in America*. She is the host of the Writers in the Sky Podcast a weekly show about the craft and business of writing in which she interviews guest authors, publishers, and book marketing experts about writing, book publishing, marketing, and a variety of topics to assist freelance writers.

Podcast Airdate:	August 21st, 2008
Podcast URL:	http://authorsaccess.com/archives/109
Author's site:	www.writersinthesky.com

7 Building Buzz with Book Reviews

Everything You Need to Know about Book Reviews
Irene Watson

Every author wants glowing book reviews with quotable sentences because a good review could entice the reader to purchase the book. But, how do authors get their books reviewed? While the process is not difficult, there are more than 400,000 titles published every year and most of those are vying for a review. Because of this, authors must designate a portion of their marketing budget and time for book reviews, and they must know how to use those book reviews to sell books.

Reasons to get reviews

- To promote books—it's the most effective way. Buyers/readers value other people's opinions when looking for a book to read.
- To gain credibility. You want to get as many reviews as possible and have them posted on Amazon.com. Many people go to Amazon.com just to get reviews.
- To post on your Web site or to link to the reviewer's Web site. Some reviewers allow you to use excerpts only and not the full review. Be sure to check.
- To include in a media kit.
- To send with publication to other reviewers.
- To add excerpts to your review/testimonial Web site page.
- To send to wholesalers, dealers, and subsidiary rights buyers.
- To use as endorsements/blurbs for back of publication.
- To give the review as much mileage as you can!

Where to get reviews

Every author strives to get a review from one of these top three reviewers: *Publishers Weekly*, *Library Journal*, and *Kirkus Reviews*. They all have strict guidelines—only accepting galleys three to four months before publication date.

Library Journal alone receives over 30,000 books every year from hopeful authors. About 5,500 are reviewed. If you are self-published it's very difficult to get your book reviewed by these companies. However, that said, it can be done.

There are many other legitimate review services available online. Be sure to check them out thoroughly and read their guidelines—twice.

Free vs. Paid Reviews

Since the beginning of book publishing, it was an industry standard to expect free book reviews; advertisements paid for the book reviews in print media. Today, however, authors must consider covering the cost of book reviews. A book reviewer spends hours reading a book and writing a review, and he or she deserves compensation for the work. Not only that, if the review is done professionally, posted on the Web site, as well as other online places like Amazon.com, there is overhead involved. Expecting someone to "give" a free review and not be compensated for his or her out-of-pocket expenses is not morally correct. Consequently, authors must budget for the cost of book reviews. Authors are recommended to budget for mailing out a minimum of twenty books for review.

How Do Paid Book Reviews Work?

Most publications and online book review services that offer free reviews do not guarantee a book review because of the volume of books submitted. Reputable book reviewers will provide a review within a specific timeline—two weeks is standard. They will also provide a review tear-sheet for your use, and give you permission to quote the review, provided you credit them. Many reviewers will also post your review online at such places as their own Web site, Amazon, Barnes & Noble, EzineArticles, Goodreads and Authors Den.

Several online book reviewers, such as Reader Views, will give you the option of a free or paid book review. Reader Views will review the book for free provided one of their reviewers is interested in it. If no one opts to review it after three months, the book is donated to a charity. If authors do not want to wait three months for a review, an express review can be purchased to guarantee a review within two weeks.

Just because you pay for an express book review does not mean a five star review is guaranteed. It is better to receive an honest review than one that gives false praise. The reviewer's reputation is at stake here; readers will not appreciate being misled to waste their time and money on a book that does not meet their expectations.

How to get a review

There are 400,000 new book titles published yearly in the USA. Reviewers get anywhere from 50 to 200 requests per week; however, in many cases review services only have one to thirty-five reviewers. When you consider how many books are received, it's not much wonder many books get passed by. When submitting your book to Reader Views or any other review service, it's important to understand that you are not the only one who needs review services. Please take the time to read the guidelines carefully (twice) before submitting your book.

Here are some other tips:

- Check to be sure the service reviews in your genre.
- If there is a request for a submission form to be filled out online, fill it out with as much information as possible. This is what "sells" your book.
- Don't ask for a review if you don't have a copy of the publication to send. If you are waiting for a shipment, wait until it arrives before you ask for a review.
- Give a thorough synopsis. This is your selling point. One-liners just don't do it. Include a sell sheet, and most importantly, your contact information. (You wouldn't believe how many books we receive without any contact information!)
- Be sure to include your Web site address. In many cases, reviewers will check the Web site for more information about the book.
- When sending in your book for review, don't put "requested material" on the envelope unless it was truly requested. Trying to get a review this way will only discredit you.

If you don't get accepted, ask yourself these questions:
- Did I follow the guidelines exactly?
- Does the reviewer work in my genre?
- Was the synopsis thorough? Did I have the hook?
- Did I include my contact information?

- Did my book look appealing? (Yes, books are judged by the cover!)
- Did I have my book edited thoroughly? (And, this doesn't mean running through a spell checker.)
- Boils down to: preparation, presentation, luck of the draw.

How to spot a scam reviewer

- Scammers do not provide tear sheets, or their review on their letterhead.
- Scammers solicit under false pretenses.
- Scammers do not have reviews or book postings on their Web site, nor do they post on other Web sites like Amazon.com
- Scammers do not read your book in order to give their honest opinions. They use the synopsis to write a review and add a one-liner to personalize it.
- Scammers collect books from authors and sell on Amazon.com, eBay.com or to used bookstores.

This is where homework is very important. There are many scam reviewers, so be wary of them. However, there are many legitimate review services available online. Check to see how many reviews they have posted, and whether or not the reviewer's name is disclosed. Also, check the formatting of the review. Is it just thrown together, or is it professionally formatted? Check, check, check.

Other important factors

- If you've sent a query and the reviewer wants to review your book, **send your publication immediately!** The reviewer has accepted your book and is ready to start—NOW. We suggest USPS Priority Mail or First Class with Delivery Confirmation. The least favored option is MediaMail, which we do not recommend, because it's too slow and there is a greater chance of loss.
- If the service requests the books be sent to their office, be sure to **read the guidelines** (again) for the correct procedure.
- **Do not send an e-mail telling the reviewer to contact your publisher** to request your book or pick up the publication at a local copy place. This is a definite "no-no." The reviewer is providing you a service; you are not providing a service for them.

- **Send a "new" copy of your book, not a used, dog eared copy.** Take pride in your creation. Every reviewer on our team that we polled told us the first thing they do when they open a package is examine the cover and the book itself. Remember, first impressions count!
- **Do not deface your publication** by writing "Do Not Sell" or "Review Copy" on it. Instead, honor the reviewer by giving them an autographed copy, making sure you personalize it for them. If you don't have the reviewer's name, just simply autograph the book. Most reviewers keep their books, donate them to libraries, or pass them on to friends to read. If you send your book to a credible reviewer, they aren't going to sell it.
- **Send a media package with the book:** bio, synopsis, other reviews, news release. Be sure your information is compact. There is nothing worse than opening a package and a bunch of "stuff" falls out on the floor. Your care in packaging gives the reviewer some insight on you. Be sure to include contact information. You wouldn't believe how many books we receive without any contact information. Those automatically go on the donate pile.
- **Enclose a self-addressed stamped post card.** Ask the reviewer to fill this out and return it, acknowledging receipt of the book and an expected review date.
- **Enclose a personal, handwritten note to the reviewer.** After all, the reviewer is volunteering a tremendous service for you.
- **Take pride in how you package your book.** Use bubble wrap to prevent any damage during mailing. I recommend an inner, clear plastic bag (from ULINE) or Ziploc™ to hold it all together. When we polled our reviewers they said the first thing they notice when a publication arrives is the packaging. So, wrap it with care!
- **Keep a log of every book you send,** including the date it was sent, the recipient, the tracking number, the mailing address and the date you receive your tear sheet. Do not send an email to the reviewer asking if they received your book – this is where your tracking number will give you the answer.

After you receive your review

- Send a personal thank you note to the reviewer. Remember, they are volunteers and have provided you a tremendous service.

- Post the review on Amazon.com if the reviewer does not. Most credible reviewers will post it for you.
- Get as much mileage as possible from the review.

About the Author

Irene Watson, MA is the Managing Editor of Reader Views, (www.readerviews.com) an online book review and author publicity service. Reader Views is located in Austin, Texas. For more information, see About the Editors on p. 215.

Podcast Airdate:	June 27th, 2007
Podcast URL:	http://authorsaccess.com/archives/63
Author's site:	www.irenewatson.com
	www.readerviews.com
	www.thesittingswing.com

Creating Bound Galleys and Advance Review Copies

Tyler R. Tichelaar and Irene Watson

Authors benefit from having their books reviewed before publication so the reviews appear simultaneously with the publication date. Book reviews can often take months to receive, and because bookstores require quick turnaround for the shelf life of new books, an author usually cannot afford to wait for post-publication reviews. Authors and publishers should send out pre-publication copies of books to ensure timely book reviews.

Bound galleys and Advance Review Copies (ARCs) are sent to pre-publication reviewers five to six months prior to publication date. Keep in mind the reasoning—not only does it take time for the mailing and reviewing process, but most publications and periodicals have editorial calendars at least four to six months prior to production. For example, Christmas themed books must be sent out for review in June or July at the latest, because by the beginning of September, the publication is already in process. Many publications will feature Christmas themes as early as in their November issues.

Whether you use a bound galley or an ARC is entirely up to you. What is important is to make the publication easy for the reviewers to use. It is extremely important that all the information listed below is included and placed in specific areas. Remember, you are competing with 400,000 other book titles annually needing reviews. Reviewers are busy people—if they don't have the information they need readily available to them, your book will be rejected or ignored. They will not take the time to "hunt down" the information. Another important reason why all information should be on a bound galley or ARC is that the publication copy will end up separated from the media kit or supporting documents, such as the sell sheet or press release.

Here are some guidelines and definitions for preparing a Bound Galley or Advance Review Copy.

Bound Galley

A bound galley looks like and is the same size as the final book but has a plain cover. The cover may be white or colored. If you are using a colored cover, be sure the black printing is easy to see on it. (Red or dark colors are not a good idea. Use white, yellow, buff, light blue). The cover doesn't indicate what the final book will look like and will still need several passes of editing. It is created at least six months prior to publication date. Bound galleys are sent to pre-publication reviewers.

The front cover should have:

- Name of book
- Author name
- Category (e.g. Fiction—Mystery; Nonfiction—Memoir)
- Size specifications (e.g. Trade paperback 6 x 9, # pages)
- Price
- ISBN
- First print run (number of copies). Keep in mind many large pre-pub reviewers will only review books of 5000+ copies on the first run.
- Promotional plan (e.g. direct mailings, book tours, bookstore displays, book release party, etc.)
- Available from (e.g. a distributor such as Baker & Taylor or Ingram)
- Publisher (name/mailing address/Web site address)
- Primary Contact (publicist, consultant, author—name, address, email address)
- Statement: "Uncorrected Proof—Not for Sale" (Make this bold and easily seen)

The back cover should have:

- Brief Synopsis (The hook—same as on the book. The synopsis will entice the reviewer to read your book. Remember, the supporting documents may get separated from the actual galley).
- Author bio

The spine should have:

- Name of book
- Name of author
- Publisher name or representative colophon (icon)

Advance Review Copy (ARC)

An ARC looks like and is the same size as the final book. It indicates what the final book will look like, but it still needs one more editing. It is created at least six months prior to publication date. ARCs are sent to pre-publication reviewers and may be used instead of bound galleys.

The front cover should look exactly the same as the final publication; however, "Advance Review Copy—Not for Sale" must be printed on it. The back cover looks exactly like the final copy, including the synopsis, author bio, ISBN, etc. The spine must include the book title, author's name, and the publisher.

The very first page of the ARC should have the following information:
- Name of book
- Author name
- Category (e.g. Fiction—Mystery; Nonfiction—Memoir)
- Size specifications (e.g. Trade paperback 6 x 9, # pages)
- Price
- ISBN
- First print run (number of copies). Keep in mind many pre-pub reviewers will only review books of 5000+ copies on the first run.
- Promotional plan (e.g. direct mailings, book tours, bookstore displays, book release party, etc.)
- Available from (e.g. a distributor such as Baker & Taylor or Ingram)
- Publisher (name/mailing address/Web site address)
- Primary Contact (publicist, consultant, author—name, address, email address)

Depending on your publisher or printer, you may receive bound galleys or ARC's, or you may request your publisher or printer send them to you to mail to reviewers.

Finally, be sure to read the submission guidelines of each individual reviewer. Some will not accept anything but the final published book. Others may accept ARC's but not bound galleys. Make sure you follow the reviewer's directions so your book gets the attention it deserves!

About the Authors

Learn more about Irene Watson, MA and Tyler R. Tichelaar, Ph.D. in the About the Editors section beginning on p. 215.

Negative Book Reviews: How to Avoid Them, and How to Use Them to Your Advantage

Tyler R. Tichelaar

All authors dream of writing a bestseller the critics will praise, causing sales to skyrocket and royalty checks to fill the mailbox. While such fame is possible, negative book reviews are just as likely. Consequently, authors must prepare for negative reviews, and more importantly, do everything possible before the book is published to make sure the book is the best it can be.

Why Books Get Negative Reviews

We've all seen movies and TV sitcoms, where a restaurant owner dreads the restaurant critic who can make or break the business. Book reviewers may not be as high profile, but they have equal power to hurt a book's sales. Contrary to popular depictions of critics, book reviewers are rarely pompous or fickle. Book reviewers love books. They want to enjoy and recommend your book. When a negative review is given, it is usually because the author failed to do the work necessary to receive a positive review. Here are primary reasons why books receive negative reviews:

Poor story line, poor character development, and choppy writing. Self-published books generally fall into this category because the authors are not professional writers or did not seek outside help, advice or reader responses. A story may be fully alive in the writer's mind, but good writing requires attention to detail, purpose, character motivation and the ability to make the reader suspend belief. Authors need a second opinion to ensure they have accomplished these goals.

Poor editing and proofreading. Nothing says "self-published" more than a book full of typos. Because self-published authors use their own funds to publish their books, many unwisely cut costs by not paying to have the book edited or proofread. Consequently, disgruntled readers give the book bad reviews. Authors must budget for editing and proofreading as well as book promotion. Until you can afford to have the book professionally edited, do not publish it. A history book with typos that include such errors as President Roosevelt's name spelled wrong or the year 1976 where 1776 is meant destroys the author's credibility. Even in fiction, typos distract the reader from following the plot.

Poor research. If a reviewer is an expert in the subject matter, he is going to notice mistakes you made or facts you left out. Do your research.

Failure to get reader responses from your potential audience. Do not publish a children's book until you let some children read it to see whether they enjoy it. If you are a senior citizen, the younger generations probably won't be interested in your book on finding romance since their views of dating are different than yours.

How Do I Make Sure I Won't Get A Negative Review?

Several services exist to help you craft a professional well-written book. The most important action is to work on your book, research all the details, write and revise several drafts, and proofread it carefully. When you are absolutely certain your book is as perfect as possible, ask others to read it. Start with a friend or family member you can trust to give you an honest opinion. If they like it, then submit it to a publisher, literary agent, or publicist for an evaluation.

Many of the print-on-demand and book review companies offer evaluations. iUniverse will provide you an editorial evaluation with many of their publishing packages, which allows you to get someone's comments on your book before it is published. Reader Views, a book review company, will provide an editorial evaluation of your manuscript for a reasonable fee. Such evaluations allow you to go back and rewrite the book with a better idea of your potential audience's reaction. Writer's Relief will help you layout your book in a manner publishers will be more willing to view.

Once you have finished all your revisions, have the book professionally edited and proofread. Hire an editor to tighten your language. Then hire a proofreader to catch the typos. No matter how perfect you think your book is, it is best to have someone else look it over because your eyes will fail to see on paper anything but the words you believe you wrote.

What If I Still Get A Negative Review?

If you have followed all this advice and you still get a negative book review, all is not lost.

- **Most importantly, don't lose your temper.** A negative review may point out weak aspects of your writing that will help you become a more effective writer of your next book or even the second edition of your current work.

- **Don't hide from the world.** The review is just one person's opinion. It's highly possible good reviews will still come.
- **Learn from your mistakes.** If you get several negative reviews, you have work to do. You can republish the book with revisions.
- **Find something good in the review.** You may still find a quotable passage to promote your book. The reviewer might not like your characters, but he might remark that the book is well researched. He may complain about the proofreading, but he may still like the story concept.
- **Build a relationship with the reviewer.** Send a thank you note and tell the reviewer you appreciate his honesty. The reviewer will be impressed by your professionalism, and this will leave open a line of communication and a possible good review for your next book.
- **Remember, even a negative review is better than no book review.** In the long run, you will become a better writer and hopefully sell more books.

About the Author

Learn more about Tyler R. Tichelaar, Ph.D. in the About the Editors section beginning on p. 215.

Elements of a Quality Book Review
Tyler R. Tichelaar

Most authors are concerned about getting a "good" or "bad" review. What is of equal if not greater importance is getting a quality book review. A reviewer may say good things about a book, but the quality of the review may still be bad. A reviewer might say bad things about a book but the reviewer may have done a good job illustrating why the book is bad. A quality book review will help sell books far more than a poorly written review that praises the book because readers will not pay attention to a reviewer's opinion if his review makes it clear he is not qualified to review the book.

To write a quality book review, the reviewer must understand a book review's purpose. A book review is not a book report, a summary of the book, or a testimonial for the book. While it may include or be similar to those, the purpose of a book review is to report on and evaluate what is published. In short, a book review is to serve as a guide to the public whether reading a book is worthwhile. Each year hundreds of thousands of books are published—no one can even read one tenth of one percent of them within a year. A quality book review will separate the chaff from the wheat, the quality from the trash, the informative from the ignorant, the entertaining from the dull. A book review should allow its readers to make an informed decision about whether to buy or read a book.

Good book reviewers who are reliable can create personal followings. If reviewers lower their standards, if they review bad books, or worst of all, if they recommend bad books, they have failed in their purpose and will lose the trust of their readers.

Good book reviews will focus on good books; flaws in a book may still be pointed out because no piece of writing is perfect, but good book reviews will bring to their readers' attention the books that truly deserve to be read, books that can help readers see life and situations in a new light while entertaining them and providing them with new and valuable information.

To illustrate the elements that compose a good book review, and how the elements are different between fiction and non-fiction, I will provide examples from two books I have reviewed for Reader Views. I enjoyed and gave positive reviews to both books. I will only briefly quote from my reviews of these books but the full reviews can be found at www.ReaderViews.com.

The fiction work is *In High Places* by Tom Morrisey (Bethany House 2007, ISBN 9780764203466). This novel is part of the Christian fiction genre, a genre I occasionally read but of which I am not particularly fond. I felt, however, that Morrisey did an excellent job of not being preachy in working Christianity into the novel, and I thought his storyline effective and his characters well-developed so it stood out for me as an example of what the Christian fiction genre should seek to accomplish.

The non-fiction book is *A South Divided: Portraits of Dissent in the Confederacy* by David C. Downing (Cumberland House Publishing 2007, ISBN 97815825879). I am always interested in history, and I thought Downing did an excellent job of bringing attention to a side of the Civil War that has not been given adequate attention previously.

The elements that should be included in a good book review are as follows:

The Purpose of the Book

Fiction—The book review will tell you what the story is about, providing enough of a plot introduction to catch the reader's interest. It will describe the content so the reader feels suspense and interest and wants to know further what happens. Mention of the author's theme is also essential. The climax and resolution should never be mentioned—the reader does not want the plot given away. Quotes may be included as an example of the author's style and approach.

Here is the description of the plot I provided for Morrisey's novel:

> *In High Places* by Tom Morrisey opens with Patrick Nolan and his father, Kevin, bonding as father and son during a rock climbing expedition at Seneca Rocks in West Virginia in 1976. The opening is a bit too filled with rock-climbing terminology, but if the reader is patient, within a few pages, the novel draws us in as Patrick and Kevin return home, only to discover Patrick's mother has died, apparently by committing suicide.
>
> Patrick and Kevin's grief is tremendous, but as men, they find themselves unable to discuss it with one another. The reader is aware both are silently suffering, not knowing how to comfort each other, and their lack of belief in God makes it more difficult for them to find solace for their pain.
>
> Unable to live in their home because it reminds them too much of their lost loved one, Patrick's father decides they will return to Seneca

Rocks and open up a shop selling climbing equipment. This new life keeps them busy and helps them forget their grief for a short time.

The plot becomes complicated when Patrick meets and falls in love with Rachel, a preacher's daughter. When the preacher and Patrick's father meet, the preacher tries to talk to Kevin about God and Heaven, but Kevin becomes angry, refusing to believe in a God who would allow his wife to commit suicide.

I introduce the characters and plot as well as the theme—grief and the question of God's existence. I make it clear the theme is essential to the conflict because the fathers have opposing beliefs about the existence of God, yet their children are in love. The reader of the review is left to understand the book will explore how God could allow suicide to happen and bring such pain to a family, and also how Patrick and Rachel will struggle to have a relationship when their fathers have different religious viewpoints.

Non-Fiction—The book review will explain what the purpose or theme of the book is. Again quotes may be included to give the reader an idea of the author's style and approach. Here is my example from Downing's *A South Divided*.

David C. Downing's new book *A South Divided: Portraits of Dissent in the Confederacy* is a fascinating and long overdue book. While he references a few books that have preceded his about divisions in the Southern States, "A South Divided" brings to the forefront a forgotten piece of American history that was far more complicated than we have been led to believe.

Downing makes the point that "the South" and the "Confederacy" are not interchangeable terms. Many people in the South did not support the Confederacy but wished to preserve the Union, and many Southerners acted subversively to support the Union during the war. Downing demonstrates that there is a lot of gray area in the battle between the blue and the gray.

Again, I stated what the book was about, what the theme was and why it mattered by explaining the importance of terminology and that history is not as black and white as it may seem.

Note that for both fiction and non-fiction, I stated quotes may be included to give the reader an idea of the author's style and approach. I recommend quoting from the book, although I did not do so with either of my above examples. In deciding whether to quote, space may be a consideration. If you are writing a review for a publication that has a word limit, you may not have room to quote. It you have the room, however, it is advisable to quote the author. It is especially recommended if the writer's style is distinctive. For example, when I reviewed *Foot Ways* by Lynn Veach Sadler (Bards and Sages, 2007, ISBN 9780615145631) I opened the review by saying:

> *Foot Ways* by Lynn Veach Sadler is one of the most creative, whimsical, and enjoyable books I have read in recent years. It is a short book, but one written with a true precision of language and thought.

Because I focused on the author's creativity and language at the beginning of the review, it was necessary to provide the reader an example to support that statement, which I did by quoting one phrase from the book, the name of an event that takes place. I also compared the book to other well-known books and literary genres so readers familiar with those works would have a better idea of the author's style.

> ...this book is remarkably unique in its humor. It reads like a fable or old wives' tale. I felt as if I were alternately reading Christina Rossetti's *Goblin Market*, James Joyce's *Finnegan's Wake*, old Scottish ballads, and Southern Gothic literature. Sadler creates moments of the grotesque such as Polly's father selling tickets for people to see her mother dying of cancer. People come from all over to see "The Woman Eaten Up," and when single men come, Polly hides for fear her father will force her into marriage with one. For me, the book's highlight was when Polly performed at the "Annual Masonic Lodge Number Fourteen Spring Jubilee Barbecue and Chicken Stew Supper and Theatrical Performance Tribute." That name alone suggests the whimsicalness of the event where people in the community go looking for a bit of culture. What happens at the (it bears repeating) "Annual Masonic Lodge Number Fourteen Spring Jubilee Barbecue and Chicken Stew Supper and Theatrical Performance Tribute" is the true climax of the novel.

What is the Book's Value

Fiction—The review will tell the reader whether the book is entertaining or whether it offers insights into life and human nature. The reviewer should briefly, without dully listing, but rather integrating them, mention the four main elements of fiction: the plot, theme, characters and style.

For example, in Morrisey's *In High Places* I listed the plot, theme, and names of the characters in the opening paragraphs I quoted above. Usually, while describing the plot, the review can also describe the theme and characters. Those opening paragraphs are largely a summary of the opening of the book. Discussion of style and to a lesser extent characters, plot and theme, focus upon the book's value—the importance of the message or theme and also how well it succeeds in its goal. With style, I focused on the point-of-view from which the story was told.

> I think Morrisey handles the difficult questions and situations he creates with great maturity and tactfulness. I especially admired his decision to tell the story from Patrick's perspective, which allowed for all the questioning of a teenage boy, making the novel a story of a father-son relationship, a coming of age story, and a love story combined.

Non-Fiction—The review will tell the reader the worthiness of the research done on the subject and also the value of the information provided. For example, the reviewer might comment upon what he personally learned from the book.

In discussing, *A South Divided* I do not mention the author's research directly, but by mentioning the many examples Downing provides of sections of the South that did not want to separate from the Union, I make it clear that the author did considerable research.

> Equally interesting were the discussions of Southern states and counties that opposed secession from the Union. West Virginia's story of division with Virginia and its own incorporation into the Union is the most notable and best known though seldom told story. However, counties in Tennessee, Mississippi, and Alabama also all sought to separate themselves from the states they were in and create their own independent states within the Union. These cases were less successful than West Virginia, but the number of them shows how much the South was divided.

What, if any, are the Book's Faults?

If a book truly is deplorably bad, it is best not to review it. A good reviewer will always find something kind and encouraging to say—for example, that the book is historically accurate or that the author clearly did his research, even if the author is a poor novelist. Overall, however, a review of a bad book is a waste of time for the reviewer and his readers. It is better not to bring attention to bad books, and especially in print media where there is limited space, to leave room for the many deserving books to receive reviews. Reviewers should always be honest because their duty is to readers who trust the reviewer to keep them from wasting their time and money on bad books.

A book reviewer should avoid being patronizing by telling the author how to rewrite the book. For example, "The book would have been better had the author developed the courtship between the characters longer" or "The author failed to mention [some interesting fact] that had a major influence on the events described." The book review is not a contest between the author and the reviewer where the reviewer is trying to show he or she is more intelligent than the author. If the reviewer knows more than the author, he should write his own book on the topic. In my own examples of pointing out flaws in the book, I try to be honest and direct, yet tactful.

Fiction—The review will describe where the book is lacking. For example, did a plot twist occur because of a character's actions but the character's motivation for the act was not clear? Was the outcome of the story unbelievable? Is the book full of typographical errors or is the writing poor?

In Morrisey's *In High Places* I found a few stumbling blocks but also pointed out that what I did not care for in the book was largely the result of my personal preferences. I quickly moved past what I perceived as the book's flaws to explain the book's greater value.

> The opening is a bit too filled with rock-climbing terminology, but if the reader is patient, within a few pages, the novel draws us in as Patrick and Kevin return home, only to discover Patrick's mother has died, apparently by committing suicide.

And later in the review:

> Some readers may be turned off that *In High Places* is clearly a Christian book, but Kevin Nolan's questioning of God made me feel the book was not trying to preach or convince the reader of the

truths of Christianity. Instead, it asked a legitimate question about why God would allow bad things to happen to good people. The book does not give easy answers; even when Patrick learns more about the details surrounding his mother's death, the novel does not seek to answer the question of why God allowed his mother to die. Rather than bring simple closure, the book opens up layers of complexity regarding the human condition and human behavior; it explores the difficulties and unanswerable reasons behind why people love and hurt each other. The book is hopeful, but the hopefulness is mixed with a strong realism throughout.

Non-Fiction—The review will describe where the book's argument is weak or the research inadequate. For example, does the author appear completely ignorant of something that is otherwise general knowledge about his topic? Is there faulty logic used by the author to bring about his main point?

When I reviewed Downing's *A South Divided*, I only found one piece of information I felt was missing, and I walked a fine line trying not to slip into telling the author how to write his book. I also gave the author the benefit of the doubt for why he did not include the information I thought was missing.

> The only information I felt missing from the book was the story of President Andrew Johnson, who was only mentioned briefly, yet I cannot help feeling he was the most important Southerner, or at least the Southerner who rose to the highest rank within the Union during the war. Perhaps Downing felt the story of Johnson and his impeachment was already well known, but I would have liked to see Johnson included. I think it would have been a good contrast, especially because Downing discusses how skeptical Lincoln and many others were about promoting General Thomas because he was a Southerner, so I would have liked to know more about why Johnson was given such a high position as vice-president.

In the end, a good book review will tell the reader why he should read the book, and good reviewers will remember that their role is not to display their own abilities, nor to patronize or applaud the author. A book reviewer's foremost purpose is to provide reliable suggestions for good reading to the reading public.

About the Author

Learn more about Tyler R. Tichelaar, Ph.D. in the About the Editors section beginning on p. 215.

8   Marketing Your Work

Promoting Your Book with a Publicist
Maryglenn McCombs

Whether you are an experienced author or a new author, you probably know you have to create awareness in order to create demand for a book. To create awareness, you have to promote your book. Some authors prefer to do their own promotion, while others prefer to seek out a publicist to represent them and their book.

What Exactly Does a Book Publicist Do?

A book publicist's job is to create awareness for your book, whether through book reviews, articles, feature stories, mentions, or radio and television interviews. Publicists work as a liaison between the author and the media with the goal of generating coverage of an author and his or her work. Publicists who are accustomed to working with books understand how to promote a book effectively, and also understand the importance of timing. Moreover, a good book publicist has strong contacts with the media.

Why Should I Consider Hiring a Book Publicist?

If you're uncomfortable with trying to promote yourself and your own product, consider hiring a publicist to do the promotion for you. Some authors are terrific promoters but freeze at the thought of trying to promote their own books. That's entirely understandable—and extremely common. If you feel uneasy about trying to do your own promotions, by all means: consider hiring someone else to do it for you.

Also, if your time is extremely limited and you don't feel you would have the necessary time to devote to promoting your book effectively, definitely consider hiring a publicist. Book promotion can be extremely time-consuming—and even more so if you don't know where to start.

What Do I Need To Do Before I Decide Whether To Hire a Publicist?

Whether you decide to do your own promotion or hire a publicist to do the work for you, it's important that you understand the importance of timing.

Before you start to look for a publicist or put together your own plan of book promotion, you should start by setting a publication date for your book. There is a great deal of confusion about what a publication date ("pub date") really is.

A pub date is an "official release" —usually at least six weeks after a book comes off press. In some ways, this is a phantom date, as it is an approximate date when books will be available in stores. A pub date is an important part of planning a PR Campaign for your books, as it facilitates coordinating media placements and in-store availability. The pub date functions as a means of tying the book promotion and distribution together.

Regardless of when you or your publisher decide to set your book's pub date, just make sure you have plenty of time to lay the necessary groundwork to ensure that your book is a success.

When Should I Start To Look For a Publicist?

Start looking for a publicist as soon as possible. In the book business, timing really is everything. Having plenty of lead time is essential when launching a new book. The PR wheels start to turn long before a book ever makes it to a bookstore shelf. In fact, many PR campaigns begin before the final edits are complete and before the final touches have been made to a book's cover design.

A great deal of advance planning goes in to the making of a PR campaign for a book. Unedited bound proofs of a book, either galleys or ARCs ("Advance Review Copies"), are widely distributed before a book is released. These ARCs make their way into reviewers' hands well in advance of when a book will be available in stores.

Publishers Weekly, one of the leading publishing industry trades, "forecasts" books by providing advance reviews of noteworthy titles. This particular magazine, and many like it, requests that advance review copies be received at least four-to-five months in advance of when a book is in stores.

Longer lead glossy monthly magazines typically operate on a four-to-six month (or longer) advance schedule. For example, come December many magazines are well into working on articles and stories that will appear the following summer.

Here is a sample timeline for a PR campaign for an as-yet-to-be-released book:

Date Range	Action Items
6-8 months in advance of pub date (or longer if possible)	Solicit long lead magazine coverage (glossy monthly magazines, journals, quarterlies)
4-6 months in advance of pub date	Solicit coverage with trade/sell-in publications (primarily book and library trade magazines), major reviewers, and larger major national shows
1-2 months in advance of pub date thru post-publication	Work to obtain shorter lead print media coverage in newspapers, news services, newsletters, Internet media, as well as broadcast (radio and television) media

The PR campaign for your book should be centered on when your book will actually be available for purchase. Media coverage creates demand, and it is imperative that there is supply to match the demand.

To hire a publicist or not to hire a publicist? That is the question.

How Do I Approach a Publicist?

Now that you understand the importance of timing, you are either prepared to put together your own promotion plan, or start the process of finding a publicist.

If you choose the latter, how do you find a publicist to represent your book? Often, the best place to start is to ask other authors or publishing industry professionals for recommendations.

When approaching a publicist, keep in mind that a publicist only needs the basic information about your book—title, publication date, publisher, and a brief synopsis. A publicist may request a copy of the manuscript or advance review copy of your book, but please do not demand that the publicist read your book in its entirety before arranging a time to talk about the project. Provide them with the basics, but understand that the publicist's time is valuable and that he or she is simply not able to read every book by every potential client that comes his or her way.

Once you have found a potential publicist, arrange a time to talk to the publicist about your project. Whatever you do, prepare for the call in advance, and do not be afraid to ask lots of questions, such as:

- What can I expect?
- What will it cost?

- How long will it take?
- When can you start to work on my project?
- Have you ever worked on a similar book before?
- Are you comfortable with the subject matter of my book?
- Do you feel your contacts align with my book's subject matter?
- How often can I expect to hear from you?
- What exactly will you be doing, and when?
- What will be expected of me?

The publicist, too, should ask questions of you, such as:
- What are your expectations?
- When is your book scheduled for publication?
- What are your plans for the distribution of your book?
- What are your goals?
- What is your availability?
- What types of media coverage would you most like to have?

Be realistic about what you are looking for, what your expectations are, and what you can afford to spend. If you know that a particular publicist's rates are more than you can budget, be upfront about what you can—or are willing to—spend. If you know you can't afford to hire a particular publicist, tell them; do not ask for a proposal from them. They will appreciate your honesty.

Expect the same honesty in return from the publicists you consider. If a publicist decides to pass on your project, do not take it personally. Often, schedules and timing are to blame, and occasionally, a publicist will decline a project because he or she doesn't have experience in working with your book's subject matter and isn't comfortable taking on the project.

How Do I Complete the Hiring Process?

Once you have found a publicist you consider to be a good fit, have a thorough understanding of what the process is, and understand what services will—and won't—be provided, ask for a written proposal. Most publicists are happy to put together proposals that outline the services they'll provide, along with the cost of those services. When asking for a proposal, you should also ask the publicist for references. Contact those references and do not be afraid to ask more questions.

Before you agree to hire a particular publicist for the job, make sure that you feel comfortable with the person you're hiring. If you feel uneasy in any way, or don't feel that you have gotten answers to the questions you've asked, it might be a good idea to keep looking.

When screening publicists, there are several red flags to watch out for. Proceed with caution:

- if a publicist agrees to take on your project before he or she knows what the project is about;
- if the publicist offers guarantees on media placements he or she promises to generate;
- if the publicist does not deliver materials, such as a proposal, on time;
- if the publicist is hesitant to give out referrals;
- if the publicist is not specific about what a PR campaign will cost, or how long the PR campaign will last;
- if the publicist refuses to put into writing the services he or she will provide; or
- if the publicist isn't able to give satisfactory answers to your questions.

Make sure you are comfortable with your decision before you sign a contract. After all, you need to trust your publicist with your book, and if you don't feel that you can do that, there is no reason to proceed.

So What Happens If I Don't Decide to Hire a Publicist?

If there is one primary downside to working with a publicist, it's easily this: cost. Book promotion is time-consuming, and there is value in a publicist's time and experience. For that reason, book promotion campaigns can be costly.

If you don't have the budget to hire a publicist, don't despair; many authors have been extremely successful at promoting their own books

If you decide to do your own book promotion, start by putting together a plan or timeline.

When you are ready to put the wheels in motion for your book's PR campaign, the first step is selecting your target media. Finding your target media requires a candid assessment of your book. Who would be interested in reading it? Make lists of potential book buyers – who they are, where they are, what topics and issues both concern and interest them, what in your book is relevant to them, and then find those potential buyers. Research magazines these potential buyers read, newspaper columns that cover issues of interest and importance to them, radio and television shows they listen to and watch, and use this information as your guide.

The more specific you can be, the better your likelihood of reaching these potential buyers.

Your book may appeal to a wide variety of different groups and you should endeavor to reach them all. Once you have an idea of who your target media is, you need to find them. Media research databases can be a terrific source of information. However, they can also be terrifically expensive. Don't despair if a yearly subscription to a media research service is cost prohibitive, as there are plenty of other ways to find media contact information. Visit your favorite bookstore, library, or newsstand and look for magazines, newspapers, and journals that might afford an opportunity for book coverage. Find magazines, journals, and outlets you think would be interested in your book.

The Internet is a wonderful source of information on specific media. Research media outlets by visiting their Web sites – read what they are writing about, note the focus of their publication or show, and research what topics specific journalists are covering. Most Web sites will include contact information for editors, writers, and staff. In addition, many Web sites even include guidelines for submitting.

Now that you've found them, it is time to make contact. Making initial contact with a member of the media can be accomplished in several ways. You can meet face-to-face, call them on the phone, write a letter, or send an email. Please do bear in mind that journalists and producers are often working on tight deadlines and may not want to disruption of a phone call. Believe me – you will know if you have caught a journalist at a bad time! On balance, email is less intrusive, as the journalist has the luxury of reading—and responding—at his or her convenience.

If you do prefer to call, be polite. Introduce yourself and ask if this is a good time for them to talk. If not, ask when might be a better time. Be brief. Explain exactly why you are calling, and offer to send more information. Use your discretion, but sometimes a follow up email thanking the journalist for his or her time, and recapping the conversation can be useful.

You've made contact, now keep in touch. Following up is crucial. Know that it sometimes takes more than one follow-up to get a response. After initial contact has been made, and you have sent the requested material, follow up in 7-10 days to confirm receipt, and offer more information or an interview. If you do not hear back within 7-10 days, follow up again. Be persistent, but follow the guideline of seven-ten days, with the exception of breaking news that relates to your book.

Whatever you do, *know thy media*. One of the most important parts of pitching successfully is researching the media outlet before you pitch. Watch for articles and columns that the journalist has written, guests the host or producer has booked on a show, and mention them when you pitch—particularly when these relate to your book. By establishing this connection, you are letting the journalist know you have taken the time to do your research and you have an understanding of what he or she is looking for. It also signals to the journalist or producer that you may be offering a great lead on an upcoming story, show or article. Doing the research does take time, but it is time well spent.

Give yourself more time than you think you'll ever need. Too often, authors rush through the process and miss important opportunities along the way. Slow down, relax and enjoy the process.

About the Author

A graduate of Vanderbilt University, Maryglenn McCombs has worked in the book publishing industry since 1993, and has been involved in the publication and promotion of hundreds of books. She specializes in offering targeted book publicity campaigns for publishers and authors. For more information, please visit www.maryglenn.com or email Maryglenn at: maryglenn@maryglenn.com

Podcast Airdate:	December 6th, 2007
Podcast URL:	http://authorsaccess.com/archives/92
Author's site:	http://maryglenn.com/

Branding: It's a Book Thing, Too
Paul McNeese

Isn't it funny how societal changes kind of sneak up on you? One day, there you are, prospect or a client, a customer or a user of a product or a service—and the next day (at least it seems to happen this quickly) you are a "consumer." You've been redefined, re-categorized, branded—but in a negative and minimizing way! Yesterday you were a person, today you're a number, one of many in an un-individuated, anonymous (but sharply defined) "group" or subset within a larger collection of statistical numbers. It's a bit terrifying (de-humanizing?) for me to think about that—and I hope you're a bit worried, too—but this chapter will look at how and why this has happened and what certain ideas about branding mean—in a very positive way—to authors who want to distinguish their creative work by differentiating their book from everyone else's.

The subject is "Branding," a concept that was developed in the advertising industry to help identify and distinguish one product from other similar items and to make it easier for people to focus on the branded item—to create an opportunity for what has become known as an "impulse buy" in the short run and a continuing loyalty over the longer term. The success of the idea is confirmed by the increasing number of products that are generically identified by their brand names; Coke, Xerox, Q-Tips, for instance, and today, hundreds of others.

Of course, there's much more to branding than simple recognition—or even the larger objective, loyalty—and we'll get there. But first, a basic definition of the word "Brand" might be helpful. Here's one that I've synthesized from a number of disparate sources but that seems to summarize the elements of the word and its application to life in today's world: **A unified, memorable name or message that communicates uniqueness, focus and values.**

As you can see, this broad definition encompasses a number of distinct notions, so let's look at each element of it and see first what it has come to mean as related to the brands you are so familiar with—names like Cheerios and such—and then we'll look at how you can apply the accumulated knowledge of some very bright people to your own marketing effort.

The Elements of Branding

The breakdown of elements in the definition of branding are most easily thought of as a set of short ideas. Here they are, one word at a time:

Element	What It Means
Unified	an image consistently projected across all activities related to the branded product or service
Memorable	a name, phrase or symbolism that is easy to think about, remember and verbalize
Communication	comprehensively, this can be words, sounds or pictures and can be transmitted over any medium that will reach the consumer
Uniqueness	what makes this brand different from all the others (not limited to the facts of it, but also taking into account the reader's, viewer's or listener's perceptions about uniqueness or differentiation)
Focus	including only the concept(s) intrinsic to the "brand
Values	what you, the producer, have to offer to your readers, listeners, users, etc., either within the product itself or within the customer's perceptions about the company as a whole.

As you can see, each of the elements stands alone as a concept, but each one relates to all the others in ways that are not always consciously understood by the receiver of the messages carried by the "brand name."

A Little Societal Background

Branding actually began a long time ago as artisans and craftsmen applied their "mark" to their work, thus differentiating it in a readily identifiable way from the work of others who created similar products such as artworks, pottery, furniture, and so forth. In truth, it was intended to be a mark of pride rather than a reason to buy, but—as the price of some rare art works would demonstrate today—such provenance might ultimately accrue great value when accepted by buyers and collectors.

In the United States, perhaps the clearest example of branding comes from the mid-continental plains during the early years of the nation's history, when the owners of livestock would burn a mark into the flank of an animal as a proof of ownership. This, of course, was a purely quantitative notion; i.e., this steer is mine because it carries my "brand." Today's brands, on the other hand, are intended to project and signify value to you the buyer—the consumer.

So pervasive has this idea of branding become that all I need to do to create a specific idea in your mind right now is to mention a generic product category; you will very likely connect with a brand. For example, I say, "facial tissue," and you think "_____."

It's not all about products, either. The same concepts can be adopted by organizations. For example: I say, "You're in good hands with . . .," and you think "_____."

Can the same principle be applied to individuals? Yes. I say, "The Terminator," and you think "_____."

It's About Relationships

How do brands work in the real world? It's much more than associations. It's relationships. And the brand relationships you've developed over the years needn't come solely from direct experience with products you may have purchased and used. They may come from the advertising you have been exposed to in newspapers, on radio and television, from billboards, or via the dozens of other media that assault our sensibilities every day—direct mail, e-mail (enough, already!). For instance, you may not be related to this particular brand, but if I were to refer to "Susan G. Komen," what would you probably think of? Almost certainly you would instantly relate to a national campaign to raise funds for research into a cure for breast cancer. Yes, it's a *relationship* because it's about more than just the identification of the product, service or person, it's about how you feel about that brand, a perception of *value* that has somehow developed in your mind, over time, and that very likely causes you to favor one maker's products over those of another.

Branding Is Inevitable

Now here's the connection between user and consumer, which is where we started. And, at the same time, here's where we can begin to switch the point of view from you as a consumer of literary product to you as a marketer of literary product.

The minute you publish a book, several important things happen.

First, other people's perception of you will change. Authorship somehow confers a certain legitimacy, and people may begin to think of you as creative who never saw that trait in you before. Or they may see you as an authority should you be writing nonfiction about, say, a certain skill set. Sure, you've always been a carpenter, but the minute you begin to show others how to do it, you become a teacher or a mentor or an authority—and that's quite a different thing. Suddenly, like it or not, you will not be exactly the same person you were before you wrote your book, and it's at this moment that your brand begins to develop.

Second, your perception of yourself may change. In fact, the change could be for better or for worse, depending upon your fundamental personal character, and that internal change will also affect the brand you will be developing from that moment on, so you need to be aware of your own changing attitudes and to incorporate the best of all that into your relationship with everyone connected with your "new" self.

Third, as a new author, you will instantly become a business (if, indeed, you plan to sell your publication). As such, you will also become the proprietor of a product line, because even a book today is a multiple product; it can be a print book, an electronic book, or a CD-based book—or all of the above. It can become the centerpiece for a speaking career, a teaching activity such as seminar leadership, or a charitable effort through which you promote your "cause" with books and other products.

From just these three standpoints, not only is branding virtually inevitable for you, but you will need to think in the very same terms that national and international branders do in order to maintain a productive, positive and perhaps profitable enterprise—the brand called YOU.

Ah, But There's More . . .

Just think about this: preliminary figures seem to indicate that over 400,000 new titles were published in 2007. Developing technology has made it easier than ever to publish a book. It won't be long before mere publication becomes relatively meaningless. Recognition, prestige, profits and public acceptance will come only from commercial success (we'll define that a bit later on in this chapter). So if you intend to create a market for your product(s), branding—setting yourself apart from the huge crowd of authors out there—will become not only desirable but also necessary for your very survival as an author. So perhaps you should learn the brand-building skill set right now rather than being left behind later, disappointed in your lack of whatever it is you currently value as the rewards of your venture into authorship.

Is there really a skill set here? Yes, there is, and it's available without undertaking a graduate degree. Granted, it's an increasingly complex effort, but a well-thought-out plan, coupled with a willingness not only to execute it but also to change and improve it as you go along and as new ideas find success in the marketplace, will bring you to a place in which you feel comfortable, even excited, with what you see developing from that original need to write a book.

The skill set starts with a tacit understanding that you must never lose sight of: **You, the author, are the primary force for progress in marketing your books and other products.** Even if you're lucky enough to find a good literary agent or to sign with a reputable publisher, there's only so much that either of those outsiders will be willing or able to do for you. In fact, it's much more likely that you will end up self-publishing your work—and that's getting to be a more and more practical idea in many respects, given the contraction of the book industry itself and the improved economics of self-publishing and online marketing of literary product. Either way, the marketing chore will probably be up to you, and the most important part of marketing in the book business is differentiation—the ability to set yourself or your product apart from everyone and everything else in the marketplace. So here comes "Branding."

Fundamental decision #1: What makes me or my book different? Implicit in this decision is to know your competition. You will need to read everything you can find that is even remotely similar to your work. By the way, you don't have to buy everyone else's book. Use your library, the Internet, and other free resources to find and figure out your competition. Once you've done this, you'll have the next decision in your gun sight:

Fundamental decision #2: Which will I brand—my book or myself? If you can truthfully say that there isn't another book in the marketplace that is like yours, or that yours is clearly the best book of its kind in current circulation, the decision goes to the book. But if this isn't absolutely true for you, don't give up hope. See what there is in you that is clearly different from, better than, or perceptually superior to every other author writing on the subject or in your genre if you write fiction. Perhaps this choice is the way you should go anyway, since once your book is published it can't change readily, whereas you can change direction or emphasis, self-investment or self-image rather quickly.

Here are two examples.

Employment consultant Joe Turner wrote a book, *Job Search Secrets Unlocked*, aimed at people searching for a job or a job change in today's uncertain economy. Well, so did lots of other people. Although his book was not clearly superior to any other book in the field, Joe had lots of experience as an employment counselor and an increasing facility with using the Internet as a marketing tool. So Joe Turner decided to become "The Job Search Guy" and to focus his branding effort on the Internet. He built a series of Web sites, created an e-book from his print book, made CDs available, then, when the economy really began to fall apart, he wrote a second book on exactly the same subject, which he titled *Paycheck 911*.

At first, sales were slow, but as a part of his promotional mix he also dissected his books and wrote articles on various aspects of job searching. Soon he was being published in many widely read blogs and on major employment web sites, always insisting that his work carry the identification "By Joe Turner, the Job Search Guy" (and, of course, a reference to one of his web sites). His name started to become familiar in employment circles, and book sales began to rise. Today, "Joe Turner, the Job Search Guy" is a known quantity, a sales success, and a "brand" that is respected by people looking for jobs all over America.

Phoenix author Jane Monachelli wrote and self-published a little book, *50 Ways to Love Your Mother*, and came up with a very simple marketing plan: do three things each weekday to promote the book. Since March of 2006, Jane has been doing just that, and in the process she has become "branded" as "the lady who writes about showing Mom how you love her." In this case, it wasn't even a conscious effort, but Jane has managed to create a brand anyway.

Now that you know what your branding object will be…

…let's look at some ways of arriving at branding strategies that could work for you.

Fundamental decision #3: What will be my brand's "look and feel?" From here on, this chapter will become something of a how-to guide, so I will begin using bullet points and other outlining techniques in the hope that you will be able to flesh them out into your own, unique branding plan. But before I lapse into my teaching mode, one more point, a very important one:

Branding is an activity that can—and should—begin before you start writing your book. Just as your marketing plan should be a function of what you are planning to do rather than a "catch-up" document that tries to make something profitable out of what you've already done (perhaps well, perhaps not, perhaps wisely, perhaps not), your branding plan should also be a document (yes, write it out) that you consult throughout the writing and publishing process as a guide to aiming at success. So if you are planning or working on a book, *stop now* and do the fundamental work that can save you a ton of agony later. Plan it out!

And if you've already written a book, *take a new look at it* from both a marketing and a branding standpoint, then write plans based on what you now know about your product. By the way, you may find it necessary to change your product, and this could be the easier, softer way; that is, you might find it more productive to rewrite and republish than to try to sell whatever mistakes you've already made.

Now, on to the steps to branding yourself and/or your work. I like the exhortation I see so often in the "green" movement and in some political campaigns: "Think globally, act locally." I believe it's a good maxim to apply to the branding process.

A visualization of the relentlessly cumulative process of branding can be found in the logo of Target Stores (talk about a well-known brand!). Their familiar symbol is, as you might think, a representation in red and white of a "target," with a bull's-eye in the center, surrounded by an area of white (which most of us think of as blank space, but in branding terms, it's not!), and circumscribed by a band of red, thus completing the "target," the logo. It's hard to think of a more evocative logotype than this one. And for me, it serves as a primary reminder of how the branding process can best be implemented for any product, service, or personality.

I see the branding process as a target, with the bull's-eye being where you are right now. Part of the equation is your current state of publication (book in development, book published, multiple books published, etc.), your level of knowledge about the marketing process in general, and the media you might wish to use to develop your product's image and sales platform. It's also, more practically, where you are geographically. There's no test market quite as accessible, affordable and applicable to your project as your own home town.

The specifics of "look and feel" include many dimensions:

Dimension	Specific details
Your copy platform	What you will say about yourself or your product(s)? *Language, copy length, copy style and other factors apply here.*
The graphics you will use	Do you have "something special" in your book cover, or perhaps an identifying categorical reference (as in the Joe Turner example above)? *If you don't have something special, can you find a special way to present something that is minimally distinctive? That's where your unique personality might take over and control the branding.*
The over-all "packaging" of your brand	Remembering that you and your book are one, how will you bring the person and the product together? *Promotional methods, plus things like devotion of personal time, energy and money, will determine this dimension of the challenge.*
One brand for all markets—or not?	Will you need more than one branding "platform" because you have more than one audience for your brand? *Example: an author I know is writing a series of books about pets, and the audience will be both children (the school venue) and adults (the pet owner venue); she is investigating different ways to bring the same story distinctly to different end-use audiences.*

Is there a set of steps to take as the branding process develops?

Absolutely, yes! And the process, as pointed out before, should start at least as soon as you begin to write your book. First off, tell people you are writing a book—and be willing to talk about it anytime, anywhere, with anyone. This will give you great motivation to finish the writing process (you don't want to fail all those friends, do you?). Moreover, you'll begin to get input from potential readers, and this may lead you to some pivotal information about what your brand strategy ought to be and how it might be developed.

Once you've declared your intention to the world, start working (yes, while you're still writing the basic material!) on the other elements that will form the skeleton of your brand, starting with a Web site. Much of what follows is most appropriate for nonfiction work, but fiction authors can also employ many of the methods, techniques and resources outlined below.

- Start with a one-page Web site, then build from there. Don't overspend or overdevelop the site on the first try.
- Think of your site as a book proposal in development; incorporate all the elements of a good book proposal (own *and read* at least one of the many good books available on this subject—it will be worth many times the cost of the book).
- Start a blog or a newsletter on your subject of expertise; advertise it on your site. Consider releasing excerpts from your forthcoming book as part of these publications—you can develop a pre-publication market for your work with people who are interested, and your own Web site is one of very few places where you can make sales and get to keep all of the profits.
- As you write chapters for your book, construct articles from the same raw material and submit these to the larger online article databases; also submit your articles to appropriate blogs written by others.
- Begin working on your cover design, back cover copy, and other promotional materials. These materials will be easier and more fun to work on while you are developing your book, and if you multi-task in this way you will be surprised, when your book is finished, that you already have on hand most of what it will take to sell it—in any marketplace, including to agents and publishers.
- Look for endorsers of your work, and read book reviews in your genre area. You'll be amazed at what you can learn from reviewers of other people's work in your subject category, and you'll probably avoid several pitfalls in style and substance that might cost you dearly later. Additionally, seek out interview possibilities on radio and TV and in local and regional newspapers and magazines. These vehicles will be easier to reach when it's time to promote, and published reviews, interviews, articles and reporter-generated stories about you and your book will pave the way to wider—possibly even national—exposure.
- Attend every book event you can find in your area. Learn how to reach those audiences by watching others do it (or fail to do it). These gigs are

fun, you meet many wonderful, new people, and you learn not only what to do and how to do it but also what *not* to do and *why not*. Also, pick up all the promotional materials you can find from other authors, then use the best aspects of these efforts in your materials.
- Start collecting mailing list information related to the various audiences for your book; also look for contacts on the Internet with whom you can partner to promote each other's work online, thus increasing your outreach without having to do as much work to develop a list.
- Make it a habit to visit local bookstores (particularly independent stores) and get to know the management people. When your book is ready, they'll be ready for you because they will already know you.
- Look for local organizations that use speakers; contact their program chairpersons and let them know that you have a book on the way—they need to plan ahead, and by working with them in advance, you can begin promoting your book as soon as it comes out rather than having to wait many months while they honor commitments to other speakers ahead of you.
- Check on local and regional book fairs and find out what it takes to exhibit; most of these events start preparation as long as a year in advance—and so should you.

This by no means covers all of the ground. There will be much to do after your book reaches print (or has become an eBook), but by allowing yourself to focus on the end result even before you have the first fruits of your authorship, you will be forcing yourself to refine your understanding of the sales and marketing process, to develop the branding approaches that will set you apart from all the others, make your name and your product more of a "household word" (at least in your local and primary target markets), and perhaps even give you some valid ideas on how best to develop, express and manage the very content of your book!

In summary, the successful author is aware from the very beginning of his or her writing process that luck isn't something that just happens. It's something one prepares for, works toward, expects, anticipates, and plans for. Then, suddenly (at least it often seems so) it happens. Always remember, whatever happens, you did it, either for yourself or to yourself.

Another thing that every successful author with a brand identity knows is that the branding process is cumulative. It may start with a seemingly insignificant event that triggers an idea. For example, an author whose original intent was to tell his own story of personal triumph over tragedy showed a portion of his manuscript to me as it was under development. This was a handsome, well-mannered young man who wasn't letting blindness stop him from living life well and enjoying every moment of it. And he could write! So I listened to him talk to me about his book and told him I thought he could, and should, begin talking his story as well as writing about it. Today he is represented by a national speaker agency and is well paid, indeed, for telling his story to audiences all over America. Incidentally, this small suggestion also changed the way he did his writing—it became storytelling rather than formal "memoir," and that style change now fits right into this man's "brand."

Could this be you? Who knows…? but part of your obligation to yourself as a writer with a message to bring to readers is to discover how best to get your message out, and the end result could be a "brand"—a well-known, generally accepted brand that might be your book, or it could be yourself.

So begin now to develop the brand called YOU; to evolve a brand for your book and the products it may spawn, and to expect that miracle that is publishing success. You can do it; just do it.

About the Author

Paul McNeese is the founder of Optimum Performance Associates, a consulting group that has been specializing in author and writer coaching, book editing, and book packaging for non-bookstore markets since 1994.

Paul has been a writer for more than 35 years and quite involved in the publishing industry as well. In 2002, he developed OPA Publishing, a publisher and packager of non-fiction e-books and "Print-on-Demand" hard-copy volumes of nonfiction for self-publishing authors and entrepreneurs. About two years ago, he expanded into fiction and now has over 60 titles in print. The company specializes in assisting both first-time and seasoned authors to self-publish and market their work. OPA Publishing also works with authors whose work has been published but has gone "out of print" for any number of reasons.

He can be contacted at pmcneese@opaauthorservices.com

Podcast Airdate:	March 8th, 2007
Podcast URL:	http://authorsaccess.com/archives/38
Author's site:	http://www.opaauthorservices.com

What Can Author and Publisher Associations Do for You?
Tyler R. Tichelaar

No matter what stage you are at in writing or publishing your book, an author or publisher association can be a great benefit to you. Maybe you only have an idea for a book but you don't know how to get started. Maybe you've published half a dozen books but you still have trouble selling them. Maybe you have sold thousands of books but now you're breaking into writing a different genre and need advice finding your new target audience. No matter how much or how little experience you have, an association can provide you with information and tools to meet your goals. Networking with fellow authors, sharing marketing ideas, receiving feedback on your writing, and learning the most cost-effective ways to self-publish your books are just a few of the many valuable opportunities to be gained from such associations.

Many different types of author and publisher associations exist. Some of the largest and best known include the Small Publishers Association of North America (SPAN) and the Independent Book Publishers Association (formerly the Publishers Marketing Association). There are also many regional associations such as the Great Lakes Booksellers Association and Florida Publishers Association. Genre specific associations include the Sisters in Crime for female mystery writers and Science-Fiction and Fantasy Writers of America. While larger associations such as SPAN are tremendously useful in helping a writer keep up with current trends in the publishing world, and the genre associations will keep you updated with news about your specific type of writing, many authors first get their feet wet by joining a smaller or local association. Many of the larger associations also have regional chapters that can fulfill this more local need.

As a resident of Upper Michigan, I am most familiar with the Upper Peninsula Publishers and Authors Association (UPPAA). Most of my discussion below is based upon my experiences and involvement with UPPAA, but most associations operate with similar goals for their members. The focus of most author and publisher associations, with some slight variations, is:

Area	How it contributes
Writing	Helping their members to become better writers.
Publishing	Teaching members how to publish books of the highest quality in the most cost-effective manner.
Marketing	How to sell and promote books in an affordable way to the widest audience possible.
Networking	Perhaps unstated, but it is the entire purpose of an association. You meet other writers and through them you make contacts in the publishing world. In the publishing world, the six degrees of separation idea is closer to three degrees. And remember what book-marketing guru John Kremer says—networking is really just making friends.

In trying to find the right group, I suggest you start with your local association. The only way you'll really know if the group is right for you is to get involved in it. Active members become happy members.

Overcoming Your Innate Shyness

Before I go further, I want to acknowledge that most writers are introverts, and our shyness may make the thought of joining an association feel like torture. I know—I've been there. For years I was a closet novelist. Only a few family members and close friends knew I wrote novels. I never showed my writing to anyone. But after years of secretly mailing manuscripts to New York publishers who didn't bother to read them, my desire to be a published writer burned so greatly that I set fear aside and self-published my first novel.

I bring up my shyness because I don't want other writers to make the same mistakes I made just because they are afraid to talk to others about publishing their books. Had I taken time to join an author or publisher association and learn from others who had already gone through the publishing process, I could have saved myself time, money, and angst, and I would have broken even on my publishing costs much sooner. No, I did not fork over tens of thousands of dollars to publish my first novel—many first time authors do make that mistake, and had I that kind of money, I probably would have. Instead, I only had a few thousand dollars, so at the suggestion of one of the few friends I spoke to about my writing, I went online to find out the cheapest (far different than cost-effective) way to publish. This search led me to the mistake of publishing with a print-on-demand (POD) company—a mistake I still see thousands of authors making each year.

If you don't know what print-on-demand means, that's all the more reason why you need to join an association. In short, a print-on-demand company will layout your book, publish it, even get it listed on Amazon for you, and for a relatively small price—to publish my first novel cost me only about $800.00. The people I worked with at the print-on-demand company did wonderful work and could not have been nicer. The problem was that to purchase copies of my novel from the POD company so I could resell them, I had to order at least 100 copies to get a significant discount. The discount was equal to what most bookstores wanted to pay me as wholesale to resell my books. Not having done my research on bookstores, I had no idea that once the shipping of my books was included in the cost, the bookstore would make a significant profit, the POD company would make a significant profit, and I would lose eight cents for each book sold! Furthermore, the POD company charged so much for books that to get a discount of just 5% more on my books—resulting in just one dollar of profit per book sold—I would have to order 250 books, the total cost of which was far more money than I had.

My dream had turned into a financial loss. Most authors give up at this point rather than doing further research. But I was determined. I created a mantra for myself: "I am a publishable, profitable, popular novelist." I brainwashed myself into believing it, and I set out to make it happen.

And So I Joined an Author's Association!

The next step on my publishing adventure was joining the Upper Peninsula Publishers and Authors Association. My shyness kicked back in so I really had to talk myself into going to that first meeting. I was afraid the other authors would not welcome me, that they would think my historical novel I had spent six years researching and writing would be considered inferior to theirs. I cannot tell you how wrong I was. I have never known such wonderful people as the friends I have made in the writing and publishing world, never known so many talented people who love what they do. Right away I decided to become involved with the association and I started asking questions of the seasoned members. I soon found out about self-publishing, working with printers, buying my own ISBN numbers, and dozens of ideas to help market my books. Had I joined UPPAA before I decided to publish my first book, I would have saved myself money, time, and frustration.

The Upper Peninsula Publishers and Authors Association's story is similar to that of most author and publisher associations. It was organized by a handful of writers in 1998 because they wanted to learn the best ways to self-publish. Today, the association has grown to eighty-five members, and believe it or not, I, the closet novelist, am currently honored to serve as its president.

The More You Give, The More You Get

I would have found little value in UPPAA, however, had I not decided to get involved. An association is only as strong as the dedication and involvement of its members. It is easy enough to join an association, and then sit at home waiting for the quarterly or monthly newsletter, and occasionally to attend the annual meeting. It only takes a bit more effort to participate. Again, I know for shy writers, participation can be difficult, but it can begin in small ways. Go to a meeting and make an effort to speak to just one other member during the day. Ask the person if he or she is writing a book and what it's about. All authors want to have people interested in their books, and they will repay the favor by asking about your book. Soon you'll be sharing ideas, and you will get excited. Trust me. Just by asking one person about his or her book, you're off to a beautiful start.

Then if the association has one, join the email discussion group or online forum. Read one of your fellow members' books and post a review of it on Amazon. Ask the other member to do the same for you. Contact the editor of the association's newsletter and offer to write an article. If you don't know what to write about, ask the editor for suggestions and do a little research on the proposed topic—you'll learn about publishing and marketing your own books in the process and the other members will start to see you as one of the experts. Volunteer to spend a couple hours selling books at the association's table at a local festival—you might even sell some of your own books that way—but the best part is you get to sit there for three or four tedious hours disappointed that no one wants your books—I'm kidding. You get to spend that time talking to the other volunteer members and getting more ideas—and you'll be bound to have people stop by to ask you about the organization because they also want to publish books. Soon you'll have dozens of author friends who will be part of your bandwagon to help you sell your book, and you'll return the favor to them. The rollercoaster ride of publishing will become faster and more joyful because your new association friends will help you smooth out some of the curves.

Tangible Benefits of Participation

If I haven't convinced you yet, here are just some of the advantages of joining an author or publisher association.

Annual Conferences and Meetings—Most associations have conferences and meetings at least once a year. Depending on the association you join, this may be your only chance to meet fellow members in person. It's well worth the cost and time to attend. I know networking is a scary word to shy writers—but networking is really nothing more than making friends. People get excited about books. They get excited hearing about your book and telling you about their books. Exchange business cards with them, recommend books to them, introduce them to writers you've already met. And then, attend the sessions at the conference. Many of these associations bring in big name speakers like Dan Poynter to do a keynote address. Usually multiple sessions are held—sessions that include experts in the field, and often member presentations. The UPPAA has had everyone from local librarians, newspaper reporters, publishing coaches, salespeople from major publishing houses, and Web site designers come in to talk about how to publish and sell books. Each session not only provides information, but the speakers are usually friendly enough to let you ask questions and even contact them after the conferences. UPPAA tends to break its sessions into three categories: publishing, marketing, and writing. Publishing has included sessions on self-publishing, editing, page layout, printing, and e-books. Writing has included sessions on writing fiction, non-fiction, workshopping your writing, and how to write an effective blog. Marketing has included sessions on how to get libraries to carry your book, how to get book reviews, how to get featured in a newspaper, and how to build an effective Web site.

Newsletters—The association's newsletter is a great way to stay up to date on the publishing world. It's also another way to get to know your fellow members. Many of the smaller associations will print notices of members' new books being released. And the newsletter editors are always looking for contributors. They will be happy to have you write an article for them, and you will learn all the more by contributing an article. Plus it's another way to get your writing published and your name known as an author.

Targeting Your Audience—As original as your book may be, there are other people who have written similar books in your genre, but that's all right. Those people can tell you what worked and didn't work for them in marketing their books. You can save countless hours of time by avoiding their mistakes. Finding your book's niche, its core audience, requires a lot of research, and when your fellow authors have already done a lot of that research through personal experience, they can serve as a tremendous resource to you. Ignore what you hear about how hundreds of thousands of books are published each year and they are all in competition with your book. The truth is that your book is unique. For example, if you've written a mystery novel, you may only have to compete with ten thousand other mysteries published that year—that's narrowed the playing field right there. Then if your mystery is set in Texas, the locals who love mysteries will want to read your book, and probably anyone who loves Texas will be interested in it—that could be thousands of book sales right in your own backyard. When I published my historical novels set in Upper Michigan, I had no idea until I joined UPPAA how many other writers lived in and wrote about Upper Michigan. But I quickly learned that those other authors were not my competition—they and their books were my greatest allies. If someone reads and loves one of their books set in Upper Michigan, that person will go looking for similar books and find mine. Networking—making friends with the other local authors and finding out how they reached their audience—is the surest way to help you figure out how to sell your books. Whenever a fellow author gives me an idea or helps me in selling some books, I guarantee I'm going to remember and want to repay the favor.

Save Money—Joining an author and publishers association may cost you as little as $20 annually. Even the largest associations do not charge much more than $100. If you learn just one thing about publishing or marketing, that $100 will repay itself tenfold. I easily made up my membership fee in UPPAA the first year by finding out from fellow members about more cost-effective ways to publish my novels. I've saved thousands of dollars just by getting advice about where to publish and where not to waste my marketing dollars.

Become an Expert—It won't take long. If you become active, in a year or two, the new members will think you're an expert. You can help new members learn the ropes of self-publishing, book marketing, or writing genre fiction. And they will be grateful for it, tell their friends about your books and build your word-of-mouth army of book promoters.

Meet Printers, Publicists, Literary Agents and Others in the Know About Publishing—These people are often invited to speak at association conferences; they would love to sell you their products and services, but at a conference, their goal is to give you the information you need. You can ask them questions about what kind of paper to use to have your book printed on, how to write a cover letter that will convince a literary agent to promote your book, how to sell yourself rather than your book to get a feature story in a newspaper, or how to book a radio interview. This information is invaluable, and these people are usually happy to assist you with finding the right information and the best services to fit your book's unique needs. People in the publishing world tend to be very open-hearted because they love what they do—they know that even if you do not use their services, you might refer someone to them who will. It's a win-win situation for everyone.

Discounts—Many associations provide special discounts. Members of the UPPAA can join SPAN (UPPAA is a member itself) and get a reduced price. Larger associations like SPAN offer numerous discounts in such areas as publicity packages, co-op marketing, healthcare options, and subscriptions to *Publishers Weekly*.

Special Events—Joining an association puts you in the know when it comes to special author events. For example, every year the UPPAA attends the Upper Peninsula History Conference. Having a book table at that event helps our historical fiction and non-fiction authors reach their audience. Other associations put together book fairs, have special booths at community events, or at national book associations like Book Expo America or the Baltimore Book Festival.

Email Discussion Lists and Online Forums—Many associations have email discussion groups or online forums where you can post a question to the association members and get answers. Often, the information provided is timelier than what you would receive in a monthly or even quarterly newsletter. If you don't join these lists, you will miss out on many opportunities.

Web site Listings—Many associations have online catalogues of all their members' books on their Web sites with links back to the individual members Web sites. Individual members may also choose to exchange links with fellow members. On my own Web site www.MarquetteFiction.com I exchange links with any other authors who live in or write about Upper Michigan.

Book Displays—Bring your book to the meetings. If there are display tables, then display your books at the conferences. (Never leave home without a copy of your book tucked under your arm). Often, associations will allow you to sell your books at the meetings to the other members. By viewing the other members' books, you will learn what others are writing about and you can make contact with members who have goals similar to yours.

Co-operative Marketing—Many associations sponsor ways to help their members advertise their books by pooling their resources. This could be by sharing space on Web sites, taking out ads in local newspapers, or sharing the cost of a table at a local craft or art show or a book festival.

So What Are You Waiting For?

Now that I've convinced you, you need to find that association you're going to join. A good place to start is to inquire at your local library or bookstore. They may have contact information for local groups. Another good place is to look online. Simply do a search with the name of your state and "publishers" and "authors" in it, or visit the list of regional affiliates at the Independent Book Publishers Association's Web site:

http://www.ibpa-online.org/pubresources/affiliate.aspx

In conclusion, I want to repeat that author and publisher associations are only as strong as the members who get involved. Writers cannot sell books if they sit at home. They need to network with other authors and market their books. Join an association and get involved. Make friends and you will sell more books.

About the Author

Learn more about Tyler R. Tichelaar, Ph.D. in the About the Editors section beginning on p. 215.

Podcast Airdate:	September 24th, 2008
Podcast URL:	http://authorsaccess.com/archives/111
Author's site:	http://www.marquettefiction.com
	http://www.superiorbookpromotions.com

Amazon Adventures: Staring Down Earth's Largest Bookstore
Victor R. Volkman

This article was adapted from my lecture "Amazon Adventures" delivered live at the Motown Writers Conference on November 9th, 2007. In this lecture, I covered a variety of Amazon programs and strategies including: Amazon Advantage, Amazon Associates, Amazon Connect, Amazon Marketplace, Amazon Mechanical Turk. I've also highlighted how to make Advanced Tactics work for you such as *Listmania!*, Search-inside-the-book, social networking, video reviews, and much more.

What is Amazon.com?

Let's talk about Amazon. We are going to look around at all the different ways we can utilize Amazon, because as I was mentioning to one participant, "There's not just one Amazon; there are several dimensions of Amazon, and you need to think about all of them." So let's start with a quick look at what Amazon is today. It's a $10 billion a year company which surprised me when I looked it up. Even though we all know it sells all over the world through the Internet, the units in Japan, Germany, the United Kingdom, and now China and France account for half the sales. So it isn't just a U.S. based company. Amazon sells *everywhere*. They have 275 acres worth of warehouses and 14,000 employees, so they really are the world's biggest bookstore. It's pretty amazing to think about.

This morning we are going to talk about all the different programs that Amazon offers: the Advantage program, Associates, Amazon connect, and Amazon Marketplace. Once you take advantage of all four of those, you are ready to go on to some advanced tactics. We'll talk about those too. The great thing is that you can enroll in every one of these programs. You don't have to choose only one or two of them.

Amazon Advantage Program

Amazon Advantage is the primary program that most small publishers and small published people use. Anything that has an ISBN or UPC number can be listed into Amazon Advantage. They are essentially giving you full seller's terms, which means they demand a 55% discount and as some of you know, is pretty harsh to deal with. Suppose your book has a list price of $20, that means a customer goes on Amazon, pays $20, and you get $9 for the sale (55% off of $20 leaves you $9). There are some exceptions available: if your book is published by a 501(c)3 charity, you can get a break on the 55% discount, and for some of the higher end books, like textbooks, they will probably cut back the discount to 25%. The best thing is that Advantage pays ninety days after sale by direct deposit; there's no invoicing to do, ever.

The great thing about Amazon advantage is when you enroll in Amazon Advantage, you get complete control over all the stuff that is displayed next to your book. You'll see that if you open that Amazon page on any given book (for example a Harry Potter book), you see the entire professional reviews, the book cover, and Search-Inside-the-Book. All of that stuff is available to you if you enroll in Amazon Advantage. Amazon Advantage is only good for selling new books or books that can pass for new. You can't sell any used materials. Generally, they put in orders once a week. They used to have a program where they would order once a quarter, but the logistics were too much of a problem for them. On Sunday night, I'll get an order for this week's books they want and they think they are going to sell in the next week or so. Weekly orders can be annoying because if Amazon orders in small quantities, it may tend to eat your profits on shipping costs.

How does warehousing work? When you sign up for Amazon Advantage, which is the traditional publisher model, you'll get an order for two books in a week to ten days. If those books sell, you'll get an order for more. They have a very sophisticated sales prediction algorithm so they don't fill their warehouses up with stuff. Eventually, orders will go up to fifty or one hundred at a time if you're lucky.

Amazon Associates

Amazon Associates program is one program that *anyone* can enroll in if you have a book in print and it's carried on Amazon. Even if you are working through a traditional publisher, you can use Associates as well. This is the program you see when you go to someone's Web page and you see a bunch of books with titles and it'll say "Harry Potter, 35% off at Amazon.com: click to buy the book." This allows you to put e-commerce on any site without having monthly fees and without having to deal with PayPal because Amazon is handling the complete transaction when you use Amazon Associates.

Amazon is still taking its 55% cut, but you don't have to worry about it (it's coming out of the publisher's pocket). What you're making on Associates is a commission of 4 to 6% depending on the item and your plan. The interesting thing here is you can list all the books similar to yours or in your genre, and you can actually make money selling competitor's books. Back when this started around 1997-98, I was making $400 to $500 per year from Associates sales. Now it's a little bit diluted because everyone is doing Amazon Associates, so it's harder to make money. Another thing you can do is put an Amazon Associates link in one of your emails. People can click on that and go buy the book. People trust Amazon, but they don't trust your Web site. Let's face it. I get a miniscule amount of direct sales on my site but Amazon will turn over hundreds of our books each month. Their reputation is gold-plated, and they deserve it because they have great customer service.

Amazon Connect

Amazon Connect is available to any author who has a book listed on Amazon by any means. So you are eligible if you had it printed by a traditional publisher and it's in print (or even out of print) or if you set it up yourself in Amazon Advantage. Amazon Connect is free blogspace where you can post messages about what you're interested in and it will show up on your book's page down near the bottom. You can use photos and links to other products on Amazon; it's very easy to write a review of someone else's book in your genre. You can get a lot of respect that way—for example if you're a Romance writer and you write about other people's books. It's not just about "me, me, me" at that point, and it's refreshing to have something to talk about other than yourself.

Amazon Marketplace

You can actually compete with yourself by using Amazon Marketplace and Amazon Advantage in tandem. Once your book is on Amazon, you can list it even cheaper on Amazon Marketplace. By having a lower price, people can buy it directly from you and you avoid the 55% discount by going through Marketplace. If your book is $20 and you list it for $14 on Amazon Marketplace, they collect $2 commissions and your profit is $12 less the cost of goods.

You can also sell used copies at Amazon Marketplace as well. You do have to relist your stuff every sixty days in Amazon Marketplace because it's a time-limited service as opposed to Half.com where your stuff will stay online for years and years and years. Amazon will automatically sell your book and expect you to ship it within two business days, so if you're out of stock or on vacation, you've got a big problem. You then have to go on to Amazon and refund the customer's money. You need to make sure you have the stock in advance. Other services like Alibris and Half.com allow you to have a confirmation step, but Amazon doesn't.

Mechanical Turk

Recently, Amazon launched Mechanical Turk, which sounds funny, but it is named after a famous mythical chess-playing robot. MTurk allows you to farm out small tasks that can be done online, just like an online service bureau, virtual assistants and all that. I came up with the idea, "Why not have somebody write blog posts about my book?" You set the commission rate, I set it around 50 to 80 cents and people will actually write a blog post about your book, post a picture of it, and put a buying link on it for that money. People have to write blogs every day and they need something to write about and this helps them. If you go to send out books, it costs a lot of money in comparison to say, 75 cents for someone to write about the book sight unseen. The only problems with using MTurk for blog publicity are that you get some awfully low quality bloggers (your post may be their very first) and you are not allowed to ask for URLs to verify their work. MTurk policy forbids them disclosing their identities or any personal information and a URL would do that, more or less.

I had somewhat better luck using MTurk to contract people to fill in Amazon tags for my books. This dramatically increases their visibility in search results and you can pay people fairly low amounts, about twenty-five cents, to go in to your book and simply reinforce existing tags. Each time someone else re-tags an existing tag, the power of that tag is increased by one increment. We'll cover keyword tagging in depth later.

MTurk will help you connect with people in an interesting way. I find it fascinating. You can also make your money yourself, although it's kind of low wages!

Print On Demand

Many people ask me, how do you deal with Print on Demand and Amazon discounts? All my books are POD and I don't price anything under $17.95. Maybe I sell less than I could, but it gives me $1 to $5 margin per book. I use Lightning Source which is the world's cheapest POD, but it's very technically challenging: you have to be able to provide PDFs that are ready for publication. You aren't really going to price people out of the market by listing your book at $20 because

Amazon tends to list everything at 30% off. It's not like you're going to frighten people away by having a high list price because Amazon, in order to make the sales, is going to mark the book down as much as it can. You might actually need to consider raising your list price. A lot of people undervalue their work!

Advanced Campaign tactics

Now we're going to talk about advanced tactics; we're going to assume you've already done a couple of these programs; you at least have an Amazon Connect blog and are using Amazon Advantage so you have control over your detail page. Actually, even if you have no formal relationship with Amazon, you can do an **Update Product Info.** Anyone who's ever even just bought one book from Amazon is allowed to submit an update product info. If there's a typo in your name, or you want to add "First Edition," or there's a Foreword by someone else and you want to give him credit, you can adjust anything except the price. It's buried at the bottom of the page and says "Something wrong here? Click on Update Product Info."

Amazon is really pushing hard on **video reviews.** I'm finally starting to take advantage of it. You can get a Flip Ultra Video camera that records directly to an embedded memory stick for $100 and it will store an hour's worth of video. I'm going to record three or four minute talks about the books and then upload them to the Amazon book page. Anyone can do this; you can talk about your favorite book in the world, upload it and once it gets going, it will be like YouTube. It's a cheap way to build buzz and it costs nothing. You've got nothing to lose.

Another interesting thing is **tagging with keywords.** That's sort of buried in the middle of a product info page. Anyone can add keywords to any book whether it's your book or someone else's book. You don't need a relationship with Amazon other than to have bought one book in your lifetime. Suppose your book is an Urban Romance but that's not in the title; the title is "How to Get a Man Without Really Trying." You can tag the book as Urban Romance, the city it takes place in, what the characters do, etc.. When someone searches for another book that happens to have the same tag that your book has, you get a link from their book to your book. You can get yourself associated with books in your genre and get known that way. People who have no idea that your book exists can click on a tag and find your book.

Now that's very similar to **Suggest-A-Search,** which is another way to pump up search engine hits. You can actually set it up so when people go to Amazon and type into a search box, you can suggest what they should see! So when someone types in those magic keywords, your book could be the #1 hit. We did that for Frances Shani Parker's book so when you type in Detroit Hospice, her book comes up as the #1 hit. I don't know how many people are going to do that but it's another way to build consciousness. The other thing I noticed is that if it's too vague or too general, Amazon will delete it. I had one of my books tagged with "self-help" and it was too general so eventually Amazon removed the tag.

Working in the Wild

There's a number of features that anyone who's ever been a member of Amazon can use. All you have to have done is just buy a single book. You can create something called a **"So You'd Like To…"** list. This is a list of books related to a single topic. One of the most popular is "So You'd Like to Survive a Zombie Attack" and it's got everything you need in that list to survive: chainsaws, shotguns, and so on. You can be really creative… "So you'd like to survive a break up"… Whatever your books are about!

The other thing that's related to this is **Listmania**, again something that anyone can create. These are more likely to be a "Top 10 best list." You could say "My 10 favorite romance books," "My 10 favorite biographies," and so on. What you are doing is associating yourself with popular titles. If you write a fantasy book, you can write a list called "My favorite fantasy books" and you can add your book and the Harry Potter book *on that same list*. If someone clicks on the Harry Potter page, they'll see "Oh someone has a list of favorite fantasy books!" and maybe click on your Listmania list. It's a way of getting free publicity by attaching yourself to other books.

Anyone with an Amazon account can beef up his or her **online profile;** you can add your photo, you can you list of personal favorite books, and there are Amazon friends so you can do social networking stuff.

Approaching reviewers who have already reviewed books similar to yours takes time but can have a great payoff. You can click on the reviewer's name and that'll take you to his or her profile. The reviewer may or may not have an email address out but a lot of them will have their own independent sites—especially if they want to become one of the Amazon Top 100 reviewers. There's some crazy people out there who have reviewed 5-6 thousand books and want to become a top reviewer. That's one way to get famous I guess. Anyway you can contact these people who have reviewed books in your genre; you will know they are favorable to your attitude, and they'll often write amazing, amazing reviews for the cost of one book. They get to meet the author so it's exciting for them and they get a free book so it's a win-win situation all the way around.

Living Outside the System

Can you contract with another warehouse fulfillment/distribution outfit and have them work with Amazon? Yes, Amazon will deal directly with Ingram, Baker & Taylor, and any other number of distributors that have a relationship with them. When you sign up with your distributor, you can ask them "How does my book get into Amazon?" They get a new list of books and upload it to Amazon every month. There's a 99% chance that they already have a relationship with them so you don't have to use Amazon Advantage.

Although, if your book goes out of print with the distributor, you can sign up for Amazon Advantage and put your book back in print. Even if your book is officially out of print (they have no more copies and no intention to print more), if you still have the right to sell your book or you have extra copies, you can unplug your books from the distribution chain and say "I'm going to have a direct relationship with Amazon." Similarly, if you start out in Amazon Advantage and get picked up later by a big distributor, you can ask to have your book de-listed from your fulfillment. This can be tricky as it could have some downtime where your book appears as "Not Available."

Links into Amazon Programs

Amazon Advantage	www.amazon.com/advantage
Amazon Associates	www.amazon.com/associates
Amazon Connect	www.amazon.com/connect
Amazon Marketplace	www.amazon.com/marketplace (or click on "Have one to sell?")
Mechanical Turk	www.mturk.com

About the Author

Learn more about Victor R. Volkman in the About the Editors section beginning on p. 215.

Podcast Airdate:	December 1st, 2007
Podcast URL:	http://authorsaccess.com/archives/95
Author's site:	http://www.lovinghealing.com
	http://www.modernhistorypress.com
	http://www.authorsaccess.com

Twenty-One Mistakes to Avoid when Publishing and Promoting Your Book

Patrick Snow

After writing and selling over 125,000 copies of *Creating Your Own Destiny*, spending ten years in the publishing industry, and coaching author-clients to get their books published, I have seen all kinds of errors made by new authors. Unfortunately, many errors are severe and completely eliminate the chance of the book having any possibility of success. Because of publishing mistakes, many new authors never see a return on their investment and their book dies prematurely.

According to the Independent Book Publishers Association (formerly PMA), 98% of authors will never sell more than 2,000 copies of their book. What are the biggest mistakes holding back this 98% from experiencing any real success with their books? How can you avoid these mistakes, end up in the 2% success category and achieve great sales with your book?

1. Writing Your Book for a Small Market Niche: Don't bother writing the book if there are not 50-100 million people interested worldwide in that book's focus. Your book must have mass appeal if you are going to sell it successfully.

2. Not Securing URL's for Your Name and Book Title: No matter what, you must own the domain name for your book title, and your first and last name dot com. If you cannot get your book title as your domain, you must change the title to make *that* title a dot com.

3. Having Your Personal Name be Part of Your Publishing Company's Name: Choose a unique name for your self-publishing company to avoid the dead giveaway that your book is self-published. You want to make a publishing imprint with no relationship to you.

4. Selecting a Publisher with High Printing Costs: Some publishers do not allow you to retain ownership of your completed book. They will force you to pay outrageous print costs. Your print costs should be $2-3 per book, instead of the $8-12 many print-on-demand publishers will charge you.

5. Selecting Your Own Book Title: Unless you are an expert at book titles, always pay a professional to help you come up with your book title. A good title makes all the difference in the world and a professional will help you make your title appealing.

6. Putting Your Own Photo on the Front Cover: Unless you are famous, under no circumstance should you place your image on the front cover of your book. This is a dead giveaway that you book is self-published. Your book is not about you; it is about your reader. Place a small photo of yourself on the lower corner of back cover.

7. Doing Your Own Cover Design: As a kid we are taught not to judge a person by the way they look. In publishing this is primarily how books are judged. Creating your own cover design is possibly the single greatest error an author can make. Hire experienced graphic designers for your cover to make that stunning first impression.

8. Forgetting to Include URL on Back of Book: Other than the book title, the most important information on your book cover is your domain name. Your domain attracts buyers to your site where you offer "Free Stuff" to capture email, and then you can sell your products to them for life.

9. Giving Away the Foreword in Your Book for Free: Only allow people to do the foreword if they are going to purchase a high volume of your books. Write one book, co-branding it with different companies with their individual forewords. Next, sell a large volume of these co-branded books to the company whose CEO foreword is in your book.

10. Skipping the Proofreading Step: After you book has been edited, type-set, and is ready to go to press, you need a professional proofreader. Hire a proofreader to read the book through cover-to-cover. Studies suggest that today's books average at least twenty errors.

11. Selling the Rights to a Major Publisher: Unless you get a six-figure advance from the publisher, you give away all your profits when you sell the book rights. Big publishers used to spend money on marketing their books; now they are nothing more than a company that pays for printing.

12. Relying on Someone Else for Publicity: Few people can do a better job publicizing your book than you can. The industry is full of authors who have spent big money on publicists and received little back in return. If you don't toot your own horn, no one else will.

13. Failing to Work with Major Distributors: It is important to land a book deal with a major distributor so that you can get your books in bookstores worldwide. Distributors can get your self-published book in stores worldwide giving you even more credibility.

14. Focusing on Bookstore Sales: Bookstores are a lousy place to sell a book because there are simply too many other books competing. Find multiple point-of-purchase locations outside bookstores to sell your books where there are no other competing titles.

15. Selling Books One at a Time: It takes the same amount of time to create an invoice for one book, as it does for 10,000 books. Focus on selling books in volumes of 10,000 at a time. There are many high volume opportunities just waiting to be created.

16. Not Following Up on Sales Opportunities: The "Rule of Seven" states that it can take up to seven bits of communication between seller and buyer before a sale transpires. When you send out a review copy, follow up with the prospects frequently to sell books, land speaking engagements, and secure new coaching clients.

17. Not Selling from Your Own Web Site: This is extremely important. You *always* want your customers to buy directly from your web site. You lose 40-60% of the profits through commissions with each outside outlet sale. Sign and ship your own books and keep all of the profits.

18. Hoarding All of Your Books: Too many authors never give out review copies, and as a result their sales suffer. You should send out 5-10 review copies per day to book buyers worldwide that have the ability to buy in volume. This is the best way to sell hundreds of thousands of copies of your book.

19. Forgetting to Leverage Your Credibility as an Author: Once published, you must also diversify into speaking, coaching, and consulting. Use your book as the "hook" to attract more clients. Your book is really nothing more than a lead-generation tool for speaking, coaching, and consulting which may become your primary sources of income.

20. Giving Up and Writing Your Next Book: A successful book is five percent writing and 95% promotion. It is better to author one book that sells 250,000 copies, than have twelve books that each only sell 250 copies. When you sell large quantities of your book, you will attract the attention of major publishers. If you decide to "sell out" to a publisher, you are now in the driver's seat and can negotiate a much higher advance.

21. Trying to Go Solo: Study people who are successful and learn from their successes as well as their failures. Hire a publishing coach and you will save time and money. Be willing to learn from others who have already been successful selling large volumes of books, picking up coaching clients, and doing lots of keynote speaking engagements.

If you can avoid these mistakes, I have no doubt you will successfully sell thousands and thousands of books. Everyone you come in contact with should know about your book. Your book cover should appear on the back of your business cards as well as on the auto-signature of your email. My best advice to you for publishing a successful book is to market it every single day and spend years and years of your time promoting it. You can contact me to schedule a free 30-minute, no obligation publishing consultation. Dream, Plan, Execute, and Soar

About the Author

Patrick Snow is the best-selling author of *Creating Your Own Destiny: How to Get Exactly What You Want Out of Life*. His book is a "success roadmap" for high achievers, and has sold over 125,000 copies in both English and foreign language editions. Patrick's "DESTINY" message has been featured in numerous national newspapers including, a cover story in *USA Today* and in *The New York Times*. His message has been featured on hundreds of radio stations throughout North America, and he has been a guest on the KOMO-TV Seattle show "Northwest Afternoon." Patrick is an entrepreneur, international speaker, and publishing coach. He has helped dozens of authors achieve their dreams of being published.

Podcast Airdate:	October 11th, 2007
Podcast URL:	http://authorsaccess.com/archives/84
Author's site:	www.BestSellerPublishingCoaching.com

Twelve Things Under Ten Bucks You Can Do
Victor R. Volkman

In the mid 1990s, I was trying to make my mark as an author of books for computer programmers. I was young and naïve and had two attitudes which I now recognize as fatal. First, the "build it and they will come" attitude which I guess essentially expected customers to magically discover and buy the books. The first year of sales reports seemed to confirm that this was inevitable. Then the returns came in, those unsold books which had been gathering dust on those oh-so-coveted bookstore shelves were being sent back to the warehouse to molder. Few things are more discouraging than a royalty statement with a negative dollar figure on the bottom line!

Second, I was convinced that my publisher should be doing everything in their power to move the book. What this Fortune 500 company ever did for me was not clear since I didn't receive any news about marketing. Now I realize that there was undoubtedly more that I could have done, even though it was a couple years before the tools which any novice can use were well known (yes, I mean blogs!). No, it was not technology or timing to blame, mostly the attitude that the publisher should be in control.

If you are a new author or are aspiring to be published soon, *ask not what your publisher can do for you* but what you can do for your publisher. Yes, I know you wrote the book, but delivery of the manuscript is NOT the finish line, merely the starting gun for the real race. Since I'm not here to just preach but to offer you some practical solutions, here are twelve things you can do to promote your book. All are under ten bucks and at least half of them are free.

1. **Send a review copy** to a post-publication reviewer: Reader Views, Midwest Book Reviews, Rebecca's Reads, TCM Reviews, Bookpleasures, MyShelf.com, etc.…
2. **Dust off that Blog!** Post something to your own blog, put in reminders into Outlook to make you get back on that horse.
3. **Contribute to other people's blogs:** ask to write a guest article on a blog related to your topic. I bet the blogger would be thrilled to have new, original content they didn't have to do completely on their own.

4. **Review books like yours:** post reviews of the five bestselling similar books in your genre on Amazon, make sure your URL appears in your posting profile. Mention that if readers liked this book, they might like yours too.
5. Get yourself a great-looking **full color poster of your book** cover from Elco Labs, starting at $9.95 www.elcocolor.com/poster_special.htm.
6. Put a **free listing of your book** up on www.Bookhitch.com
7. **Record the Introduction** or Chapter One of your book on headset microphone attached to your PC, upload it to www.podiobooks.com
8. If self-published, **upload your book** to print.google.com or if not then badger your publisher to do so or explain why they can't.
9. **Use your video camera** to record a 4 minute video about you and your book. Add music from PodSafeAudio.com. Upload it to YouTube, Broadcaster.com, and post it as an Amazon video review
10. **Schedule an event** at a local school, church, civic organization where you can be an expert about the subject of your book, get kids interested in reading or writing, or raise awareness for a charity.
11. **Become an official author** at LibraryThing.com, Amazon.com (www.amazon.com/connect), and RedRoom.com. Update your profile, fill in missing book details, post a blog item.
12. **Post a free Press Release** at any of the sites below.

www.pr.com	www.ecommwire.com
www.openpr.com	www.express-press-release.com
www.24-7pressrelease.com	www.free-news-release.com
www.newswiretoday.com	www.free-press-release-center.info
www.pressmethod.com	www.freepressindex.com
www.clickpress.com	www.freepressreleases.co.uk
www.free-press-release.com	www.prlog.org
www.pressbox.co.uk	www.prurgent.com
www.i-newswire.com	www.przoom.com
www.pr9.net	www.theopenpress.com
www.pr-inside.com	www.free-press-release.info
www.prfree.com	www.prlog.org

9 Making the Most of Technology

Successfully Selling Your Book Online
Brad Grochowski

The Best Place to Sell Your Book

I have often been heard repeating the quote, "The worst place to sell a book is in a bookstore." I attribute that nugget of wisdom to the great skydiver and publishing guru Dan Poynter. And I think that, for many reasons, this is a mighty good thing to keep in mind when developing a marketing plan for an independently published book.

But I would follow it with my own personal belief; the best place to sell a book is online.

Note that I am not saying it's the easiest place to sell a book. You have to do all the work yourself. Indeed, there is a lot of work to be done and so much to learn. In fact, there is more that *could* be done than you will ever be able to do for a book. What a wonderful problem to have.

Doing business online can be daunting, especially if you aren't a web savvy kid who has grown up living and breathing the Internet. Even if you do affiliate yourself with Generation X, Y or especially Z, there is a lot to know. It can be overwhelming: Web 2.0; social networking; streaming video; Content Management; search optimization; blogging; vlogging; wiki-this and wiki-that.

The world does seem to be catching up. That list of web buzz-words will ring more bells with more people than it would have even one year ago. You may even feel like you have the web in your pocket. But figuring out how to put all of these things together and wielding them to sell your book can be a daunting enterprise indeed.

Daunting, yes, but it is worth it. Clearly, the Internet offers an amazing opportunity. Never in the history of the world have we been able even to dream of a global sales and distribution system such as this. Add the fact that it's in the hands of every person, and entry costs are relatively negligible, and you can teach yourself to master it. We take these things for granted...but holy cow...stop and think of what you have access to.

You can write your book in Cleveland, have it printed in China, and sell it to a fan in Denmark, who deposits her payment directly into your bank account in Delaware. And doing it this way, as remarkable as it is, is *more cost effective* than any other method mankind has devised.

I'm not going to claim to understand how all of this came to be. But I marvel at the Internet as I would any of the wonders of the ancient world, a testament to the greatness of mankind's unbounded ingenuity. Only unlike the Pharaoh's Pyramid, or Nebuchadnezzar's hanging gardens, this wonder of the world was built for you. And it can help you sell your book.

All you have to do is learn its ropes. If you learn what tools are out there and how to use them, you are well on your way to tapping into this Wonder of the World.

Get Their Eyeballs on Your Book

Getting your book online is one thing. There are lots of ways to do that—we'll cover this to some degree in a bit—but getting people to find your book once it's online is the real trick. Actually, getting them to find it—then convincing them to buy it—is the real trick.

Fortunately, there are a lot of tools that you can use to take advantage of the Internet. You just need to know what they are and have some idea of how to use them.

Before we begin looking at some of these tools, let's talk a little strategy.

Primary Point of Sale

There is a lot of web out there. There are many places to list your book online. I encourage you to take advantage of as many of them as possible. If there is a Web site, online bookstore or book database that will list your book—list it with them. If there is a small fee, pay it. If there is a medium fee, consider paying it. If there is a large fee, ask yourself why the fee is large. If there is some reason that warrants paying a large fee, then pay it.

Understand that even the biggest online booksellers, such as Amazon.com, won't charge much to list your book. To register as a bookseller, it generally costs under $50 per year. Some of the more indie-book friendly Web sites, such as

Making the Most of Technology

AuthorsBookshop.com, charge much less than that, and you will only have to pay one time.

So by all means, go crazy. List your book everywhere and anywhere you can. You never know who or when or where or how or on what Web site someone is going to stumble upon your book and want to buy it. (To help you in this, I have included a list of online booksellers in the resource section at the end of this chapter).

You can look beyond bookselling sites as well. Your book is about something—whether it is fiction or nonfiction. Contact Web sites that are related to your book, and ask them to list your title. If you wrote a book about improving your golf swing, look for web sites that list and sell golf-related equipment.

You might think that selling through your own Web site may offer the best financial return. However—and take it from someone who runs an online bookstore—packing and shipping book orders everyday takes a lot of time and work. This is time and work that you could spend marketing your book, or writing the next one. When you also consider the cost and effort of accepting credit cards and dealing with all the taxes and extra paperwork—not to mention the inevitable unhappy customer—you may quickly realize that this isn't the best option for you.

Conversely, selling through bookstores or other Web sites may cost a bit—or a lot—depending on the terms. There will likely be an up-front listing fee and/or a consignment of up to 60% of the selling price. The upside is that they handle everything. They manage the secure credit card transactions, packing, shipping, returns, customer satisfaction, etc. so you don't even have to think about all of that.

Consider also that not all online bookstores are the same. Some of the major online bookstores can be pretty hard to deal with. Their consignment is high—often as much as 60%—and Amazon, in particular, has a widespread reputation for treating independent publishers poorly.

On the other hand, there are online bookstores that adore the variety and passion that can be found in the independent publishing community. This is primarily what led me to create AuthorsBookshop.com. I wanted to create a place that celebrated independent publishing, and offer terms that were really to the advantage of the small publishers and self-published authors.

It is worth it to look around and look closely at all of the options when deciding where you are going to send people to buy your book. Disadvantageous as it is for you, you have to list your book with Amazon. They are the king of online book sales, and you will get some credibility for having your book listed on their site. It would be irresponsible of you to ignore Amazon. However, is this really where you want to send people to buy your book?

This brings me back to my point. Pick the online seller that makes the most sense to you and that benefits you the most. We are going to designate this sales point as your Primary Point of Sale.

Any time you mention your book, online or off, list this Primary Point of sale as *the* place for people to go to buy your book. You want to link to this Primary Point of sale from as many online places as you can. We are going to talk about how to do that in a bit. But first I want to explain why.

You want to designate a Primary Point of Sale, and funnel as much traffic as possible to it, for two reasons:

1) You have already decided that this is the place that benefits you the most, and

2) Search engines.

Let's take a glimpse at search engines, to see why this is a good idea.

The Search Is On

Google rules the web. For reasons that are beyond the scope of our mission here, they control a huge percentage of online activity. Before Google, it was Yahoo. Before Yahoo, well, the web as we know it did not exist.

What do Google and Yahoo do? Search. Or rather, help you search.

Why is this so powerful? The power isn't in the searching, but in the finding—as in, are people going to find your book online?

Think about it; imagine if Google suddenly decided that it wasn't going to list your book anymore. Effectively, it would suddenly cease to exist. That may be a slight exaggeration, but it is only slight. If customers can't find you by search, then you are going to lose a very large percentage of traffic.

If you are going to play the game of online bookselling, you have to understand one thing: It is Google's game.

So what do you do? Learn the rules to Google's game, and play it as diligently as you can. I want to lay out a few things here that will help you understand a few things about how Google (and other search engines) work. This will help you tune your online strategies to optimize your Primary Point of Sale, and bring more eyeballs to your book.

The most important thing you need to understand, the yardstick with which Google measures all sites, and the currency with which it trades, is called a "linkback."

What is a linkback? It's simple. It's a link on one site, pointing back to another site. Every time a site has a linkback pointing to it, Google counts it as a vote. The more linkback votes a Web site has, the more important Google assumes it must be. The more important Google thinks a site is, the higher it will list it in its search pages.

So you want your Primary Point of Sale to be as important as possible so that Google will put it close to the top of the search results for anything related to your book.

You now understand what linkbacks are, and it's really pretty simple. But it gets more complicated. More important sites get more votes. So, if SuperOnlineWebsite.com (a very important site) links to your Primary Point of Sale one time, it gets a lot of these "linkback votes." However, if JoesBoringBlog.com points to the same page, it may get very few (if any) votes.

Add to this the fact that there are "bad" linkbacks. Bad linkbacks usually come from people trying to cheat Google. These linkbacks can actually take away votes—or get a site banned from Google altogether.

You can steer clear of creating bad linkbacks by avoiding activities that are meant to fool Google into thinking your site is more important than it is. Bad practices include things such as:

- "hiding" links or text on web pages by making the text the same color as the background;
- listing your link with "linkfarms"—collections of computer generated Web sites that post hundreds of links;
- joining "link sharing" programs that promise to post thousands of linkbacks to your site; or
- any other of the dozens of tricks people use to try to fool Google into giving a higher search placement.

So, it gets a little involved. But still, all you need to know is which sites count for how many votes, get those sites to link to yours, and you're all set, right?

The problem is that there is no way to know which sites count for how many votes. Google uses a special algorithm to determine the value of a Web site. It guards that algorithm like a top-secret cold-war-era military-super-spy chocolate chip cookie dough recipe. No one knows what it is. Well, obviously a few eggheads at Google understand it, but no mortals do.

Web marketers are pretty clever though. We have found many ways to surmise what is going on inside of that algorithm. This has helped us to develop strategies to optimize Web sites to take the most advantage of the algorithm without falling afoul of what Google considers to be legal.

Oh SEO Can You See?

Search engine optimization (SEO) is the arcane art of tweaking a Web site to make it as friendly to Google as possible. This is a *huge* topic. It could (and does) fill whole volumes. There is also a lot of debate of what is and is not effective. I'm not going to wade into that stream here, as it would pull us off track. But, as it is vital to selling your book successfully online, I want to discuss the number one thing you can do to increase your standing in Google searches.

First, a word of caution. There is a lot to understand here. It can be very tempting to offload a lot of this stuff onto a third party that will charge money to do it for you. There are legitimate Search Engine Optimization companies out there —but there are many more that are just out to get your money. Since this is such an arcane art, it is easy to fleece an unsuspecting webmaster of thousands of dollars without any measurable results. Be cautious of companies that:

- Contact you out of the blue. They will email you, and they will call you. If you want to use an SEO service, do your research, gather recommendations, and select one that looks good to you.
- Guarantee results. Because of the nature of SEO, there are no guarantees. If they promise you a specific rate of traffic, they are not being honest with you. Or they are using methods that Google will eventually punish you for.
- Won't reveal their methods. They should be able to give you a general idea of the strategies they will employ. Remember, bad strategies can do more harm to your site than good.

So what can you do to leverage Google and its super secret algorithm? That question brings us back to...your Primary Point of Sale.

If your book is available for sale on ten different Web sites, imagine if you do not designate a Primary Point of Sale. One link may point to one point of sale, another link may point to another, and another link may point to yet a third. You are diluting all of these linkback votes across many different points of sale—and not all of them are to your best advantage even if they sell one of your books.

So, by picking one point of sale, and directing as many links to that one point as possible, you will optimize the number of linkback votes, and thus it's value to Google. With all of these linkbacks to your Primary Point of Sale, it will quickly begin to push its way upward in the search rankings.

It will do one other thing, too. It will increase the non-Google-search traffic to this point of sale. Because there are all these links out there pointing to your book in this one place, that's where everyone will end up when they want to buy it. This means that you will be getting the most out of every book sold online.

So that's Google search. Selecting a Primary Point of Sale and optimizing it are clearly important. But what else can you do to help people find your book online?

Paying For Clicks

We aren't done with Google yet. Search made them powerful, but the thing that made them rich is online advertising. Google advertising is unlike any other advertising option we have ever had in the past. It is highly targeted, flexible, inexpensive and easy. This is a revolution.

How has Google (and other similar services) managed to do this? The answer is "content based advertising."

They allow you, and anyone else who has something to sell, to create an account. You may then pick some keywords that pertain to your book, and agree to pay a little bit each time someone clicks on your ad. Google will then place your ad on Web sites that seem to pertain to the keywords you have chosen.

So for your book about improving a golf swing, you choose the keyword "golf swing." Now your ad will appear on Web sites across the Internet that are all about golf. When browsers visit these Web sites, and they are clearly interested in golf, they will see your ad. If they click through it—and **only** if they click through it—you will pay what you have agreed to pay.

Because click-throughs can cost as little as $0.10, this can be an effective way to bring interested buyers to your Primary Point of Sale. These are the most likely people to order your book.

The Web, redux

What is the "Web 2.0?" Well, it means different things to different people. But for the sake of our purposes, we can think of it as a web that does four important things:

- Allows extensive user interaction with Web sites.
- Fosters large online communities of like-minded people.
- Provides online applications that assist in many of life's activities.
- Leverages high traffic volumes to allow no- or low-cost to the users.

Put these four things together and you have created an environment very suitable for the small-fry publisher getting the word out about an unknown book.

What does all of this mean though, in a practical sense? How does this Web 2.0, and the four things that it consists of, help you sell your book?

It does this by allowing for things such as MySpace, Facebook, blogging, vlogging, eBay, Paypal and hundreds of other tools. These things allow you to do things that you couldn't do before and most of them are free. If they are not free, then there is usually a low or no upfront fee, allowing you to work on a micro scale.

If you are interested, I cover many of these Web 2.0 tools in greater detail in the resource section at the end of this chapter—in the list of *10 (almost) free things you should be doing to market your book online*.

"Design for online"

The last thing I want to discuss in regards to the marketing end of selling your book online has more to do with how to present your book than how to market it.

Displaying your book online brings a list of considerations that had never been an issue in the pre-web days. We are all still learning what does—and what does not—make a good impression with online shoppers. There are, however, some things that we generally recognize as best practices and you would do well to understand them. You should consider these things well before your book appears online.

In fact, you should probably start to consider your online strategies before your cover is even designed. Why? Because your cover should be designed for the web. Why? Because that is where 90% of the people who will ever see it, will see it.

When a book is presented online, you usually see it as a thumbnail. There is an old idea in book design called the "15 foot" test. If you can't understand what a book is about when viewing the cover from 15 feet away, it's time to head back to the drawing board. Well, the modern corollary would probably be the "100 pixel" test. You should be able to recognize the cover art and read the title of your book even when it's shrunk down to 100 pixels. Pictures should be clear, typeface should be large and contrast should be high.

When you list your book, you will also post a synopsis. Make it good. Make sure it is tight, well written and I am sorry to have to say...spell checked.

Moving Forward

We have covered a lot of ground here. I think I have made a pretty strong case for selling your book online and how to succeed at it. I've outlined a pretty straightforward strategy that should get you started and discussed some of the tools and elements that will help you succeed.

But one of the best things about the web is how young it is. To call it a frontier is not an exaggeration. It really is the Wild West all over again. Because of this, the rules and best practices are still being written. I encourage you to take the leap and try new things. Much of what I describe here was unknown to anyone five years ago. Five years from now, we will be talking about strategies that haven't even occurred to anyone yet.

The techniques and strategies for successfully selling online that we understand today were devised by folks like you and I. Just as we are, they were looking for new ways to get more people interested in finding their products online and hitting that "buy" button. And just as they did, perhaps you will come up with some new trick that will create a nice bump in the sales of your book. If you do, let me know! I'm always looking for new ways to help independent authors succeed at selling their books online.

10 (almost) free things you should be doing to promote your book:

1) Online bookstores: Online bookstores aren't free. You will usually have to pay a bit up front as a setup and a consignment on book sales. But with very little effort you can get your book listed in a place where people are going to buy books. You would be very fortunate to have distribution that will place your book in brick-and-mortar stores in every city in the country. But barring that, this is the best way to get your book broadly distributed. And my advice—get your book in every online outlet that you can. You can pick one and call it a day, but why limit yourself? Your book should be everywhere.

2) Blog: It's almost a cliché now. Everyone and his dog has a blog. But it is free, and it can make a difference. Besides, you're a writer. Blogging leverages the thing that you do best, in a format that you get to control. You don't have to become a hardcore, twenty posts-a-day blogger, but you should post a few times a week.

A blog can do several things for you. It puts fresh content online, with your name on it, and links to your book. Search engines love that. It can bring new people to your book's subject matter and attract new readers who are already interested in it. It can also bolster your reputation as an expert on your subject matter.

What are you going to blog about? It's like any other writing you have done; write about what you know. You don't want to write about your book. Write about what your book is about. Link to other blogs, and comment on other writers' blogs. Certainly, link to your own book whenever it is prudent.

3) Email signature: this one is so easy I hesitated to include it. But it's such a good way to spread the word about your book. It's so completely effortless and free, I couldn't leave it out. In your email settings, set your signature with your name, the title of your book and a link to its primary online sales point. You will be surprised by the people who notice and follow the link to your book.

4) Seek out online communities related to your book: you are an expert about something. You wrote a book about it. There are other folks online who are talking about that very subject. Find them and get to know them. Discussion lists and forums, as well as niche social networking sites have popped up for even the most esoteric interests.

Let me caution you though. Join these communities in good faith and in good form. Talk about the subject, not your book. Form new friendships and relationships. Your book will come up and, if it does naturally, you are much more likely to gather interest.

Of course, make sure you have a link to your book in your signature or profile. That way, people will find out about your book on their own. You won't even have to mention it.

5) Social networking sites: social networking sites barely existed just a few years ago. But they have quickly become one of the best, "free-est", most exciting ways to market your book online. Simply put, social networking sites aggregate people—many people—into online communities. The people in these communities

Making the Most of Technology 187

are tied to each other into networks of relationships. These people share with each other information that they find interesting. Because they are all connected, this information can spread through large numbers of people very quickly.

The latest generation of sites doesn't even require people to pass information along. It's done automatically. Anything you add or post to your page will automatically be broadcast to all of your friends' pages. With the click of a button, you can promote your book on hundreds of pages to be seen by thousands of viewers. This is very powerful.

6) Write Articles: You are a writer. That gives you some great advantages for marketing online. Musicians can do most of the things you can do, but most of them would be hard pressed to write really good copy about their album. You on the other hand write great things before breakfast.

Write short, well-edited articles about what you know. Don't write about your book—write about what your book is about.

There are many online article databases to which you can submit your articles. They are free and they accept articles almost automatically. Submit to as many as you have time for. Once your articles are accepted and published, they are placed in a searchable database. I have listed a few of them in the resource section at the end of this chapter.

These databases are used by journalists, publishers, writers, bloggers and webmasters as copy to fill their publications. They get the article for free, you get the byline...including info such as your Web site, your book and where to buy it.

So, though you are writing articles for free, you are building broad exposure while bolstering your reputation as an expert in your area of knowledge.

7) Write reviews and blurbs for other authors: As an author, you know full well how hard it is to get good reviews and blurbs. Well, get by giving and pay it forward. Reviewing other authors' work does two things. It helps out a fellow writer, who may very well reciprocate for your next book. It also gets your name out there. The reviews you write will be published on Web sites, in online bookstores, quoted on book covers and printed in publicity material.

8) Your own Web site: this one isn't free either. In fact, having your own Web site designed and hosted can cost thousands of dollars. But it doesn't have to.

I would advise against asking a friend, relative, friend of a relative or relative of a friend to do it for free. These days, a Web site must look and behave as if it were professionally designed. If someone is able to do it for free, they aren't likely to do a professional quality job. If they were, they would be too busy to work for free.

Fortunately, there are great options that are free or nearly free. Content management software such as Joomla, Wordpress and Drupal can be downloaded and installed for free. You need only pay for a hosting service, and a few hours of time with a knowledgeable person who can show you how to use it.

There are an untold number of free and low-cost templates that you can download and install. They will give your site a very professional appearance and should offer enough flexibility to keep you happy for quite a while.

Additionally, online services such as Blogger, Wordpress, MySpace and many others can be used as a Web site and they are all free.

Even better, many online bookstores and social networking communities offer web pages that you could use as your "homebase" on the web. You can usually sell your book directly from that page.

9) Regular Newsletter: It is good to remind people that your book is out there. A good way to do this, without being too intrusive, is to send out occasional email newsletters.

Your newsletters should be short, informative and well-written. Let people know what you have done since the last newsletter, let them know what you have coming up, give a refresher synopsis of your book and point them to your Primary Point of Sale. Consider posting material from your blog or articles you have written. Invite other authors to write for your newsletter in exchange for a byline and a link to their own Web sites.

For your email list, start with friends and family. From there, you can build your list by asking recipients to forward the newsletters on to their friends. You can collect emails from your Web site and your own networking efforts.

You can start by sending email directly from your own email account. However, once you get to about fifty recipients, this can be a bit cumbersome. Look for an email host that specializes in email lists, or sign up for one of the many low-cost mass email services. You will find a list of some of these services in the resource section at the end of this chapter.

Be aware of spamming, however. Make sure you are using legitimate practices and following all of the etiquette and laws for mass emailing.

10) Send out press releases: Press releases have become an online activity, and this is a really great way to get press and attention for your book. There is a lot of information out there on how to write a great press release. Do some research, and look at some examples of successful press releases.

Start your press list by looking up every local media outlet you can think of—TV, radio, print and online media. Use the web to find the contact information of the pertinent editor. Once you have a good local list, start to move outward by looking at towns and cities near your own. Also look at national media outlets—major television, radio and print networks. You're sending your releases out by email, so it costs the same to send it out to 10 as it does to 1000. You might as well hit as many media outlets as you can.

As you build out your media list and send out your press releases, pay attention to who seems to be interested. If you get an outlet that prints a reference from your release, send them a thank you email. The next round, make sure you send a personal note to that outlet. In doing so, you will start to build a relationship with their editor. The next time they need an expert's opinion on your book's subject, they are more likely to call you.

Additional resources

Online booksellers	
Alibris	http://www.alibris.com
Amazon.com	http://www.amazon.com
AuthorsBookshop.com	http://www.authorsbookshop.com
Barnes and Noble	http://www.barnesandnoble.com
Borders Books	http://www.borders.com

Social Networking sites and Online Communities	
AuthorsDen	http://www.authorsden.com
Facebook	http://www.facebook.com
MySpace	http://www.myspace.com
The BookMarketing Network	http://bookmarket.ning.com/
The *Self-Publishing* Yahoo Group	http://finance.groups.yahoo.com/group/Self-Publishing

Blogging and Free Web site services	
Blogger	http://www.blogger.com
Homestead	http://www.homestead.com
Squarespace	http://www.squarespace.com/
Weebly	http://www.weebly.com/
Wordpress	http://www.wordpress.com

Email list management Web sites:	
Constant Contact	http://www.constantcontact.com
EzineDirector	http://ezinedirector.com
iList	http://www.ilist.com
Yahoo Groups	http://www.groups.yahoo.com
YesMail	http://www.yesmail.com

Article databases	
ArticleBase	http://www.articlebase.com
Article City	http://www.articlecity.com
Article Geek	http://www.articlegeek.com
Ezine Articles	http://www.exinearticles.com
Submit Your Article	http://www.submityourarticle.com

About the Author

Brad Grochowski is the founder of AuthorsBookshop.com, an online bookstore dedicated to selling independently published books. He is also the author of *The Secret Weakness of Dragons*, published by his own imprint, Eepie Press. In addition to writing and selling books, Brad is a web developer, happy husband and proud father. His blog, IndieBookMan, covers daily news, thoughts and ideas about independent publishing. You can find it at www.IndieBookMan.com

Podcast Airdate:	February 7th, 2008
Podcast URL:	http://authorsaccess.com/archives/97
Author's site:	http://indiebookman.com
	http://authorsbookshop.com

Promoting Your Book with Social Media and Web 2.0
Deltina Hay and Neil Kahn

The Internet as we know it is evolving quickly. However, these changes are in favor of entrepreneurs and small businesses, including authors and small presses. This "new" Internet is often referred to as Web 2.0, and "social media" are the tools and technologies that power it.

The beauty of Web 2.0 is that it is driven by the people who use it. Unlike the old Internet, Web 2.0 relies on a site's true popularity among the masses, as opposed to search engine algorithms. Incorporating social media optimization alongside Search Engine Optimization (SEO), then, enables anyone to establish a truly optimized Web presence— especially if paired with a meaningful message.

The tools available to achieve this optimization are numerous and can undoubtedly seem overwhelming. However, once armed with a general knowledge, it is easy to select the appropriate tools and technologies to maximize one's presence in the social Web.

According to Wikipedia, Web 2.0 describes:

> "...changing trends in the use of [Internet] technology and Web design that aim to enhance creativity, information sharing, collaboration, and functionality of the Web." This *new* Internet has "led to the development and evolution of Web-based communities and hosted services, such as social networking sites, video sharing sites, wikis, blogs, and folksonomies."

Additionally, Wikipedia defines social media as "activities that integrate technology, social interaction, and the construction of words, pictures, videos and audio" using technologies like blogs, picture sharing, crowd-sourcing, social networking, video sharing, microblogging, etc.

Web 2.0 and social media optimization, then, means optimizing one's presence on the Web in three general ways: interactivity, sharing, and collaboration.

Interactivity

The essential premise of social media is that information, or media, offered to users is interactive. Social, in a word, means interactive, and interactivity can be accomplished in various ways, whether by allowing readers to comment on or share your content, subscribe to your blog or RSS feed so they can have your content on hand, or display your content on their own site.

To make online content interactive, Web users can implement the following tools and technologies:

- Blogging using Wordpress, Typepad, or similar
- Really Simple Syndication (RSS) Feeds
- Podcasting and vidcasting
- Wikis
- Social media news releases
- Social media newsrooms
- Image tools such as site snapshots

Sharing

Sharing in the social Web means offering content to others through blogging indexes and media communities; by tagging interesting blogs or Web site on social bookmarking sites; or by developing mini applications like widgets or mash-ups. Don't forget that everything that can be posted to a Web site can be shared in some type of social media community.

To begin sharing content in the social Web, Internet users can:

- Include their blog, podcast, or vidcast in directories like Technorati, Google Blog Search, Podcast.com, or BlogPulse.
- Tag their favorite blogs and Web sites on social bookmarking sites like Technorati, del.icio.us, and StumbleUpon.
- Share and tag multimedia in media communities like Flickr and YouTube.
- Use Collage tools or Webcasting like SplashCast Media or blogTV.
- Create and distribute widgets or mash-ups using services like Widgetbox, Open Social, or Yahoo Pipes.

Collaboration

In order for collaboration to occur, Web 2.0 and social media users need to be willing to give back. Collaborating can be as simple as commenting regularly on other users' content, joining and contributing to social networking sites, contributing to crowd-sourced news sites, or becoming an avatar in virtual reality.

Specifically, these efforts can include:
- Commenting on blogs (and use co.mments to track them).
- Contributing to crowd-sourced news sites like Digg and NowPublic.
- Creating profiles or business pages on social or professional networking sites like Facebook, LinkedIn, or MySpace.
- Creating a presence in author networking sites like Shelfari and Goodreads.
- Participating in microblogs like Twitter or Jaiku.
- Posting events in social calendars like Upcoming.org and eventful.com.
- Creating and sharing a wiki.
- Becoming an avatar in a virtual world like Second Life.
- Creating your own social networking site using Ning.

Participating in the new, social Web is ultimately about connecting with people. Armed with a conversational and information-rich message and a general understanding of social media tools and technologies, anyone can participate in the new Internet and garner tremendous benefits from their efforts.

Social Media Newsroom

One way to demonstrate these efforts is with a social media newsroom (SMNR). A SMNR is a place to send the media, prospective clients, book reviewers, or anyone who wants to know all about you, your business, or your book. It's a place where they can:

- View all of your major media coverage.
- See all of your past and present press releases.
- Look up all of your past and future events.
- Read and link to all of your book reviews.
- Download multimedia material like photos, company logos, podcasts, vidcasts, etc.
- View biographies on each key person in the company, along with links to their social or business networking profiles in Facebook, MySpace, or LinkedIn.
- Check out your own purpose-built del.icio.us page linking to other sites relevant to your business.
- Subscribe through RSS feeds to any portion of information on the site.

- Share any content on the site with their friends or colleagues via email or by posting to social bookmarking indexes like del.icio.us or StumbleUpon with one click.
- Send you an instant message using AIM, Yahoo Messaging, MSN, Skype, etc.
- Link directly to your latest blog posts.
- Search the site or the entire Web using Google or Technorati.
- Link to other blogs or Web sites that are relevant to your message.
- See all Technorati tags related to your content.
- Comment directly on your media coverage, press releases, and events.

Similar to a traditional online newsroom, an SMNR houses media coverage, media contact information, news releases, events, and so forth, but it also includes social media and Web 2.0 elements that allow visitors to share and interact with the content.

An SMNR fulfills a traditional purpose while simultaneously taking advantage of the tremendous indexing opportunities that social bookmarking and RSS feed services like Technorati, del.icio.us, Digg, and Feedburner provide. Imagine that every entry made in your newsroom, including *all* of your media coverage, press releases, biographies, photos, vidcasts, podcasts, events, etc., was not only indexed in Google and all of the other search engines, but also in popular social bookmarking sites and RSS feed services, which are accessible to millions of bloggers and Web users. This is the true power of the SMNR—exposure.

Don't I have most of this already?

Internet users who already have a functioning Web site that incorporates most of these social media features may wonder why they need a newsroom. First, a newsroom tells the media and prospective clients that you are making a serious effort to make their jobs easier. A social media newsroom is akin to a press release, in that standardization is essential to allow for easy navigation and content extraction by the media.

Second, as mentioned earlier, a social media newsroom, built using a blogging platform such as WordPress, means that each entry in your newsroom, from a press release to a simple image, can be automatically indexed in search engines, RSS feed indexes, and social bookmarking services. This means someone can find your site by coming across your company logo image, by searching for a blog on the subject of your business expertise, by looking up relevant sites tagged in Technorati or del.icio.us, or by searching for RSS feeds. Think of it like this: you can have one lottery ticket in the pot or one hundred—you figure the odds.

But, a social media newsroom should not replace your existing Web site. You still want a place for blogging and to present other information. You will also do all of your "selling" on your Web site. Your SMNR is not a sales tool; it is meant to be a neutral place to present all of your media materials.

Many small businesses, entrepreneurs, and authors may not have enough media coverage yet to justify a complete newsroom, but that does not mean they can't take advantage of a social media and Web 2.0 optimized Web site. Using the blogging platform WordPress as a content management system (CMS) provides all of the benefits of social bookmarking and RSS feeds, and makes it easy to place widgets and badges from other social sites. It is a surprisingly easy way to build and maintain a feature-rich and easy-to-maintain Web site.

An optimized Web site and social media newsroom—if applicable—coupled with a healthy presence in the social Web, as discussed above, will give entrepreneurs, authors, and publishers an edge in this new Internet arena. But keep in mind that these tools require fresh content in order to yield successful results.

Resources Mentioned in this Article

BlogPulse	http://blogpulse.com/
blogTV	http://www.blogtv.com/
co.mments	http://co.mments.com
del.icio.us	http://delicious.com/
Digg	http://www.digg.com
eventful	http://eventful.com/
Facebook	http://www.facebook.com
FeedBurner	http://www.feedburner.com
Flickr	http://flickr.com
Goodreads	http://www.goodreads.com
Google Blog Search	http://blogsearch.google.com/
Jaiku	http://www.jaiku.com/
LinkedIn	http://linkedin.com
MySpace	http://www.myspace.com

Making the Most of Technology

Ning	http://ning.com
NowPublic	http://www.nowpublic.com
OpenSocial	http://code.google.com/apis/opensocial/
Podcast.com	http://podcast.com/
SecondLife	http://secondlife.com/
Shelfari	http://shelfari.com
SnapShots	http://www.snap.com/
Splash Cast Media	http://web.splashcast.net/
StumbleUpon	http://www.stumbleupon.com
Technorati	http://technorati.com
Twitter	http://twitter.com
Typepad	http://www.typepad.com/
Upcoming	http://www.upcoming.org
widgetbox	http://www.widgetbox.com/
WordPress	http://www.wordpress.com
Yahoo Pipes	http://pipes.yahoo.com/pipes/
YouTube	http://www.youtube.com

Optimized Web site Examples

Dalton Publishing	http://www.daltonpublishing.om
Social Media Power	http://www.socialmediapower.com
Accolades Public Relations	http://www.accoladespr.com
Les McGehee	http://www.lesmcgehee.com

Social Media Newsroom Examples

Pure Soapbox	http://www.puresoapboxnewsroom.com
Joe O'Connell	http://www.joeoconnellnewsroom.com
The Hidden Lands of Nod	http://www.hiddenlandsofnodnewsroom.com
Owen Egerton	http://www.owenegertonnewsroom.com

About the Authors

Deltina Hay is the founder of Social Media Power and Dalton Publishing, a literary press based in Austin, Texas. She has been programming and doing Web development in one form or another for twenty-five years. Her love of media and publishing, coupled with her passion for open source programming led her naturally to social media and Web 2.0 consulting. She knows firsthand the amount of traffic that social media optimization and marketing can drive to a Web site, as well as the millions of potential customers and readers it can reach. She created Social Media Power to offer ways for entrepreneurs, small businesses, authors, and publishers to improve greatly their own Web presence using social media and Web 2.0 tools and technologies. Her graduate education includes computer science, applied mathematics, numerical analysis, fluid dynamics, and psychology. You can find Ms. Hay's eBook, *A Step-by-Step Guide to Social Media Marketing and Web 2.0 Optimization,* on SocialMediaPower.com. Look for her upcoming print book, *A Survival Guide to Web 2.0 and Social Media Optimization: Strategies, Tactics, and Tools for Succeeding in the Social Web*, due out in November 2008 from Wiggy Press. You can reach Ms. Hay via email at deltina@socialmediapower.com.

Neil Kahn earned a bachelor's degree in English from the University of Texas at Austin in 2006. She interned with The Texas Medical Association, gaining writing and editing experience through interaction with contributors and editors for *Texas Medicine* magazine. Neil has always been an avid writer and reader, which lends naturally to her proofreading and editing skills. In her current position as Assistant Publisher at Dalton Publishing, she utilizes and hones those writing and editing skills daily. She is only beginning to tap into the power of social media and Web 2.0 optimization; however, her strengths in writing and editing lend to the production of polished written content for all of Social Media Power's optimized sites, newsrooms, and generated online content.

Podcast Airdate:	September 27th, 2007
Podcast URL:	http://authorsaccess.com/archives/82
Author's site:	http://www.socialmediapower.com http://www.daltonpublishing.com http://www.plumbsocial.com http://www.bookproposalpower.com http://www.empoweredbywordpress.com

Revolution: Audiobook
Toby Heidel

Revolution.

That's a big word, isn't it? Sure, it gets thrown around a lot, invoked at the slightest hint of change, pressed into service when somebody wants you to buy into something, but there's a reason for that. It's a big word. It speaks to people. The founding fathers knew it. Lenin knew it. Heck, even the Beatles knew it! Sometimes, using the term revolution isn't hyperbole. When things in a given industry or culture are changing rapidly with far-reaching consequences, it's the right word to use.

Right now, there's a revolution brewing in all facets of the audiobook world. It's primarily being driven by one single technological advancement, but the implications and reach of that advancement's influence can't be understated. There are other important factors in play, as well. Things are changing at a breakneck pace, and the audiobook landscape in ten years is poised to look dramatically different than it does today.

Of course, every industry is constantly evolving and changing, but there are a few elements that make change within a given field "revolutionary." First, in a revolution, the changes that occur are extremely rapid. Second, many of the principal players, the "old guard," are blindsided. Their methods are outdated and they don't anticipate change until it's too late. And lastly, those deep, fundamental changes look obvious in hindsight. All of these elements are in place in the audiobook publishing industry right now.

The audiobook revolution has begun.

Let's examine the changes occurring in the industry point by point and see if we can make some sense of what's going on, where this audiobook revolution is headed, and how authors, small publishers, and audiobook professionals can benefit.

The Emergence of AudioBooks

To understand the changes that are happening now, we'll have to look first to the past. Let's briefly examine the industry from a historical perspective. Audiobooks didn't appear on the scene in a really meaningful way for the majority of consumers until the early 1980s. This era could be considered the infancy of audiobooks as a viable industry. Of course, audiobooks existed before this time, but they weren't widely used by consumers. Instead, the industry was focused primarily on "special populations" such as the visually impaired. Audiobooks were unwieldy and cumbersome as the majority of them were distributed on vinyl records. They weren't portable in any sense of the word. Many of them were available only at libraries, and they weren't marketed for sale to the general population.

Things began to change when cassette tapes appeared on the scene, but it was slow going in the early years. The Books on Tape Corporation opened its doors in 1970, but for the first decade of its existence the company concentrated on selling its products mainly to libraries and institutions. Although portable tape players existed, they weren't driving audiobook sales. Most people were content to consume their reading content as they always had, via traditional print books.

All that changed in the waning years of the decade. When the oil crisis of 1979 hit, sales of Japanese cars in America exploded. A standard feature of many of those cars that their American counterparts lacked? A cassette tape player! In the early 1980s, tape players rapidly became a standard feature on many automobiles. In addition, another cassette-related product appeared on the scene in 1979: the Sony Walkman. As people started adopting this new portable audio technology, they began looking for novel ways to use it. What could be more "novel" than a book on tape? The audiobook consumer industry was born.

Several traditional print publishers, along with a growing number of independent, audio-only firms, realized the potential for this new technology and began ramping up production of audiobooks. By the mid-1980s, audiobook companies were recording several billion dollars a year in retail sales. In 1986, six major audiobook companies joined together to form the Audio Publishers Association to promote the industry and increase consumer awareness of the format. The first real golden age of audiobook production had begun, launched in large part by Japanese automakers!

And then... nothing much happened. The major players were established, the industry stabilized, and things pretty much stagnated for twenty-five years! Publishing is a notoriously staid, conservative, and slow to change industry. One might think that a segment of that industry that relies so heavily on technology might be a bit different, but that's just not the case. Although technology has become more and more integrated into our lives and the formats consumers use to listen to audio have changed, the traditional audiobook publishers have continued to operate as if it Reagan is still in the White House.

Want an example? According to the Consumer Electronics Association, sales of cassette tape players peaked in 1994. As late as 2005, a full 16% of audiobooks sold were on cassette tapes! That means that more than a decade after the zenith of the format's popularity, audiobook publishers were still cranking out content on it. In fact, as of 2008, some industry leaders such as Blackstone Audio and Recorded Books still offer each and every one of their titles on cassette.

Using Today's Technology

Of course, even audiobook executives have begun to notice that it's been a long time since they've seen anyone popping and locking as they walk down the street listening to a Sony Walkman! There has been a slow shift over the last decade to distribution via compact discs in the industry. By 2006, 77% of audiobooks sold were compact discs. The marketing and distribution approach taken by the major publishers hasn't changed much, though. Audiobook publishing is approached by most of the industry "leaders" using the same outdated, nineteenth-century models that print publishers use. If you're familiar with any facet of the publishing world, you know what I mean: lots of buying on credit with a high percentage of returns, middlemen, unnecessary shipments of product from publisher to distributor to bookstore and back again, meager royalty percentages for content creators, the works. One wonders whether there are publishing executives who think their products are shipped across the Atlantic by the Dutch in wooden ships!

This brings us to the current state of affairs. A few stuffy companies steadfastly clinging to cassette tapes, most major publishers slowly transitioning to compact discs, and everyone seemingly sitting in armchairs smoking big pipes while wearing tweed jackets with elbow patches. It's enough to drive a Twitter user mad!

"Wait a minute!" you might be thinking. "You said that one of the tenets of 'revolution' is rapid change. If nothing has substantially changed in the audiobook world in twenty years, what gives?"

Well, remember that technological advancement I mentioned way back in the second paragraph? The one poised to shake the industry up dramatically? It's the mp3 player, of course, and its widespread adoption by consumers has enormous implications. In 2007, 90 million MP3 players were sold in the United States alone. 30% of the US population listens to an mp3 player weekly. Those numbers grow by leaps and bounds every year. The iPhone has taken the world by storm, and it is, at its heart, primarily an MP3 player.

Meanwhile, audiobook publishers are hawking cassette tapes.

There's some irony here. Technological advances that put portable audio within reach of a large percentage of the buying public launched the consumer audiobook industry. This cycle is repeating itself. After a few years of dominance by compact disc players that didn't have the true portability of cassette players like the Walkman, devices such as the iPod Nano and the Creative Zen are making audio available anywhere, anytime, a lot like Japanese cars in the 1980s! Factor in widespread broadband Internet access making large file transfers a snap, and it becomes obvious that the audio distribution game has fundamentally changed. No more shipping physical product from place to place while the middlemen take their cut. And yet, amazingly, the traditional audiobook heavy-hitters don't seem to realize it yet!

But why not? Sure, the industry is conservative and slow to change, but audiobook producers are still in the business of making money. If the trend is toward digital distribution, why aren't they jumping on board as innovators and leaders in the industry? Well, remember the second tenet of revolution? The old guard is blindsided. Their methods are outdated and they don't anticipate change until it's too late. Why does this seem to happen during revolutionary periods, again and again in different settings, be they industrial, political, or cultural?

There are a number of reasons, of course, but the most important may be that as those in control get bigger and more beholden to the status quo, their ability to react to, or even recognize, change, is compromised. The sheer size and percentage of market share of a few of the companies who currently control most of the audiobook industry can't be understated. As in a lot of entertainment industry segments, the last decade in publishing has been marked by a significant amount of consolidation. Huge conglomerates have risen to the fore and gobbled up a lot of smaller publishers. In fact, a mere ten companies publish 80% of books released today! And if there's one thing that giant corporations do poorly, it's handle change. They've invested enormous amounts of time and resources to fine-tune their operational systems. There are layers of bureaucracy that are good at doing one thing: keeping things going in the direction they're already headed for as long as possible. Equipment and technologies have been acquired over the years that would be difficult and hugely expensive to re-vamp or scrap.

A good analogy for these conglomerates is that of a cruise ship. It's an enormous vessel, and it has the ability to get a lot of people from one place to another. But if rough waters are ahead, if a storm or an iceberg appears unexpectedly, it takes a significant amount of time and energy for that cruise ship to change direction. So a lot of these companies stay the course. Even if they do recognize the difficulties ahead, they believe that their organizations are simply too massive, too strong, too powerful, to sink. The captain of the *Titanic* probably believed much the same thing about his ship.

This is very good news for small publishers, self-publishing authors, and technology-oriented audiobook, well, revolutionaries! It means that, even seven years after the appearance of the first iPod, digital audiobook distribution is still wide open. As the big companies struggle to guide their "cruise ships" into favorable waters or ignore altogether the sea changes occurring in the industry, smaller, smarter companies can rocket ahead with their "speedboats" and come out on top.

Digital Download Revolution

The digital revolution is still nascent. In 2004, 6% of audiobooks were sold as digital downloads. By 2006, that percentage had more than doubled to 14%. That's an enormous percentage increase in just two years, but digital downloads still represent a small share of overall audiobooks sold. That number will increase dramatically over the next few years. There's no way around it. It simply remains to be seen exactly who will be offering those downloads for sale.

In addition to distribution opportunities, technological advances on the production end mean that great-sounding results are within reach for companies that could once only dream of in-house production. Audiobook production was once an overwhelmingly expensive affair. A well-outfitted production studio used to cost hundreds of thousands of dollars to assemble. With recent advances in affordable recording, editing, and mastering equipment, small companies can assemble the right personnel, add a healthy dose of creativity, and achieve professional studio sound with as little as a few thousand dollars.

Perhaps the best example of the possibilities present in the current digital revolution is the world's best-known digital audiobook distributor, Audible.com. Audible has seen exponential growth over the last few years. The company went public less than ten years ago. At the beginning of 2003, it had yet to turn a profit. By the end of 2005, annual revenues were estimated to be $63 million.

Audible isn't the only company with revolutionary ideas about audiobooks. Red Planet Audiobooks offers self-published authors and small presses turnkey packages that include production, manufacturing, as well as physical and digital distribution for as little as $899. By leveraging new technology and incorporating "print-on-demand" manufacturing practices similar to those used by independent print publishing companies, Red Planet puts audiobook revenue within reach of even the smallest publishers and content creators.

As for the final tenet of revolution, it's apparent that the fundamental changes occurring in the audiobook industry are not only going to be obvious in hindsight, but indeed are very evident right now, even as they are happening! Consumers are shifting to digital formats. That fact is inevitable. Digital audio is more convenient, it's cheaper, and it's more durable and portable. Compact discs are going the way of the cassette tape and the Dodo bird.

The only real questions that remain are those regarding who will flourish in this rapidly evolving environment and who will perish, and how those who succeed will do so. Will it be great customer service that rockets a company to the forefront of the industry? Will it be a smaller technical advance within the larger framework of digital distribution that consumers find they just can't live without? Will it be a streamlined business model that leverages the Internet or social networking in new ways?

These questions remain unanswered, but if you are a publisher or author with content that you feel would make a great audiobook, now is the time to be daring, to take chances, to run with that oversize, crazy, wonderful idea for producing or distributing your content digitally. Now is the time to seek out those companies whose philosophies and business practices speak to your soul, make you smack your forehead and think, "Why isn't everybody doing it like this?" Don't fall into the trap of believing that there is security or a future for the cruise ships of the industry. Trust your instincts. Believe in change. Hop aboard a speedboat.

Because this, friends, is a revolution.

About the Author

Toby Heidel is a futurist with Red Planet Audiobooks in Austin, TX. As such, he is in charge of long range planning for the company, implementing new technologies and responding to developing trends in the audiobook industry. In addition to his work with Red Planet, Toby has a solid background in spoken word entertainment as the long-time Executive Director for the Violet Crown Radio Players, a radio drama re-creation troupe based in Austin, Texas

Podcast Airdate:	April 24th, 2008
Podcast URL:	http://authorsaccess.com/archives/102
Author's site:	http://redplanetaudiobooks.com/

Book Marketing on MySpace
Tyler R. Tichelaar

We have all heard that online social networking is a great way to get a book noticed. We've also heard negative things in the media about MySpace as one of the premiere social networking sites.

I have actively marketed my novels on MySpace since February 2006. I am here to vouch that I have had nothing but a positive experience (despite some occasional spam). MySpace can be a fantastic way to get attention for your book, to network with other writers, and to make friends in the book world and among readers.

If you haven't tried out MySpace yet, it is extremely user-friendly. By following my suggestions below, you can have a rewarding book marketing experience.

Build an Effective MySpace Profile

1. PROFILE SETUP—On your profile, link to your Web site. Write a description of yourself and synopses of your books. The profile is an intimate way to know an author beyond the capabilities of a regular Web site or listserv, and it provides viewers an interactive experience to write or post comments to the author. MySpace is a great place to promote your author image.

2. PROFILE PHOTO—Make your profile picture your book cover. If you have more than one book, rotate your book covers periodically.

3. PHOTOS—People want to know what the author looks like, so in your "pics" have some pictures of yourself as well. In your various photo albums, have different albums devoted to different subjects relevant to your books, your writing, and your life as an author. Also, MySpace has the option to flash or play your photos in a slideshow on your profile page. Don't miss this opportunity. I like to have my book covers alternately flash for everyone to see.

4. ADD EVERYONE—When you get friend requests, don't turn anyone down (except the occasional spam girls who hit on you—MySpace will delete them right away). More friends, more exposure. I recently added friend # 1,000 and I'm sure I have thousands more to come. Many of my friends will list

me as a top friend, which increases my visibility and my book covers' exposure.

5. COMMENTS—Leave comments on all friends' pages when you add them. That way, your book cover (your profile picture) appears on their pages and people can click to your page. More than 8,000 people have viewed my page, primarily from clicking on comments I left on other people's pages, and the number who have seen my book covers on friends' pages has to be in the hundreds of thousands by now. You don't need fancy comments—something as simple as "Have a Nice Day" or "Thanks for the Add" will do, or a personal comment if you choose to leave one. In addition, copy and paste your URL to your Web site below each comment you make. You will be amazed how many people click through to your Web site. My Web site traffic nearly doubled once I started adding my Web site to each of my MySpace comments.

6. BLOGS and BULLETINS—Post blogs frequently. People will read your blog when they view your page. Encourage people to subscribe to your blog as well. Whenever you add a friend, send them a message requesting they subscribe to your blog. You can also post your blog as a bulletin that goes to all of your friends. There are plenty of topics for an author to blog about. My blogs include quotes from my novels, reviews of books I've enjoyed reading, announcements of author events, updates on topics included in my novels, humorous lists of reasons to buy my books. Whatever you think might remotely stir interest in your book is worth becoming a blog.

7. EVENTS—Make an event posting for every appearance, book publication date, book signing, and speaking event. All your friends will be notified of your event. MySpace also includes a calendar option where you can list the place, date, and time of each book signing, speaking engagement, or other public appearance you are going to make.

8. GROUPS—Over 5,000 book groups are on MySpace. Join and participate in the ones most relevant to your book. Every comment you leave makes people see your book cover and they may go to your profile, then Web site. My favorite group is the self-publishing group where I can talk to other authors. However, many book club groups also exist. Join the clubs where people are reading books similar to your book. You don't need to plug your

book, but do join in the discussions about the books there. Everyone will know you're an author because with every comment you leave, your book cover will appear. Some of the book club members are bound to click on your icon to view your MySpace page.

MySpace Results

1. BOOKSALES—MySpace has not resulted in huge sales for me that I know about directly, but I don't know how many people saw me on MySpace and then bought my books at Amazon or in stores. At least a couple dozen MySpace members have directly told me they have bought my books. Book sales are what authors most want, but my book would not have been visible to millions of people if not for MySpace.
2. NETWORKING—Perhaps MySpace's greatest advantage

   - Several hundred self-published and traditionally published authors have added me as a friend—some famous like Kurt Vonnegut (since deceased). Many have traded books with me.
   - I have befriended some of the MySpace book reviewers who have reviewed my book and the reviews have been read by their thousands of friends and blog subscribers. One reviewer said she would be my "fan for life." What more can an author want?
   - Reader Views is a member. They list, among other things, their book video trailers, a great new way for authors to market books and which has made me rethink how to present my novels to the public. Many other authors, publishers, and book promoters' profiles will help you come up with your own marketing ideas.
   - I added Authorsbookshop.com, an independent bookstore—they now carry my books and displayed them at Book Expo America. The owner, Brad Grochowski, moderates the MySpace self-publishing group.
   - *The World of Myth* ezine approached me for an author interview, then agreed to publish two of my short stories in different issues.
   - If you offer other services beyond writing, such as editing, you can also promote these services on MySpace to other authors. It's a great way to get potential clients.

- Movie star, Casper Van Dien and I had an email conversation about the Tarzan novels. You don't know who might talk to you on MySpace. Now if only Oprah would talk to me….

MySpace is an enjoyable marketing experience. Thousands of authors, publishers, reviewers, editors and especially readers are members. You may get a good idea of who your potential readers are by who sends you a friend request.

Many other social networking sites are out there. Among the ones I've tried are LinkedIn, Facebook, Shelfari, Library Thing, and Authors Den, but I find MySpace the most fun and entertaining as well as the best-organized. It is the only one I actively log into and I highly recommend it.

MySpace is free, easy and fun. Sign up now! Then visit www.MySpace.com/tylertichelaar. I'll be happy to add you as a friend.

About the Author

Learn more about Tyler R. Tichelaar, Ph.D. in the About the Editors section beginning on p. 215.

Amazon Kindle: Lighting a Fire on eBook Sales
Victor R. Volkman

It's hard to conceive that it's only been twelve months since the Amazon Kindle eBook reader was released on November 21st, 2007, just a few days shy of Black Friday: the infamous mega-retail (and now e-tail) day of the year in commemoration of the beginning of the holiday shopping season. The first production run was sold out in 5.5 hours after the announcement according to CEO Jeff Bezos. Shortly thereafter, it could be found on eBay for $100 over list price. Despite being extremely short in supply during its first six months of life, it is back in stock and often has free delivery from Amazon.

This despite all reasons to the contrary, the industry wags branding it with various epithets from ugly[1] to zany[2] to "a bit sad"[3]. That hasn't discouraged consumers, who have been wanting something like this for a decade or more: an eBook reader that made sense. They've been voting with their pocketbooks to the tune of 6% of Amazon total book revenues[4]. The Kindle can deliver your blogs and newspapers to you without ever leaving the comfort of your own bed—not even your dog can do that for you.

Really, once again, it's the content, stupid! The Kindle launched with 90,000 titles and by all accounts is adding an astonishing 3,000 titles per month. As of June 2008, there were 130,000 titles online. Now I'm going to say something really controversial: the Kindle has leveled the playing field for self-published authors and small presses in a way that has not been since the introduction of the Internet itself. There is no fee for authors to get their books up on Kindle; once they are on Kindle they look just the "same" as all other books by any of hundreds of other publishers. Yes there are some apocryphal success stories of people selling 20,000 copies on Kindle, but the average Kindle title probably moves a hundred copies of itself per year. It's a revenue stream that's only going to grow. Also, consider that Kindle users can download a free preview of your book. That itself could result in a sale.

---

[1] "Credit For Amazon's Ugly Kindle Should Go To E-Ink Maker." *Information Week*. Alexander Wolfe, Nov 26, 2007.
[2] "Amazon's Kindle won't spark your e-book fire." Salon.com, Nov 28, 2007.
[3] "Amazon Kindle 'a Bit Sad,' Designer Says." James Niccolai, *IDG News Service*. Dec 11, 2007.
[4] "Amazon kindles hope after e-reader interest explodes" Guy Dammann. *The Guardian*. June 3, 2008.

You can get onboard yourself as an author through their do-it-yourself site, or you can get an experienced team to optimize the reading experience for you, as is offered by Reader Views. In this article, we'll look at some basics of the do-it-yourself approach, the workflow, and limitations of the platform.

The Do-It-Yourself Approach

If you've made it this far into the book, odds are you are at least willing to consider things like self-publishing and rolling up your sleeves to get the job done. Let's take that as our working assumption and try to figure out how we get started. Best of all, you can pretty much do everything you need to do without ever laying out the money to buy a Kindle unit!

All of this presupposes that you still retain the rights for eBook publishing and that you haven't signed away these rights to a publisher. If your book exists in any printed form, it is imperative that you review your contracts to see whether the publisher left you any eBook rights. Generally, if you signed your contract after 2003, the odds are very low that you have eBook rights for your own books. In that case, your job becomes that of lighting a fire under your publisher to get them put it on Kindle. Your royalty will probably be quite a bit lower in this case.

The first, and most important, decision you will make is how to upload your content into the Amazon Digital Text Publishing (DTP) site (http://dtp.amazon.com). The Kindle system will take a variety of inputs, and I'm listing them here from most desirable to least desirable (roughly):

1. Microsoft Word documents (BEST)
2. Mobipocket (.mobi files)
3. HTML files
4. Raw text (ASCII) files
5. PDF files (WORST)

Getting into HTML

Why are PDF files ranked last when you might think these are a "natural" eBook format? That's a very interesting question that gets us into the heart of Kindle technology. The bottom line is that everything gets converted to HTML. Period. Basically, the Kindle is a handheld Web browser and all the documents it (or you) are ever going to see have to be converted to HTML syntax. If the thought of working with or learning HTML frightens you, it's time to forget about the do-it-yourself method and consider farming this job out to a contractor. A poorly formatted Kindle book is worse than no Kindle book at all. In fact, if customers complain that your book is poorly formatted, Amazon will refund their money and yank the book right off the shelf; you will have to re-list it under a new ASIN.

Relax, there isn't much HTML that Kindle does support so if you only know a little HTML you're actually better off than an experienced webmaster because you won't know enough to try things that will backfire on you! Mainly what's missing is HTML tables, so if your document has a lot of tables, you're in trouble. The main thing you can do at that point is to build screenshots of your tables; by converting them to graphics, you can get around this limitation. This only works if your tables are not overly large or contain a lot of fine print.

The next question that should leap to your mind is: HTML doesn't have page breaks so how does it know where to insert page breaks? The answer is: it doesn't. You manually have to add page break tags everywhere you want to force a page break. This tag is written as `<mbp:pagebreak/>`. The most common place where page breaks belong, ironically enough, are in the front matter of the book. So this is the first problem you will hit. Suggested areas for page breaks are:

- Title page
- Copyright page
- Table of Contents
- Introduction
- Before each new chapter
- After final chapter (before bibliography, etc.)

Another problem that can crop up is PDF files that contain characters with ligatures. A ligature is a fancy bit of font business used to make letters look better when they appear in consecutive special sequences such as "ff," "fi," "fl," "oe," and "oa." These are in fact combined into a new character which is on the Unicode map and may not display correctly on the Kindle. You'll eventually learn to recognize these issues as they come up. The Kindle may reject HTML files with Unicode characters in them so you will have to watch closely for this error condition.

Last, PDF users will need to be wary of "drop caps". This is the big first letter on the first word of the first page of a chapter. For example, if you had a story book that started out "Once upon a time...", the initial letter "O" might be three lines tall as a giant drop caps. Unfortunately, these look rather awkward when converted into HTML so you'll want to drop-kick the drop caps.

Understanding the Workflow

The Kindle workflow follows a process that only a programmer could love. In a nutshell, it goes like this:

1. Upload initial document type (prefer Microsoft Word)
2. Preview the results on Amazon Kindle simulator
3. Download the HTML file from the Kindle simulator
4. Edit the HTML to add page breaks, fix funny spacing, and font issues
5. Put in hyperlinks for the Table of Contents items
6. Re-upload the HTML file to DTP site
7. Continue doing Preview, Download, and Re-upload steps until it's perfect!

And that's about it! I could draw any number of interesting diagrams with pictures and arrows, but it would still be just window dressing on the seven magic steps I've listed above.

When you come to achieve the perfect state of a Kindle document with no flaws, there are just a few last minute things to do before hitting the Publish button. You need to pick appropriate content categories (up to five) for subjects that your book relates to. These seem to be largely similar to the BISG BISAC codes that bookstores use to classify content. Also, if your Kindle book duplicates a printed book title, you need to enter that ISBN as the reference ISBN to use. Unlike other eBook systems, Amazon Kindle eBooks don't really have to have their own ISBN but they can "refer" to an ISBN of an existing printed book. This is how it links the printed edition with the Amazon Kindle edition of your book. Last, you'll need a high-quality image of your book cover to stand-in as the placeholder book cover on the Amazon Kindle book purchase page.

I also highly recommend you go in and add a book "cover" inside your book so when users download it and open the book they see the same cover they would on a printed book (not just the title page). You can do this by simply adding an HTML <img> tag into your document ahead of the title page and followed by a page break.

It ain't perfect but it's the best we got

Never before has there been such a groundswell of support for an eBook platform as we have seen for Kindle 1.0. Nobody knows what the future will hold with Kindle 2.0—perhaps color, perhaps support for tables or PDF files; we shall see. But if you start developing by using my workflow suggestions for today's Kindle, you're guaranteed to get a great result for generations of Kindle to come.

About the Author

Learn more about Victor R. Volkman in the About the Editors section beginning on p. 215.

About the Editors

Tyler R. Tichelaar is a novelist, freelance writer, scholar, editor and book reviewer. Tyler holds a Ph.D. in Literature from Western Michigan University, and Bachelor and Master's Degrees from Northern Michigan University. He has lectured on writing and literature at Clemson University, the University of Wisconsin, the University of London, and at Best-Seller Publishing Institute seminars. Tyler is a regular guest host of *Authors Access* podcasts, and the President of the Upper Peninsula Publishers and Authors Association. Tyler is also the Associate Editor at Reader Views, one of the fastest growing book review services today. He has written more than fifty book reviews, interviewed over two hundred authors, and written dozens of press releases during his tenure there.

Tyler's expertise comes from being an author himself. He has published the regionally bestselling *Marquette Trilogy*, a family saga covering seven generations between 1849-1999 and centering on the pioneers who settled Upper Michigan. The trilogy consists of the novels *Iron Pioneers, The Queen City,* and *Superior Heritage*. He is also the author of *Narrow Lives* and *The Only Thing That Lasts*, the latter of which will be published in Spring 2009. Tyler is a seventh generation resident of Upper Michigan, and he lives in his native Marquette where the roar of Lake Superior, mountains of snow, beautiful scenery, and sandstone architecture inspire his writing. For more information about Tyler and his books, visit www.MarquetteFiction.com

Irene Watson is an author, entrepreneur, and former therapist and educator. She currently is the owner and Managing Editor of Reader Views, Reader Views Kids, and Inside Scoop Live, and a co-host on *Authors Access* podcasts. Irene holds her Master's Degree from Regis University in Denver, CO and a Bachelor's Degree from St. Edward's University in Austin, TX. She is the president of Higher Power Foundation, Inc., a non-profit organization dedicated to awarding scholarships to people seeking recovery.

Irene's expertise in the publishing industry comes from being an author herself as well as managing an online book review service. Reader Views offers book reviews, author publicity, and many other elements needed by authors and writers. Irene also coaches authors to write book proposals and is a literary agent. Irene lives with her husband in Austin, Texas. For more information about Irene visit www.irenewatson.com or Reader Views www.readerviews.com

Victor R. Volkman began his writing career in the late 1980s writing for computer programming journals such as *Windows Developer's Journal, The C Gazette, C/C++ Users Journal*, and many other print publications that have been obsoleted since the Web was born. He authored two computer programming books in the mid-1990s before finding out that writing for Fortune 500 companies was not terribly rewarding. In 2003, he formed Loving Healing Press out of a community project in the Self-Expression and Leadership Program (SELP) course at Landmark Education.

Since then, LHP has gone on to publish dozens of cutting-edge books that promote its mission of "redefining what is possible for healing mind and spirit." As such, he has produced a series of books on Traumatic Incident Reduction (see www.TIRbook.com) as well as empowering other authors in a wide range of helping areas including trauma recovery, self-esteem, physical disabilities, sexual abuse recovery, and much more. He produces regular podcasts for *Authors Access*, *Authors Airwaves*, and the *Unbreak Your Health* show. In 2007, LHP spun off a new imprint, Modern History Press, dedicated to empowering authors to speak about surviving conflict and seeking identity in modern times. When not publishing, he enjoys spending time with his wife Marian K. Volkman, a formidable author in her own right.

Bibliography

Bilanich, B. (2008). *Straight talk for success: common sense ideas that won't let you down.* Denver, CO: Front Row Press.

Calvani, M., & Edwards, A. K. (2008). *The slippery art of book reviewing.* Kingsport Tenn: Twilight Times Books.

Campbell, A. (2000). *Forensic science: evidence, clues, and investigation.* Crime, justice, and punishment. Philadelphia: Chelsea House.

Campbell, A., & Ohm, R. C. (2002). *Legal ease: a guide to criminal law, evidence, and procedure.* Springfield, Ill: C.C. Thomas.

Campbell, A. (2002). *Making crime pay: the writer's guide to criminal law, evidence, and procedure.* New York: Allworth Press.

Daoust, B. (2005). *Networking: 150 ways to promote yourself.* Pleasanton, CA: Blueprint Books.

Denbow, C. (2008). *A book inside: how to write, publish, and sell your story.* North Bend, Ore: Plain & Simple Books.

Dodd, P., & Sundheim, D. (2005). *The 25 best time management tools & techniques: how to get more done without driving yourself crazy.* Ann Arbor, MI: Peak Performance Press.

Dunsky, M. (2007). *Watch your words: the Rowman & Littlefield language-skills handbook for journalists.* Lanham, Md: Rowman & Littlefield.

Flowers, P. W. (2006). *Underdog advertising: proven principles to compete and win against the giants in any industry.* Dallas, Tex: Brown Books.

Fry, P. L. (2006). *The right way to write, publish and sell your book: your guide to successful authorship.* Ojai, Calif: Matilija Press.

Gerson, M. D. (2008). *The voice of the muse: answering the call to write.* Santa Fe, NM: LightLines Media.

Harper, S. (2005). *The ripple effect: maximizing the power of relationships for your life and business.* Austin, Texas: SWOT Publishing.

Hay, D. (2008) *A step by step guide to social media marketing and web 2.0 optimization* (Kindle Edition).

Hoenig, C. (2007). *The author's guide to planning book events: tips and tools for bookselling success.* Lincoln, NE: iUniverse.

Howard-Johnson, C. (2007). *The frugal editor: put your best book forward to avoid humiliation and ensure success.* Branson, Mo: Red Engine Press.

Jagoe, A. L. (2006). *Next in line: everyman's guide for writing an autobiography.* New York: iUniverse.

James, L. (2006). *Ten commitments of networking: creative ways to maximize your personal connections.* Bandon, OR: Robert D Reed Pub.

Josephson, D., & Hidden, L. (2005). *Write it right: the ground rules for self-editing like the pros.* Hilton Head Island, S.C.: Ground Rules Press.

Josephson, D. (2003). *Putting it on paper: the ground rules for creating promotional pieces that sell books.* Hilton Head Island, SC: Ground Rules Press.

Kurek, M. (2007). *Who's hiding in your address book?: introducing the ideal network for successful women.* Bandon, OR: Robert D. Reed Pub.

Levine, M. L. (2006). *The fine print of self-publishing: the contracts & services of 48 major self-publishing companies--analyzed, ranked & exposed.* Minneapolis, MN: Bridgeway Books in association with Bascom Hill Pub. Group.

Poynter, D. (2006). *Dan Poynter's book publishing encyclopedia: tips & resources for authors & publishers.* Santa Barbara, CA: Para Publishing.

Roerden, C. (2006). *Don't murder your mystery: 24 fiction-writing techniques to save your manuscript from turning up D.O.A.* Rock Hill, S.C.: Bella Rosa Books.

Sampson, B. (2007). *Sell your book on amazon: top-secret tips guaranteed to increase sales for print-on-demand and self-publishing writers.* Denver, Colo: Outskirts Press.

Snow, P. (2002). *Creating your own destiny: how to get exactly what you want out of life.* Snow Group.

Terrell, P. M. (2006). *Take the mystery out of promoting your book.* Richmond, VA: Palari Pub.

Styne, M. M. (2007). *Seniorwriting: a brief guide for seniors who want to write.* West Conshohocken, Pa: Infinity Pub.

Wuebben, J. (2008). *Content rich: writing your way to wealth on the Web.* Fallbrook, Calif: Encore Pub.

Index

A

Advance Review Copy. *See* ARC
Amazon Advantage, 96, 162–63
Amazon.com, 162–68, 210–14
   book reviews, 115, 120
   print-on-demand, 156
ARC, 136, 137
   defined, 122
   vs. bound galley, 121
audiobooks, 199–204
author visits, 62
Authorsbookshop.com, 208

B

backstory, 2, 16
blogging, 150, 186, 194, 195
book cover, 89–90, 95, 171
book pricing, 98
book promotion
   campaign, 139
book proposals, 36, 150
book reviews
   by print media, 137
   galleys and ARCs, 121
   how to get, 117
   negative, 126
   where to get, 116
   writing, 133, 187
book title writing, 87–88, 170
bookstores
   online, 177–85
bound galley
   defined, 121
branding, 142–52

C

Cather, W., 39
chain stores, 96
character
   action, 1–2
   description, 4
   development, 16
   introducing, 21
   voice, 75
characterization, 35
children's books
   reviews, 64–68
   rules for writing, 61–62
co-authoring
   defined, 102
collaborating
   defined, 102
competitive analysis, 15
conflict, 6–7, 22
   resolution, 25
content editing, 69
criminal law, 31–36

D

dialect, 44
dialogue, 75
distributors, **172**

E

eBook, 151, 210–14
editing, 88–89
   vs. criticism, 77
editors, 89

F

Facebook, 184, 194, 209
Field Expert
   defined, 102
flashbacks, 16, 61
forensic science, 31–36
forewords, 171
freelancing, 110–14

G

galley proof, 80
gay and lesbian fiction, 49–58
genre
   crossing, 47
ghostwriting, 101–8, 112–13
   contract, 108
   defined, 102
grammar, 11, 71, 77
Grochowski, B., 208

H

Hubbard, S., 47

K

kindle eBooks, 210–14
Kohl, J., 99

L

line editing, 69

M

manuscript
   submission, 13–14
media kit, 119
media releases. *See* press releases
memoir, 102
modifiers, 17
motivation, 9
MP3, 60, 201
MySpace, 184, 206–9

N

newsletter, 150, 188
noir era, 34

P

pace, 11
plot, 16, 21, 22
podcasting, 110, 193, 194
Point-of-view. *See* POV
POV, 5, 84
    changes, 8
Poynter, D., 177
press releases, 69, 110, 111, 189, 194, 195
printing, 91–92
proofreading, 80, 171
publication date, 136
publicist, 135–41
    defined, 135
publicity. *See*
publishing associations, 154–61
punctuation, 5, 73, 77

R

read-aloud, 10, 70, 74
regional fiction, 38–45
Roerden, C., 20
romance, 47
RSS, 193, 194, 195, 196

S

Search Engine Optimization. *See* SEO
self-publishing, 17, 93–100
SEO, 182–83, 192
setting, 3
showing vs. telling, 72
SMNR, 194–95
social bookmarking indexes, 195
Social Media Newsroom. *See* SNMR
social networking, 186–87
story
    vs. chronicle, 21
structure, 84

T

theme, 9, 10
true crime, 35–36
T-shirts, 99
typesetting, 87, 91, 92, 93, 94, 96

V

voice, 11

W

Web 2.0, 177, 184, 192–96
Writer's Ego, 104
writer's block, 28–29

Y

Young Adult, 59

www.ingramcontent.com/pod-product-compliance
Lightning Source LLC
Chambersburg PA
CBHW081916170426
43200CB00014B/2744